Clean, Green
and Blue

Advance Praise for Clean, Green and Blue

I welcome this book as an inspiring how-to guide for any city seeking to improve its environment, and particularly its management of water resources, in sustainable ways. It goes beyond a description of technical innovations to document the importance of forward-looking policies, partnerships, economic planning, and a willingness to invest for the future. Above all, the book shows that investment in environmental sustainability can indeed be fully compatible with economic growth.

The expertise, experience, and practical wisdom embodied in this report are well worth study and replication on a broad international scale. This is especially true at a time when climate change increases the certainty of water scarcity in many regions of the world, and adds urgency to the quest for efficient and sustainable solutions.

The book's overarching message is clear: with political commitment supported by good planning and technical innovation, any city can achieve a clean environment. By soundly substantiating this conclusion, Singapore makes an admirable contribution to some of the most pressing challenges facing the world, today and into the future.

Dr Margaret Chan
Director-General, World Health Organisation

Behind the clean and green environment that Singaporeans enjoy today lies a story of strong political will, sustained effort and a committed citizenry. Tan Yong Soon and his team at MEWR give a comprehensive account of how Singapore turned "green" before it became the fashion. Their account also reminds us that Singapore's achievements are the result of far-sightedness and hard work.

Peter Ho
Head of Civil Service, Singapore

No city in the world has done a better job than Singapore at planning for and managing environmental quality. Their success in this very complex task is reflected every day in the lives of its citizens who benefit from clean air and water. This book is a useful guide to cities, governments and their people on learning from the experience of Singapore over several decades on how to build more sustainable cities.

Peter Schwartz
Chairman, Global Business Network

If you always wanted to know how a government could develop a sustainable water strategy, this is the book to read. It is a remarkable story well documented with references to official government publications and a record of vision, strategy and implementation. It is commended to all administrators and policy analysts as both source material and a model.

Dr David Garman
President, International Water Association

While other nations talk about climate change and environmental issues like clean air, water and waste management, Singapore implements sustainable solutions. This little gem of a book explains what they are doing, how and why to preserve their ecosystem. The associated management actions position the city state of Singapore at the forefront of world's best practice. Moreover, the lessons contained herein are readily applicable in other cities and nations.

Dr Allan Hawke
Chairman of the MTAA Superannuation Fund, Australia and
Chancellor of the Australian National University (2006–2008),
Secretary of Defence, Australia (1999–2002), and
Secretary to the Department of Transport and Regional Services (1996–1999)

When Singapore became a sovereign state in 1965, the fledgling nation faced very similar problems as most other developing countries: high unemployment, low standard of living, and poor environmental conditions. In a scant four decades, it has become the sixth wealthiest country in the world in terms of per capita GDP and has managed its environment so well that it is now considered to be one of the best in the world. In this remarkable book, Tan Yong Soon authoritatively and objectively analyses how the environmental conditions were radically transformed within this period, and the enabling conditions which made this extraordinary transformation possible. This book will unquestionably make all Singaporeans proud of their environmental achievements, and at the same time enable other countries, both developed and developing, to learn many lessons from a most remarkable success story. This book is a must read for any individual interested in environment-development issues.

Professor Asit K. Biswas
President, Third World Centre for Water Management, Mexico and
Distinguished Visiting Professor, Lee Kuan Yew School of Public Policy, Singapore

With our planet in peril, not least from the looming crisis of freshwater scarcity worldwide, this book is sounding a timely call to action. Yong Soon's exposition of Singapore's response to the challenge of balancing "can-do" economic development with environmental and water sustainability makes fascinating reading, even for readers beyond the shores of the tiny city state. The coverage of water desalination, recycling and management would hold special interest for those in arid land masses such as Central Asia, Australia, the sub-Sahara, and the Middle East.

Professor Shih Choon Fong
President, National University of Singapore (2000–2008) and
President designate, King Abdullah University of Science and Technology

The Ministry of the Environment and Water Resources of Singapore has been doing very interesting and useful work in the field of environment and water sustainability. I have been visiting and participating in the different international conferences held in Singapore. Providing infrastructure and using modern technologies and processes which are environmentally friendly to fulfill water needs of the population is key to their success in achieving the goal of clean environment and water sustainability. Now again this attempt to write a book on Singapore's journey towards environment and water sustainability to bring awareness among populace is another step forward to achieve clean environment not only for Singapore but for humanity in general world wide.

H.E. Fehied F. Alshareef
Governor, Saline Water Conversion Corporation, Kingdom of Saudi Arabia

This is a comprehensive and unique record of how Singapore approaches the environmental issues in development. It is recommended reading for those who wish to rise to the challenge as we — public, private and people sectors — better understand the opportunities ahead for sustainable development.

Lee Tzu Yang
Chairman, Shell Companies in Singapore

Water is truly the lifeblood of society. Recognizing this imperative, Singapore continues to demonstrate innovative approaches to sustaining this vital resource for its citizens. The country's leaders also play a significant role in providing a roadmap for others by balancing social, economic, environmental, government and public interests for the benefit of current and future generations.

Len C. Rodman
Chairman, President and CEO, Black & Veatch

Singapore's environmental aspirations and achievements are presented with clarity and insight in this book. Its inclusive perspective recognizes not just the government's major role but the importance of community and NGO participation/ partnerships in attaining the vision of environmental sustainability.

Dr Geh Min
President, Nature Society of Singapore (2000–2008)

This book illustrates the magnitude of Singapore's achievement through foresight and prudent planning. It comprehensively captures Singapore's commitment to environmental sustainability, recounting the unprecedented challenges this nation has overcome in the past and the possible challenges it will face in the future. Reading this book is essential for understanding how Singapore has managed its environmental resources, not only for ensuring national security but also for creating a cleaner and greener home for the people of Singapore.

Eugene Heng
Chairman, Waterways Watch Society, Singapore

The surge in interest in climate change has resulted in many publications on the whys and wherefores of environmental issues. Yong Soon and his team have rightly sought to reach out to everyone who is concerned with the sustainability of our planet and who wishes to play a role in improving the living environment. I congratulate them and their collaborators for their noble and outstanding endeavour which is based on Singapore's experience but relevant to others who are also interested in promoting sustainable development and living.

Lim Chee Onn
Executive Chairman, Keppel Corp

Singapore's Ministry of the Environment and Water Resources has shown global leadership in many areas. For example, in water recycling, a critical area in a water short world, Singapore managed to grab world leadership in record time. The planning and the flawless execution of the whole program were far beyond anything I have ever seen. It was also of great service to the world because Singapore's health studies and full-scale installations removed the fear that others felt in proceeding with large-scale water reuse. Thanks to this book we can now learn the way one can organize so that such great successes happen systematically.

Dr Andrew Benedek
Founder of ZENON Environmental Inc. and
Winner of the 2008 Lee Kuan Yew Water Prize

This book is much more than a history of how Singapore has achieved its unique combination of environmental and economic prosperity. It is also a thoughtful explanation of the policy considerations, trade offs, and constraints faced by Singapore's leaders in making strong environmental stewardship an integral part of the nation's economic development strategies. In today's world of rapid urbanization, environmental stress, and sustainability concerns, Singapore's remarkable environmental success story sets the world standard for sustainable economic growth in the twenty-first century.

Ralph Peterson
Chairman and CEO, CH2M Hill

Singapore is one of the twentieth century's most successful development stories. I am proud to say that the Asian Development Bank is working very successfully with Singapore in both the water and urban management sectors, with the aim of spreading best practices throughout developing Asia and the Pacific. Now is the time for inspired leadership to improve water governance, performance and knowledge management.

Haruhiko Kuroda
President, Asian Development Bank

The **Institute of Southeast Asian Studies (ISEAS)** was established as an autonomous organization in 1968. It is a regional centre dedicated to the study of socio-political, security and economic trends and developments in Southeast Asia and its wider geostrategic and economic environment. The Institute's research programmes are the Regional Economic Studies (RES, including ASEAN and APEC), Regional Strategic and Political Studies (RSPS), and Regional Social and Cultural Studies (RSCS).

ISEAS Publishing, an established academic press, has issued almost 2,000 books and journals. It is the largest scholarly publisher of research about Southeast Asia from within the region. ISEAS Publishing works with many other academic and trade publishers and distributors to disseminate important research and analyses from and about Southeast Asia to the rest of the world.

Clean, Green and Blue

Singapore's Journey

Towards Environmental and

Water Sustainability

TAN YONG SOON

WITH

LEE TUNG JEAN • KAREN TAN

INSTITUTE OF SOUTHEAST ASIAN STUDIES
Singapore

First published in Singapore in 2009 by
ISEAS Publishing
Institute of Southeast Asian Studies
30 Heng Mui Keng Terrace
Pasir Panjang
Singapore 119614
E-mail: publish@iseas.edu.sg
Website: http://bookshop.iseas.edu.sg

The responsibility for facts and opinions in this publication rests exclusively with the authors and their interpretations do not necessarily reflect the views or the policy of the Institute or its supporters.

ISEAS Library Cataloguing-in-Publication Data

Tan Yong Soon.
    Clean, green and blue : Singapore's journey towards environmental and water
    sustainability / Tan Yong Soon with Lee Tung Jean and Karen Tan.
    1.   Water supply—Singapore.
    2.   Water resources development—Singapore.
    3.   Environmental protection—Singapore.
    I.   Lee Tung Jean.
    II.   Tan, Karen.
    III. Title.
TD299 S6T23   2009

ISBN 978-981-230-860-3 (soft cover)
ISBN 978-981-230-861-0 (hard cover)
ISBN 978-981-230-862-7 (PDF)

The cover illustration shows Lower Peirce Reservoir, in Singapore.
Photo courtesy of PUB.

Typeset by Superskill Graphics Pte Ltd
Printed in Singapore by Utopia Press Pte Ltd

 This book is printed on recycled paper.

This book is dedicated to
Mr Lee Kuan Yew,
Prime Minister of Singapore (1959–1990),
whose vision and leadership have made Singapore
a clean, green and blue city.

CONTENTS

PART IV — APPLYING ECONOMICS AND
WORKING WITH THE COMMUNITY

PART V — LOOKING AHEAD TO FUTURE CHALLENGES

APPENDICES

PREFACE

The idea for this book originated from my first day in the Ministry of the Environment on 1 January 2004. It was a dream job. Singapore has had a wonderful record in environment protection. The staff of the Ministry, including its two Statutory Boards, the Public Utilities Board (PUB) and National Environment Agency (NEA), are passionate, competent, and professional. The job is also a constantly evolving one, as new environmental challenges such as climate change and sustainability issues continue to confront us. One never gets bored. And the work is rewarding, as we know that what we do will leave a lasting impact on future generations.

I wanted to produce a book to explain how Singapore came to choose the environmental path it did. Not just what we did, but how we made our calculations and reached our decisions. And through reflecting on the past, I wanted to synthesize the principles that would lead us forward into the future.

But like many good ideas, this book had a long gestation period. Over the years, I have become engrossed in my work. The Ministry was renamed the Ministry of the Environment and Water Resources (MEWR) in August 2004 to better reflect its work, which is not just about environment, but also water resource management. At the time when I was discussing names with my Minister, other names being considered were "Ministry of Resource Conservation" and "Ministry of Environment Sustainability" as these were longer-term challenges that we would have to grapple with. However, we eventually agreed to recommend the more straightforward name, as ideas such as resource conservation and environmental sustainability would not have resonated as well with the public until we could gain their understanding and buy-in on these issues.

As Permanent Secretary of the Ministry, I have included increasing the investment on environmental infrastructure as well as environmental ownership among my priorities because while it is critical to ensure that the necessary infrastructure is in place, it is only by actively involving people that we can hope to achieve the goal of resource conservation and environmental sustainability. We continue to embark on public education and consultation and open up our water and environmental resources for the community to enjoy as these steps can spur them onto taking better care of the environment. In addition, promoting and developing a vibrant environment and water industry is important, in order to grow the economy and increase employment, as well as facilitate the transfer of Singapore's expertise and solutions to other parts of the world. This is done through outsourcing environmental services to the private sector and public-private partnership (PPP) projects, helping companies to internationalize and grow, as well as developing technology and manpower for the sector and within the Ministry. In preparation for the impact of climate change, Singapore acceded to the Kyoto Protocol and put together a National Climate Change Strategy, among other initiatives, to anticipate the risks and opportunities posed by climate change, as well as to adopt suitable mitigation and adaptation measures.

The Ministry has received numerous delegations from countries all over the world, ranging from Australia to China to the Middle East, who came to Singapore to learn more about our environment and water management practices. Many wondered how Singapore could have achieved so much in such a short span of time. A few understood immediately when I told them that the simple and straight answer was "Mr Lee Kuan Yew". But I realized that several others would have benefited from a more detailed explanation. I was thus reminded of the book and started work on it at the end of 2007. I assembled a team of officers to carry out extensive research in order to enable us to recount the work of the Ministry, as well as our partner and predecessor agencies in delivering the environment all of us enjoy today.

I hope this book will be read by Singaporeans who wish to play a role in improving the living environment, whether they are working in the government or the environment and water industry, or are just concerned members of the public. The latter group is especially important because the environment is everyone's business, and is too important to be left to only the professionals and policy-makers. It will be an added bonus if professionals in other cities also find the book useful to their work. Since more than half of the world's population live in cities and all of us live on the same earth, each person taking action to improve his local environment will collectively result in significant improvements for the global environment.

Tan Yong Soon
September 2008

ACKNOWLEDGEMENTS

This book is the work of a team from MEWR, NEA, and PUB, led by myself, and ably managed by Karen Tan. It has benefitted from tight editing by Lee Tung Jean. It is made possible only because of the hard work and achievements of past officers in the Singapore Ministry of the Environment and PUB (since 1972 and 1963 respectively), and the continuation of the good work by existing officers in MEWR, NEA, and PUB.

I would like to express my appreciation to the following Ministers and past Permanent Secretaries, Ministers Mah Bow Tan, Teo Chee Hean, Lim Swee Say, and Dr Yaacob Ibrahim, as well as Permanent Secretaries Lee Ek Tieng, Tan Guong Ching, and Tan Gee Paw, who despite their many commitments and busy schedules, generously shared their time and insights and provided their comments which have helped to improve the book.

My appreciation also goes to an extraordinary team of dedicated officers who spent many hours and days conducting research and writing the draft. The following officers helped in the research and writing, or acted as key resource persons:

Chapter 2: Achieving Clean Air Quality — Ang Jian Zhong, Policy Executive, Clean Air, MEWR; Chen Jia'en, Policy Executive, Climate Change Office, MEWR; Chua Soon Guan, Director, Strategic Policy Division, MEWR; Foong Chee Leong, Director-General Meteorological

Services, NEA; Joseph Hui, Director-General Environmental Protection, NEA; Tan Chun Kiat, Assistant Director, Clean Air, MEWR; Tan Quee Hong, Director, Pollution Control Department, NEA; Karen Tan, Deputy Director, Strategic Policy Division, MEWR.

Chapter 3: Cleaning the Land and Rivers — Chan Wai San, Director, Hawkers Department, NEA; Chua Soon Guan, Director, Strategic Policy Division, MEWR; Foong Chee Leong, Director-General Meteorological Services, NEA; Khoo Seow Poh, Director-General Public Health, NEA; Lai Kim Lian, Head, Planning and Development, Hawkers Department, NEA; Andrew Low, Senior Assistant Director, Clean Land, MEWR; Ng Lee Ching, Head, Environmental Health Institute, NEA; Tan Han Kiat, Assistant Director, Public Health, MEWR; S. Satish Appoo, Director, Environmental Health Department, NEA.

Chapter 4: Integrated Solid Waste Management — Chan Chee Wing, Assistant Director, Clean Land, MEWR; Chua Soon Guan, Director, Strategic Policy Division, MEWR; Eng Tiang Sing, Director, International Relations Division, MEWR; Goh Hong Boon, Assistant Director, Clean Land, MEWR; Joseph Hui, Director-General Environmental Protection, NEA; Low Fong Hon, Director, Waste Management Department, NEA; Ong Seng Eng, Director, Resource Conservation Department, NEA; Ong Soo San, Chief Engineer, Waste Management Department, NEA; Mohd Fadil Bin Supa'at, Senior Manager, IP Industry Regulatory Unit, Waste Management Department, NEA.

Chapters 5 and 6: Ensuring Water Sustainability: The Supply Side & Water Demand Management — Chan Yoon Kum, Assistant Chief Executive, PUB; Chong Hou Chun, Director, Water Supply (Network) Department, PUB; Stanley Fong, Deputy Director, Water Studies Division, MEWR; Louis Goh, Assistant Director, Water Studies Division, MEWR; Koh Boon Aik, Director, Water Supply (Plants) Department, PUB; Lee Tung Jean, Director, Water Studies

Division, MEWR; Harry Seah, Director, Technology and Water Quality Office, PUB; Tan Yok Gin, Director, Policy and Planning Department, PUB; Melanie Tan, Engineer, Policy and Planning Department, PUB.

Chapter 7: Managing Used Water — Ridzuan Bin Ismail, Deputy Director, Water Studies Division, MEWR; Lin Jing, Policy Executive, Water Studies Division, MEWR; Lee Tung Jean, Director, Water Studies Division, MEWR; Harry Seah, Director, Technology and Water Quality Office, PUB; Tan Thai Pin, Director, Water Reclamation (Network) Department, PUB; Tan Yok Gin, Director, Policy and Planning Department, PUB; Wah Yuen Long, Director, Water Reclamation (Plants) Department, PUB.

Chapter 8: From Flood Prevention and Flood Management to ABC Waters — Stanley Fong, Deputy Director, Water Studies Division, MEWR; Ruth Khan, Engineer, Catchment and Waterways Department, PUB; Lee Tung Jean, Director, Water Studies Division, MEWR; Lydia Loh, Executive, Environment and Water Industry Development Council, MEWR; Moh Wung Hee, Director, Best Sourcing Department, PUB; Tan Nguan Sen, Director, Catchment and Waterways Department, PUB; Jeremy Tay, Policy Executive, Water Studies Division, MEWR; Evelyn Tee, Policy Executive, Water Studies Division, MEWR; Yap Kheng Guan, Director, 3P Network Department, PUB.

Chapter 9: Applying Economic Principles to Environmental Policy — Chan Chee Wing, Assistant Director, Clean Land, MEWR; Benedict Chia, Senior Assistant Director, Strategic Issues, MEWR; Chua Soon Guan, Director, Strategic Policy Division, MEWR; Ridzuan Bin Ismail, Deputy Director, Water Studies Division, MEWR; Lee Tung Jean, Director, Water Studies Division, MEWR; Lin Jing, Policy Executive, Water Studies Division, MEWR; Philip Ong, Director, Climate Change Office, MEWR.

Chapter 10: Working with People and the Community — Edrick Chua, Assistant Director, 3P Network Division, MEWR; Dalson Chung, Director, 3P Network Division, MEWR; Derek Ho, Head, North West Regional Office, NEA; Paula Kesavan, Senior Assistant Director, 3P Partnership Department, NEA; Angela Koh, Senior Assistant Director, 3P Network Division, MEWR; Lau Yew Hoong, Deputy Director, Community Relations, 3P Network Department, PUB; Ng Meng Hiong, Deputy Director, 3P Partnership Department, NEA; Tan Wee Hock, Director, 3P Network Division, NEA; Yap Kheng Guan, Director, 3P Network Department, PUB.

Chapter 11: Linking with the Global Community — Chua Yew Peng, Director, Policy and Planning Division, NEA; Chong Teng Sheng, Assistant Director, International Relations Division, MEWR; Eng Tiang Sing, Director, International Relations Division, MEWR; Foong Chee Leong, Director-General Meteorological Services, NEA; Khoo Seow Poh, Director-General Public Health, NEA; Koh Joon Hong, Senior Assistant Director, International Relations Division, MEWR; Ng Han Tong, Director, Industry Development, PUB; Terence Siew, Director, International Affairs Unit, MEWR.

I would like to thank Ong Ho Sim, former CEO PUB; Loh Ah Tuan former DCEO and Director-General Environmental Protection, NEA; Daniel Wang, former Director-General Public Health, NEA; Goh Chin Tong, former Director, Hawkers Department, NEA; and Koh Hee Song, former Head, Engineering Services Division, NEA, who despite having retired, made time to meet with me and the team to recount their experiences and other perspectives from their many years in the environmental field.

The book has also benefited from the insightful comments of Tommy Koh, Chair of the Asia Pacific Water Forum Governing Council and UNEP Champion of the Earth; Lord Ronald Oxburgh, Chairman of the House of Lords Select Committee on Science and Technology (2000–2004); Asit K. Biswas, President, Third World

Centre for Water Management, Mexico; Chew Tai Soo, Ambassador-At-Large; Koh-Lim Wen Gin, Chief Planner, URA; Leong Chee Chiew, Commissioner of Parks & Recreation; Chua Mui Hoong, Senior Writer, *Straits Times*; Ong Choon Nam, Professor, Department of Community, Occupational and Family Medicine and Director, Life Sciences Institute, NUS; Ng Wun Jern, Professor and Executive Director, Nanyang Environment and Water Research Institute, NTU; and Malone-Lee Lai Choo, Senior Lecturer and Programme Director, MSc (Environmental Management), NUS.

I would also like to thank the following from MEWR, NEA, and PUB who assisted the team in the production of this book: Khoo Teng Chye, Chief Executive, PUB; Lee Yuen Hee, Chief Executive Officer, NEA; Rosa Daniel, Deputy Secretary, MEWR; Ong Eng Kian, Director, Singapore Environment Institute, NEA; Eng Wee Hua, Deputy Director, Water Reclamation (Plants) Department, PUB; Fong Peng Keong, Deputy Director, Regional Cooperation Department, International Relations Division, MEWR; Foo Chee Sai, Deputy Director, NEWater Business Development, Water Supply (Network) Department, PUB; Ho Cheng Hoon, Deputy Director, Policy and Planning Division, NEA; Hazri Hassan, Deputy Director, International Cooperation Department, International Relations Division, MEWR; Lim Chee Leong, Executive Engineer, Water Supply (Network) Department, PUB; Lim Meng Check, Deputy Director, Planning, Modelling and Hydrology Division, Catchment and Waterways Department, PUB; Lim See Gan, Deputy Director, Project Management, Best Sourcing Department, PUB; Lye Wing Kai, Manager, North East Regional Office, NEA; Martin Nathan, Head, North East Regional Office, NEA; Ng Cheng Tong, Senior Manager, North East Regional Office, NEA; Ngaim Hai Guan, Deputy Director, Strategic Planning, Policy and Planning Department, PUB; Ong Hian Hai, Deputy Director, Project Management, Best Sourcing Department, PUB; Ong Puay Son, Engineer, Chemical Control, Pollution Control Department, NEA; Sam Ow, Assistant Director, Planning, Modelling and Hydrology

Division, Catchment and Waterways Department, PUB; Indrani C. Rajaram, Chief Scientific Officer, Environmental Monitoring and Assessment Unit, Pollution Control Department, NEA; Ramahad Singh, Deputy Director, Water Demand Management and Inspectorate, Water Supply (Network) Department, PUB; Arasu Sivaraman, Assistant Director, Strategic Planning, Policy and Planning Department, PUB; Soh Suat Hoon, Senior Assistant Director, International Relations Department, Policy and Planning Division, NEA; Francis Tan, Assistant Director, 3P Network Division, MEWR; Tan Eng Keong, Assistant Director, Manpower, Environment and Water Industry Development Council, MEWR; Teo Eng Dih, Senior Assistant Director, Climate Change Office, MEWR; Wong Nung Sim, Deputy Director, Water Reclamation (Network) Department, PUB; Wong Wai Cheng, Senior Manager, Water Demand Management and Inspectorate, Water Supply (Network) Department, PUB; William Yeo, Assistant Director, Central Watershed Division, Catchment and Waterways Department, PUB; Young Joo Chye, Deputy Director, DTSS Project, Best Sourcing Department, PUB; Yuen Sai Kuan, Deputy Director, Finance and Admin, Environment and Water Industry Development Council, MEWR.

Finally, I would like to thank Triena Ong, Head of the Publications Unit at the Institute of Southeast Asian Studies and her colleagues for their professionalism in putting this book together.

INTRODUCTION

The high priority that Singapore has placed on the environment since the early days has endowed it with reliable environmental systems and practices. The Singapore Government spent a vast amount of money on the engineering and provision of environmental infrastructure and services even at a time when the country was poor and had to attend to pressing economic, social, and security development programmes.

Achieving environmental and water sustainability is a strategic goal. As Prime Minister of newly-independent Singapore, one of the first things Lee Kuan Yew did was to give water top priority — setting up a unit in his office to coordinate this at the whole-of-government level. At a dialogue session with delegates of the inaugural Singapore International Water Week in June 2008, he recalled that "This (water) dominated every other policy. Every other policy had to bend at the knees for water survival."

Attaining a high environmental standard is never a waste of time, energy, or resources. In planning the sewerage system for instance, the government decided to put in place a comprehensive sewage network with proper used water treatment facilities, even though many countries had been discharging their used water without treating it. Subsequently, as Singapore had well-equipped used water treatment plants and island-wide sewer coverage, it was able to harness the used water for the production of NEWater through the reclamation of treated used water. Hence, having taken care of the environment in the early days (at a considerable cost even when it did not seem necessary at the time) has proved rewarding for Singapore decades later.

Singapore's approach to better environment management may be summed up by the 5Es of Engineering, Economics, Education, Enforcement, and Engagement. Engineering provides the foundation. Singapore invested heavily on environmental infrastructure such as sanitation and flood alleviation schemes, water production capacity, and incineration plants, as well as on technology improvements and the necessary manpower development. Economics is applied to ensure services are produced efficiently and scarce environmental resources are priced right. It would be tempting to subsidize environmental services, but that would lead to over-consumption and compound the problem for the future as it would be difficult, if not impossible, to wean people off the subsidies after that. Education is important to help people change their behaviour to look after the common good, but education must be complemented by enforcement as there must be consequences to irresponsible behaviour. Finally, it would be costly and unsustainable if the government was to be relied upon to do everything to protect the environment. There must be engagement. People can and must want to take ownership of the environment.

While such sound environmental practices have served Singapore well, it would not suffice to merely maintain the status quo. Unless there is strong will and commitment to safeguarding and enhancing the environment, it would be increasingly difficult to tackle the challenges ahead.

In the early post-independence period, Singapore faced severe environmental problems that threatened its survival, ranging from the spread of diseases to the prospect of not having sufficient water for its people. These national crises served to galvanize the people and lent strong support to the government's call for action. However, as environmental standards have improved and people now enjoy a high quality of life, will Singaporeans become less conscious of the need for a good environment, and let complacency creep in?

There is a need for Singapore to be responsive to the growing affluence of society and the effect this will have on the environment: Do rising income levels point towards a society which, having satisfied its more basic needs, will be increasingly conscious of the importance of the environment and the shared responsibility of safeguarding it? Or do rising income levels paint a bleaker picture — one where material goods become more desirable? As the world becomes more globalized and markets more competitive, certain trade-offs may become harder to make. In such a situation, the environment could be at a distinct disadvantage, particularly when the benefits that accrue to those who care for the environment are often non-monetary, or cannot be realized immediately.

Cognizant of the scale of the challenges ahead, the government has formed a Ministerial Committee to review Singapore's strategies for sustainable development. For Singapore, sustainable development means achieving growth without sacrificing the quality of our living environment. Because of rising resource prices, a key priority area will be studying ways to improve overall resource efficiency — whether in energy and water, or in minimizing waste — and increasing recycling, since this not only optimizes the use of scarce resources, but will also boost overall economic competitiveness.

As in the past forty years, keeping pollution in check will continue to be important since ensuring clean air, clean water, and clean land is critical to safeguarding public health in Singapore. Given further population and industrial growth within Singapore's limited land area, the government will have to look at more innovative ways of managing the pollution load, without imposing unreasonable costs on businesses and the economy. Finally, maintaining Singapore's clean and green living environment, where public spaces are pristine, and green spaces and waterways are lifestyle attractions for all to enjoy, will allow Singapore to be a vibrant and liveable city. A city where residents will enjoy quality of life alongside vibrant economic growth for generations to come.

This book traces how Singapore has arrived at the good environment it enjoys today. However, rather than just recording chronologically the key milestones in its environmental history, the book attempts to highlight the policy considerations, constraints and trade-offs in each area of the environment, explain how decisions were made, and discern the key learning points.

Part I reflects on Singapore's environmental journey, beginning from the early days of post-independence Singapore, and discusses the fundamental principles and success factors that have guided environmental policy-making in Singapore from the onset:

- Clear Vision
- Long-term Planning
- Constant Innovation
- Practical and Effective Approach

Part II considers how Singapore has controlled and managed air, land, and water pollution, and achieved a clean environment.

Chapter 2 describes the challenges to air quality Singapore faced in its early days of industrialization and explains how Singapore's strategies of air quality monitoring and long-term integrated urban and industrial planning and development control have enabled the government to pre-empt pollution and put in place preventive air pollution control measures. The chapter also touches on how practical legislation and enforcement measures have helped the government to ensure that air quality standards are maintained in the long run.

Chapter 3 details Singapore's experience in cleaning up the land and rivers, explaining the motivations behind this clean-up programme — to improve the standard of living for its people — and how cleanliness was elevated to a national and nationwide priority as the government understood that success could not be achieved without the understanding and participation of all residents. The chapter also explains how achieving clean land and rivers requires a long-term perspective and long-term programmes based on practical solutions which are implemented effectively.

Chapter 4 explains how Singapore has put in place an integrated solid waste management system — from waste collection and disposal to incineration and landfill — that also encourages recycling and waste minimization. It highlights the importance of both leveraging on technology and investing in environmental infrastructure, ranging from mechanized refuse collection vehicles to incineration plants and an offshore landfill, as well as addressing the behavioural people-related aspects through programmes to increase recycling and waste minimization. The chapter also describes Singapore's experience in opening up its waste collection and disposal sector to private-sector participation, and the lessons learnt from that process.

Part III encapsulates Singapore's water story, and how Singapore has managed to close the water loop, ensuring long-term water sustainability.

Chapter 5 traces the development of Singapore's sources of water supply — the Four National Taps of water from local catchments, imported water, NEWater, and desalinated water. It explains how integrated planning has allowed land-scarce Singapore to set aside sufficient land for water catchments, and how the upfront implementation of pollution control measures allows the city state to tap on unprotected and urbanized catchments. The chapter also describes how Singapore has managed to turn vulnerability, in terms of lack of local water sources, into a strategic advantage, through successfully developing NEWater technology, which effectively doubles water sources through recycling, and piloting desalination.

Chapter 6 describes how long-term sustainability in water cannot be achieved by boosting water supply alone. Complementary to this is the management of water demand, which has been a key thrust of Singapore's water management policy from its early days. The chapter explains the government's holistic approach to managing water demand — both domestic and non-domestic water demand — which ranges from national-level campaigns and the provision of water efficiency information to encourage voluntary efforts to conserve water, to pricing water at the correct level, to imposing mandatory performance standards. It also touches on the government's efforts to improve water supply quality and reliability through improving service reliability and keeping unaccounted-for-water low.

Chapter 7 considers Singapore's efforts to provide effective modern sanitation and used water management systems for its population as it regards this as being critical not only to improving the standard of living, but also to supporting further economic growth and industrialization. The chapter describes how the country has progressed from the early days of the night soil collection system to the present-day water reclamation plants and integration of used water management under the Deep Tunnel Sewerage System (DTSS), achievements which were only possible with long-term planning, coupled with technological innovation and the willingness to invest up front in capital-intensive infrastructure.

Chapter 8 details Singapore's strategies to manage and prevent flooding, which have been successful due to the long-term approach adopted. For instance, anticipating drainage challenges early and making land-use provisions to cater for possible solutions up front allows the government greater flexibility in implementing these solutions subsequently. The chapter also reflects on how the government is moving beyond just flood control and flood management to transforming utilitarian reservoirs and waterways into Active, Beautiful and Clean Waters. This is a bold and long-term programme through which the government hopes to encourage greater public ownership and responsibility for keeping the waterways clean by bringing people closer to the water.

Part IV discusses some of the cross-cutting strategies and approaches that have been applied to Singapore's environmental and water policies.

Chapter 9 highlights the role economics plays in guiding environmental policies and legislation in areas such as decision making, setting prices, introducing market competition, and dealing with market failures. While we value the environment, government decisions must be made on the basis of stringent analysis as the government has to prioritize competing demands in the face of limited resources. The full environmental cost of a certain initiative should, therefore, be factored into the decision-making process in order to arrive at the correct decision. In practice, this is seldom straightforward, due to the inherent complexity in environmental issues, such as quantifying intangibles and externalities. Through the use of various case studies and examples, the chapter discusses how economics has been applied in some of Singapore's environmental policies and decisions.

Chapter 10 discusses Singapore's experience in engaging the public to achieve shared environmental outcomes. It traces the evolution in Singapore's approach over the past decades in response to changes in the national context as well as in social attitudes and demographic characteristics, which ranges from targeting individuals to communities. The chapter also introduces the concept of 3P or Public, Private, People sector partnerships, in which the focus is not just on building public awareness of environmental issues, but engaging and empowering the public to act to address these challenges.

Chapter 11 covers the external angle, explaining the considerations underpinning Singapore's interactions with the international community on the environmental front. It moves from the early days, when Singapore benefited greatly from the technology and expertise of more developed countries, to the present day when Singapore is fortunate to be in a position where it is able to share its expertise with others and assist in bringing foreign technology into the region. The chapter also touches on Singapore's efforts to play its part in contributing to collective efforts to respond to global challenges such as sustainable development and climate changes.

Finally, Part V considers upcoming environmental challenges which are confronting not just Singapore, but, in fact, the entire global community, and the steps which the Singapore Government is taking today to prepare itself to deal with them.

Even as this book is being written, there are new chapters in Singapore's environment story that are unfolding. Emerging challenges such as climate change and increasing scarcity of resources are forcing the world to pay more heed to the environment. Environmental problems are also becoming increasingly regional and global, requiring strong international cooperation and long-term vision. Singapore itself must learn the lessons from its past, in forging a better world for all of us.

PART **I**

DRAWING LESSONS FROM SINGAPORE'S ENVIRONMENTAL JOURNEY

I

REFLECTIONS ON SINGAPORE'S ENVIRONMENTAL JOURNEY

We have built, we have progressed. But no other hallmark of success will be more distinctive than that of achieving our position as the cleanest and greenest city in South Asia. For, only a people with high social and educational standards can maintain a clean and green city. It requires organisation to keep the community cleaned and trimmed particularly when the population has a density of 8,500 persons per square mile. And it requires a people conscious of their responsibilities, not just to their own families, but also to their neighbours and all others in the community who will be affected by their thoughtless anti-social behavior. Only a people proud of their community performance, feeling for the well-being of their fellow citizens, can keep up high personal and public standards of hygiene.

> Prime Minister Lee Kuan Yew at the launch of the
> inaugural Keep Singapore Clean campaign in 1968

Residents in Singapore breathe in clean air, drink clean water direct from the tap, live on clean land, and enjoy good public hygiene. However, Singapore is not a green utopia with zero carbon emissions, large-scale renewable energy sources, or cutting edge zero-energy buildings. What it does have is a practical, cost-effective, and efficient approach towards sustaining its environment, which contributes to the high quality of life in Singapore.

In a world where rapid industrialization and urbanization have led to tremendous pressures on environment and water resources, visitors to Singapore often ask: how is it possible that a small city state sitting on barely 700 sq. kilometre of land, housing close to 5 million people, and bustling with a world class airport, the world's busiest port and many other industries, can remain clean, green, and environmentally sustainable? They want to understand how Singapore has achieved this and hear about Singapore's experience.

CLEAR VISION

The answer is that it starts with a clear vision from the very top that a clean and good quality living environment is important, and a strong commitment to implement that vision. Poverty, economic uncertainty, and a living environment defined by night soil buckets, polluted rivers, water rationing, unhygienic street hawkers, and smoke-emitting/effluent-discharging industries may seem like a distant memory today, but they were a reality faced by many Singaporeans as late as the 1960s and 1970s. The transformation of Singapore from a poor, developing nation to a vibrant and prosperous city state has taken place over a relatively short period of three to four decades.

Singapore is a small country with no natural resources. In the 1960s, it had a small, but rapidly growing population of 1.6 million. The economy was highly dependent on entrepôt trade and the provision of services to British military bases in Singapore. The country had only a small manufacturing base, with little industrial know-how and domestic capital. When Singapore gained independence in 1965, its per capita gross domestic product was barely US$1,525 (S$4,700). As a fledgling nation, it faced problems such as ensuring national security and defence, mass unemployment at rates of 10 to 12 per cent, housing shortages, and a low standard of living. It also had to grapple with the lack of resources and land. This was further compounded by the challenges posed by the planned withdrawal of the British troops from the late 1960s.[1]

To survive, economic development was paramount as it held the key to providing resources to improve Singapore and better the lives of the people. Singapore invested heavily to promote economic growth, embarking on an aggressive strategy of export-oriented industrialization and attracting foreign investment, backed by government incentives and tax holidays. Education was also viewed as a critical factor, with many schools built in the early post-independence years. Through these efforts, Singapore's per capita gross domestic product in 2005 reached nearly US$27,000 (S$45,000).

However, what is perhaps even more noteworthy is that despite its unrelenting industrialization, breakneck growth, and rapid urbanization over its relatively short forty-year history, Singapore has managed to turn itself into a clean and green city with a high-quality living environment. (Refer to Appendix I: Key Statistics of Singapore for the economic, social, and quality of living indicators.)

Building Up the Environmental Infrastructure

The government recognized the importance of a good environment, and hence the need to balance economic development with a good environment, very early in Singapore's development. It has always believed that a clean and green environment is necessary to provide a good quality of life, not just for the present generation, but for generations to come. The government also realized that a clean and green environment helps to attract investments and retain talents, supporting further growth. A poor environment and a lack of water will cause health and other serious problems. If the environment and water resources are managed well, quality of life and even economic competitiveness will be greatly enhanced.

The government, therefore, invested in critical environmental infrastructure from the early days, despite competing demands for funding. S$2 billion was spent on drainage development projects over the past thirty years; S$1.8 billion on sewerage and used water treatment infrastructure in the 1970s and 1980s, and another S$3.65 billion on the construction of the Deep Tunnel Sewerage System (DTSS); over S$300 million on cleaning up the Singapore River from 1977 to 1987; S$270 million on constructing the Marina Barrage; S$100 million on Singapore's first incineration plant in 1973, a further S$1.6 billion on its other incineration plants, and S$600 million on an offshore landfill island. The heavy investment in the environment was all the more visionary as the new nation did not have enough money, especially in the early years. The benefits were long term while the costs were immediate, but Singapore was prepared to borrow from the World Bank to develop its environmental infrastructure, where necessary. For Singapore, it was never a case of pursuing growth at all costs and cleaning up afterwards. Investing in the environment continues to be of high priority today, to upgrade Singapore's environmental infrastructure and improve its efficiency.

Communicating the Vision

The Singapore Government has always made clear to the public the national priority placed on the environment so that its vision for the environment can be shared and supported by everyone. The first yearly "Keep Singapore Clean" campaign was launched in October 1968, by then Prime Minister Lee Kuan Yew to educate all Singaporeans on the importance of keeping shared public spaces clean. This annual campaign took on an additional dimension in 1971 with the launch of Tree Planting Day. Far from being just one day in a year, Tree Planting Day symbolized the government's vision for Singapore to be transformed into a tropical garden city — both clean and green — and became a tradition spanning the next twenty years. In 1990, the first Clean and Green Week was launched, incorporating both the Keep Singapore Clean campaign and tree-planting activities. In addition, Clean and Green

Week also aimed to increase community awareness of global environmental concerns and encourage community participation in caring for the environment. In 2007, Clean and Green Week was rebranded Clean and Green Singapore, in order to send a clear message that environmentally-friendly lifestyles and habits should be practised all year round. Each successive prime minister, from Lee Kuan Yew to Goh Chok Tong to Lee Hsien Loong, has strongly signalled the importance attached to keeping Singapore clean by personally launching the campaign nearly every year for the past forty years. On the few occasions when the prime minister could not do this, it was the deputy prime minister who officiated at the event.

Building Capabilities

The importance that Singapore has long placed on the environment is underscored by the fact that the Anti-Pollution Unit (APU) formed in 1970 to combat air pollution was placed under the Prime Minister's Office (PMO) at the outset. Not long afterwards, in September 1972, the Ministry of the Environment (ENV) was established. This was immediately after the United Nations Conference on the Human Environment in Stockholm in June 1972. The Stockholm Conference was the first international forum aimed at addressing global environmental challenges, and Singapore was one of the first countries to form a Ministry dedicated to creating and sustaining a good environment for its people.

Prior to the formation of ENV, there were, of course, other organizations responsible for public health and environment-related services in Singapore. Two local authorities, the Rural Board and the City Council, together with the Government Health Department provided both personal and environmental health services in the 1950s. These included water supply, sanitation and sewage disposal, cleansing services, as well as vector and disease control and food hygiene. Drainage was overseen by the Public Works Department (PWD).

Local government was abolished when Singapore gained self-government in 1959. Administrative changes were made to integrate the City Council and the Rural Board with the various ministries. The PWD came under the new Ministry of National Development (MND). The City Engineers Department from the City Council was merged with the PWD. The City Health Department and the Rural Health Department were integrated into the Ministry of Health (MOH).[2]

When the City Council was dissolved, the Public Utilities Board (PUB) was set up as a Statutory Board[3] under the Ministry of Trade and Industry (MTI) on 1 May 1963 to succeed the City Council in coordinating the supply of electricity, piped gas, and water for Singapore. Specifically in relation to water, the PUB was handed the mission of ensuring that Singapore's industrial and economic development and its population's well-being would be sustained by the provision of an adequate and dependable supply of water. It was entrusted with improving and extending the existing water distribution systems, planning and implementing new water schemes to meet projected water needs, and spearheading public campaigns to conserve water.[4] As a result of these changes, the MOH was in charge of public health services, except for sewerage and drainage, which were carried out by the MND. PUB was responsible for water supply.

When ENV was formed in 1972, the departments under the MOH and MND which dealt with pollution control, sewerage, drainage, and environmental health, were absorbed into the new Ministry. The APU was also subsequently transferred from the PMO to the Ministry in 1983. In 2001, recognizing that Singapore's water catchment and supply systems, drainage systems, water reclamation plants, and sewerage systems are part of a comprehensive water cycle, the PUB was reconstituted to become Singapore's national water authority, overseeing the entire water loop. The sewerage and drainage departments from the Ministry were transferred to PUB. PUB itself was transferred from the MTI to the Environment Ministry. The regulation of the electricity and gas industries, formerly undertaken by the PUB, was transferred to a new Statutory Board, the Energy Market Authority (EMA), under MTI.

In 2002, a new Statutory Board, the National Environment Agency (NEA) was formed under the Environment Ministry through integrating the Environmental Public Health and Environmental Policy and Management Divisions of the Ministry with the Meteorological Services Department (MSD), formerly under the Ministry of Transport (MOT). The aim was to create a leaner, more policy-focused Ministry and a more streamlined, operations-focused Statutory Board. The division of responsibility between policy formulation and operational implementation would allow the Ministry to focus on setting strategic policy directions and addressing key policy concerns. NEA on the other hand would direct its efforts towards the effective implementation of policies.

Environment and water as well as public health issues in Singapore today are, therefore, comprehensively overseen by the Ministry of the Environment (renamed in 2004 as the Ministry of the Environment and Water Resources) and its two Statutory Boards, NEA and PUB.

LONG-TERM PLANNING

To turn its vision for the environment into reality, Singapore relies on long-term and integrated planning. This is critical since the environment is a long-term issue. Moreover, while the effects of poor planning may not be immediately observable, they can have longer term repercussions. Policies and measures to protect and improve the environment may oft-times result in short-term costs. Without a clear vision and the adoption of a long-term perspective, it would be difficult for any city to take actions which incur short-term costs in order to achieve long-term environmental gain. For example, requiring industries to satisfy good air emission standards can increase the cost of doing business and may thus turn away some investments, with the resultant loss of jobs. Restricting vehicular usage and setting high emission standards may be unpopular, especially when coupled with an increasingly affluent population's desire to own cars. Providing proper sanitation and sufficient water incurs heavy infrastructural expenditure. Such environmental policies and developments will often have pay-offs only decades later.

That said, having borne the short-term costs in support of its vision, Singapore is enjoying the benefits of many of its past policies and actions today. For instance, the Marina Barrage, which was completed in 2008 to form a reservoir in the heart of the city, is the outcome of cleaning up the Singapore River, which started way back in 1977. Ranked as the most liveable city in Asia[5] and Asia's most competitive economy,[6] Singapore is an example of a bustling city that can be both environmentally "liveable" and economically vibrant.

Integrated Planning and Development Control Process

The formation of the Environment Ministry did not mean that the Ministry and its Statutory Boards operated in isolation to meet and safeguard their own interests. On the contrary, an integrated approach has been adopted in formulating and implementing environmental policies. This is a structured framework in which all government agencies work together to identify a clear vision and shared outcomes, and coordinate the efforts required by agencies to achieve these goals. Such an approach also allows trade-offs to be objectively discussed and deliberated on, with decisions made in light of overall national interest.

Perhaps the best illustration is Singapore's integrated planning and development control process. With limited land, land-use planning is of utmost importance in ensuring that the best possible use is made of Singapore's land without compromising its development needs.

At the macro level, Singapore's development is guided by the Concept Plan, which was introduced in 1971 and updated every ten years. Through the Concept Plan process spearheaded by the MND and the Urban Redevelopment Authority (URA), representatives from all the relevant government agencies come together to map out the land-use vision for Singapore over the next forty to fifty years. It ensures that land resources are used well so that quality of life improves even as Singapore continues to develop and its population to grow. One level down, the Master Plan translates the broad, long-term strategies of the Concept Plan into detailed plans, even to the extent of specifying the permissible land use and density for each parcel of land. It guides Singapore's development in the medium term, over a period spanning ten to fifteen years, and is reviewed every five years. Similar to the Concept Plan, the Master Plan is a collaborative effort, taking inputs from a whole gamut of ministries, which together with their Statutory Boards, oversee the various key areas, from national development, to the environment, to trade and industry, and to defence.

Land adequacy aside, proper land-use planning also plays a major role in protecting the environment. First, land is set aside for critical environmental infrastructure such as sewerage as well as waste disposal and incineration facilities. Projections of future land requirements for such infrastructure are also factored into the Concept Plan so that adequate land is safeguarded for these needs. Selected areas that are ecologically rich are also safeguarded.

Second, with limited land space, it is not possible to provide a large buffer between incompatible developments such as industrial centres and residential areas. Environmental controls are, therefore, factored into land-use planning to ensure that developments are properly sited. Thus, major pollutive land-users are grouped together and located as far away as possible from residential areas and population centres. Through the process of development control and planning approval, a project has to satisfy the planners and technical agencies of its limited environmental impact and compatibility with the surrounding land use. Where necessary, environmental pollution control requirements have to be incorporated into the design of the development, particularly with regard to environmental health, drainage, sewerage, and pollution control. Highly pollutive industries and major developments that are likely to be detrimental to the environment are required to carry out pollution control studies covering all possible adverse environmental impacts, as well as the measures recommended to eliminate or mitigate these impacts.

These practices have their roots from the days of the APU that was established by then Prime Minister Lee Kuan Yew who was very concerned about the impact of industrialization on Singapore's environment. Soon after its inception in 1970, one of the top priorities of APU was to study how industries contributed to air pollution. One industry of particular concern to APU was petrochemicals as it involved many complex processes, each of which had the potential to emit smoke and various gases that could cause severe air pollution if not contained or burnt off properly. Hence APU, with advice from overseas consultants, proposed measures to control pollution from such factories.

One example was the flare system.[7] Elevated flares (where the waste gas is combusted at the tip of a tall stack) are most commonly used in refineries and chemical plants. However, they can give rise to glaring flames at the stack tip or prolonged emissions of dark smoke and soot if the combustion at the flare is incomplete. Hence, in addition to the elevated flares, APU required petrochemical factories to install a ground flare system. This consists of a supplementary set of enclosed furnaces at ground level, allowing for more complete combustion and reducing the need for excess gases to be flared at the stack. However, putting such a measure in place could be very costly. So it was not surprising that APU often met with resistance from the Economic Development Board (EDB), which was responsible for attracting multinational corporations (MNC) to invest in Singapore.

Lee Ek Tieng, the first head of APU (and subsequently Permanent Secretary (ENV) and Head of Civil Service), recalled an early incident involving a big MNC which was planning to build a petrochemical facility here. It was a major investment, very important to Singapore's economic development. The MNC was not prepared to incur the expenditure for a ground furnace (assessed at that time to cost S$5 million), and hence garnered EDB's support to appeal against APU's decision. Nevertheless, APU reported directly to the Prime Minister and he understood that putting in place such preventive measures was better than cleaning up after industries retroactively. Hence, the appeal was rejected and the company had to install the ground furnace. This set the stage for subsequent pollution control measures that the APU introduced, so that all industries had to obtain APU's approval first before they could get the go-ahead to build their factories. The same applies today — a project will only be given the green light to proceed if environmental authorities have been satisfied that its location would not affect the environment adversely, its emissions are within the required standards, and wastes generated are safely managed and properly disposed.

Third, land-use planning also factors in the need to protect Singapore's water catchments. For instance, the Water Catchment Policy was put in place in 1983 to control developments within the unprotected catchment areas.[8] The overall urbanization cap[9] was set at 34.1 per cent and a population density limit of 198 dwelling units per hectare was imposed on anticipated developments up to 2005. Less intensive development, coupled with stringent pollution control measures, enabled Singapore to ensure the good quality of water collected even from these unprotected water catchments. Subsequently, PUB could adopt advanced water treatment technology to upgrade treatment plants to cater for water from increasingly urbanized and unprotected areas. Hence, in 1999, the urbanization cap and population density limit were lifted, subject to the continuation of stringent water pollution control measures.

The 1983 Water Catchment Policy demonstrates how planners and engineers worked alongside one another to review and improve a policy as technology advanced and pollution management practices evolved. Adopting an integrated approach thus ensures that each agency understands the considerations and constraints of its partner agencies, and where possible, reviews and tweaks its own plans to the net gain of Singapore.

Singapore River Clean-up

This integrated and inter-agency approach spans not just planning, but also extends to the efficient and effective execution of environmental policies and plans. Perhaps the most notable example of inter-agency cooperation is the Singapore River clean-up which took place from 1977 to 1987. The Singapore River is located in the heart of the city. It was here that Stamford Raffles landed in 1819 and established a British trading settlement. Since the early days, the river has been the lifeblood and centre of commercial activities of Singapore, around which the central business district grew. Together with its Kallang Basin catchments, the river covers about one-fifth of the total land area of Singapore, and by the 1960s had become very polluted. As can be imagined, the clean-up programme was an enormous undertaking, involving the development of infrastructure such as housing, industrial workshops, and sewage systems; massive resettlement of squatters, backyard trades, industries and farmers (including pig and duck farms); resiting of street hawkers to food centres; and phasing out of pollutive activities along or close to the river banks by offering them development incentives.[10]

Implementing this action plan required the joint efforts of the Environment Ministry together with the URA, PWD, Housing and Development Board (HDB), Port of Singapore Authority (PSA), Jurong Town Corporation (JTC), and the Primary Production Department (PPD). In 1987, the results of these inter-agency efforts could be seen and enjoyed by everyone. The river was flowing freely. Its banks, once cluttered with boatyards, backyard trades, and squatter premises, were transformed into riverside walkways and landscaped parks. Fish returned to the river, and people could engage in activities such as boat races and river cruises. Today, outdoor eateries, entertainment outlets, and waterfront housing line the riverbanks, creating a vibrant buzz. The river mouth has also been dammed with a barrage to create a unique reservoir in an urban environment.

CONSTANT INNOVATION

Cleaning up a country's environment and sustaining it goes beyond a clear vision and long-term, integrated planning and implementation. Another essential ingredient is continuous improvement and constant innovation on both the policy and technology fronts. To remain ahead of emerging environmental challenges, Singapore has continually searched for innovative solutions and leveraged technology to tackle such challenges. It is prepared to learn from the good practices of other countries where they exist, or innovate if there is no existing model. Two examples of innovations that have served Singapore well are NEWater and its offshore landfill, Semakau Landfill.

NEWater

Produced using advanced membrane technologies, NEWater allows each drop of water to be used more than once, and so multiplies Singapore's effective supply of water. It is a key pillar of the Environment Ministry's efforts to ensure a secure and sustainable supply of water for the long term.

Where other countries have faced resistance in the use of recycled water, public acceptance of NEWater in Singapore is high. One contributory factor was the intensive publicity programme that accompanied the launch of NEWater in 2002. It culminated in the toast with NEWater by 60,000 Singaporeans and foreigners led by then Prime Minister Goh Chok Tong and the entire Cabinet at the National Day Parade on 9 August 2002. The strong support by Singaporeans can also be attributed to their understanding of the safe technology behind NEWater. Demand for NEWater has increased several fold since its launch, especially from industries such as wafer fabrication plants who value NEWater for its ultra pure properties.

Singapore's investment in R&D and the conscious efforts to involve the private sector in the production of NEWater have also led to the development of a vibrant water industry in Singapore. More importantly, it is now able to share the solutions it has developed with other cities, as many will, otherwise, face water shortages in future. It also hopes to build on this good start to develop Singapore as a global hydrohub, with the inaugural Singapore International Water Week (SIWW) in 2008 as a platform to advocate best practices in water management and the successful application of water technologies.

Semakau Landfill — the "Garbage of Eden"

Singapore's limited land area has made it necessary for the Environment Ministry to find innovative solutions to meet the country's waste disposal needs. All incinerable waste in Singapore is incinerated since this reduces waste volumes by 90 per cent. Despite having four waste-to-energy incineration plants, Singapore still requires landfill space for the disposal of the remaining waste volumes as well as non-incinerable waste. To avoid using up space on mainland Singapore, the idea of an offshore landfill was conceived. This gave rise to Semakau Landfill, which is the world's first offshore landfill created entirely from sea space.

The care put into the design and operational work at the landfill, as well as the environmental protection and conservation measures taken by the NEA, have ensured that Semakau Landfill is not only clean and free from smell, but is also a green natural environment thriving with rich biodiversity. It is open to members of the public for recreational activities such as birdwatching, sport fishing, and intertidal walks to allow everyone to enjoy the biodiversity of the island. The April 2007 issue of the *New Scientist* featured Semakau Landfill, dubbing it the "Garbage of Eden".

PRACTICAL AND EFFECTIVE APPROACH

The government's firm belief in the importance of constant innovation also means that policy solutions and approaches evolve over the years in response to changing needs, demands, and attitudes so that the vision for the environment can be realized in a pragmatic and cost-effective manner. In Singapore, practical standards are legislated and enforced. Sound economic analysis is applied and economic pricing are adopted to allocate scarce environment resources. Use of the private sector and market players to bring costs down is encouraged wherever it makes sense.

The right policies will not produce the right results without the awareness, understanding, and support of the people. The public sector must, therefore, forge common goals with the people and private sectors. Only through working together, known as the 3P[11] approach, can sustainable results be achieved.

As we go forward, the pressures of economic and population growth on our environment will become more acute. Major challenges such as tackling climate change and grappling with sustainable development are now key concerns of governments and peoples around the world. Singapore is no different. Recognizing the scale of the challenges, the government has set up two Ministerial Committees to drive efforts to deal with climate change and ensure sustainable development for Singapore.

While the challenges may be new, the fundamental beliefs and principles which have served Singapore well remain unchanged.

The country stands firm in the belief of the importance of the environment as a key contributor to ensuring a good quality of life in Singapore. Thinking and planning will continue to be carried out in a long-term and integrated manner, backed up by effective, inter-agency implementation. The private and people sectors will be involved in the government's plans in order to tap their knowledge and expertise. Through these strategies and actions, Singapore will not only be in a better position to overcome the challenges of climate change and sustainable development, but will also be able to create opportunities from necessity.

SHARING THE SINGAPORE ENVIRONMENT EXPERIENCE

The Singapore environment is far from perfect. There are still challenges to be overcome, higher standards to be achieved, as well as greater awareness and better behaviour to be fostered among its residents. But it is an example of the kind of clean environment that can be achieved by any city, and it is a model that can be scalable and replicated in many cities. This is especially pertinent since the United Nations estimates that by 2008, more than half of the world's population live in cities; and between now and 2030, 90 per cent of global population growth will take place in cities. This population explosion in the urban context will put a huge strain on the environment. Nevertheless, if it is properly managed, people living in cities throughout the world should be able to enjoy a good living environment and have access to clean air, sufficient drinking water, and proper sanitation.

The Singapore experience is also useful as Singapore has not always been clean. It was not too long ago when Singapore roads were dirty and its rivers stank, just like in many parts of some developing countries and even some more developed cities. Singapore has shown that a clean, green and blue environment can be achieved within a generation.

EARLY YEARS

In Singapore's developing years, its environment left much to be desired. The air, land, and waters were polluted. Furthermore, water scarcity was a major concern. Examples are shown in the photos that follow.

1. Unhealthy air then (1964): Smoky vehicles and industries such as the plywood factory shown here polluted Singapore's air during its developing years.
Source: MICA.

2. My bin runneth over (1963): Irregular and unsanitary waste disposal often led to overflowing garbage by the roadside.
Source: MICA.

3

4

3. The way they were (1970): Hawkers along Singapore River raised public health concerns because they operated in unsanitary conditions.
Source: Hawker, A.J.

4. Soiled waterways (1950): Polluting activities and dumping of waste into rivers led to unsightly scenes such as this on the Singapore River.
Source: MICA.

5. Not a drop at home (1959): Rural homes obtained their drinking water from the Rural Board's water wagons in the early years.
Source: NAS.

6. By the bucket (1961): Sanitation systems were rudimentary, with the use of the night soil system.
Source: SPH — *Straits Times.*

5

6

THE TRANSFORMATION

Recognizing the importance of a good environment, the Singapore Government launched large-scale, national-level efforts to clean up Singapore's land and rivers towards the greening of Singapore. These campaigns also aimed to educate Singaporeans on the importance of water and the environment and instill in them the right mindsets and behaviour. Examples are shown in the photos that follow.

7. Hosing down: PM Lee Kuan Yew led thousands of volunteers during a one-week mass drive to spring clean Singapore in 1969.
Source: SPH — *Straits Times.*

8. Cherished flow: Environment Minister Lim Kim San at the opening of the "Water is Precious" Exhibition at the Victoria Memorial Hall in 1972.
Source: SPH — *Straits Times.*

9. Sowing green habits: PM Lee Kuan Yew planting a Tembusu sapling for the third annual Tree Planting Day in 1973.
Source: SPH — *Straits Times.*

10. Job well done!: PM Lee Kuan Yew presents a gold medal to Lee Ek Tieng in 1987 for completing the ten-year Singapore River clean-up.
Source: SPH — *Straits Times.*

9

10

11. Helping hand: Former Environment Minister Mah Bow Tan receives a little assistance watering a sapling at the Tampines Festival Park durir the "Towards a Gracious Living Environment" eve on 2 June 1996.
Source: SPH — Strai Times.

12. Marking Worl Environment Day: Environment Minister Teo Che Hean launches an underwater clean-up at East Coast Park on 2 June 1996.
Source: SPH — Strai Times.

11

12

Through its concerted efforts to clean up its land and waterways, Singapore has transformed its environment into a clean, green and healthy one. Singapore has also built up a sustainable water supply, and its waterways are being opened for all to enjoy. Examples are shown in the photos that follow.

13. Clear and crisp air now: Pollution from transport vehicles and industries such as those located on Jurong Island shown here is well under control. *Source:* JTC.

14. Waste to energy: Singapore now has an integrated waste management system with waste disposed of in waste-to-energy incineration plants such as Tuas South IP shown here. *Source:* NEA.

15. Haven for biodiversity: Non-incinerables and incineration ash are disposed of at offshore
Semakau Landfill (aerial view illustrated here), the ecosystem of which is home to rich marine life.

16. Tunnelling a way out: The DTSS system comprises two large, deep tunnels criss-crossing the island, with two centralized water reclamation plants, deep sea outfalls, and a link-sewer network. The deep tunnels are designed with diameters of up to 6 metres and are at depths ranging from 20 to 50 metres below ground.

Source: PUB.

17. Turn on the tap: PM Goh Chok Tong (middle) officially launches NEWater at Bedok NEWater Factory on 21 February 2003. Also present were Environment Minister Lim Swee Say (left) and PUB Chairman Tan Gee Paw.
Source: SPH — Berita Harian.

18. Tapping the sea: PM Lee Hsien Loong (second from left) at the opening of the SingSpring Desalination Plant on 13 September 2005. Also present were Environment Minister Dr Yaacob Ibrahim (left) and PUB Chairman Tan Gee Paw (second from right).

Source: SPH — Straits Times.

19. Brave new project: Minister Mentor Lee Kuan Yew (fourth from left) and Minister for the Environment and Water Resources Dr Yaacob Ibrahim (third from left) at the ceremony marking the start of construction of the Marina Barrage/Reservoir in March 2005. Also present (from left) were Permanent Secretary for the Environment and Water Resources Tan Yong Soon, Chairman of PUB Tan Gee Paw, and CE of PUB Khoo Teng Chye (behind MM Lee).
Source: PUB.

20. Active, beautiful, and clean: The ABC Waters project at Kolam Ayer entices canoeists to put paddle to water.
Source: PUB.

21. The way we are: Modern, upgraded hawker centres such as the Adam Road Food centre shown here offer a comfortable and hygienic dining option.
Source: NEA.

22. Water rapport: Singaporeans are now encouraged to get "close to water" through water sports as the waterskiing performance at Marina Reservoir during Singapore International Water Week 2008 attests.

Source: PUB.

PART **II**

ACHIEVING A CLEAN ENVIRONMENT

2

ACHIEVING CLEAN AIR QUALITY

Clean air is a basic requirement of human health and well-being. Air pollution, however, continues to pose a significant threat to health worldwide. According to a WHO assessment of the burden of disease due to air pollution, more than two million premature deaths each year can be attributed to the effects of urban outdoor air pollution and indoor air pollution (from the burning of solid fuels). More than half of this disease burden is borne by the populations of developing countries.

Margaret Chan, Director-General for the
World Health Organization (WHO), and
Marc Danzon, WHO Regional Director for Europe,
in the Foreword for the WHO Air Quality Guidelines
Global Update 2005

Among the first impressions that a new visitor acquires of a city is often its ambient air quality. Polluted air is not just unsightly and uncomfortable to breathe. Inhaling polluted air can make a person sick and, in the extreme, lead to death. Air pollution also damages the natural and built environment. Because clean air improves both the health of the population and the quality of life in the city, national environmental protection authorities such as the United

States Environmental Protection Agency (USEPA) as well as international organizations such as the World Health Organization (WHO) have established ambient air quality guidelines and legislation which prescribe standards to reduce the effects of air pollution on human health.

Maintaining clean air quality so that residents enjoy a healthy and pleasant living environment has been a priority for the Singapore Government. As a result, the air quality in Singapore compares favourably with that in other major cities, despite the presence of industrial centres within the city state. However, this achievement did not come easily. As a small urbanized city state, Singapore finds maintaining clean air quality a challenge, especially in view of its many constraints. These include its dense population, limited land and airspace, and vulnerability to transboundary pollution.

In addition, there are many trade-offs to be considered, and difficult choices to be made. While emissions from industries can potentially cause the air quality to deteriorate, these developments contribute significantly to the economic growth of the nation. Introducing air pollution control measures, such as the legislation of emission standards to ensure a minimum standard of air quality and safeguard public health, also invariably imposes costs on industry. In order not to hinder Singapore's economic growth and competitiveness, legislative and regulatory measures must take into consideration the effectiveness and cost of measures to reduce emissions. Over the years, the government has had to balance industrial and economic growth consciously, even as it keeps air pollutants such as sulphur dioxide, oxides of nitrogen, carbon monoxide, ozone, lead, hydrocarbons, and particulates within acceptable standards.

BACKGROUND — THE BEGINNINGS OF AIR POLLUTION CONTROL

When Singapore gained independence in 1965, smoky chimneys and vehicles were widespread. Existing factories such as sawmills and canneries polluted the air, and the influx of new industrial developments threatened to exacerbate the poor environmental situation.

These factories could not simply be got rid of, as the young nation needed these industries to survive. The first foreign multinational corporations (MNCs) set up operations in Singapore in 1968, and by the 1970s, its industrial base had grown rapidly to include chemical and electronic industries. The government realized that rapid industrialization would have an adverse impact on air quality, and in the long term, this would be extremely harmful to the health of the people. With this realization came the commitment to ensure that air quality was not sacrificed in the rush for rapid industrialization and infrastructure development.

In April 1970, the Anti-Pollution Unit (APU) was formed under the Prime Minister's Office to look into air pollution control. The urgency of mitigating air pollution problems in Singapore was such that the APU was first established on an *ad hoc* basis and only formally approved by Parliament on 1 April 1971, a year after its formation.[1]

The APU was subsequently transferred from the Prime Minister's Office to the Ministry of the Environment on 1 April 1983. Three years later, the Pollution Control Department (PCD) was formed within the Ministry of the Environment, from the amalgamation of the APU and Water Pollution Control Section of the Sewerage Department. The PCD, which today is a department under the NEA, is responsible for the prevention and control of air and water pollution, the management of hazardous substances, and the disposal of toxic industrial wastes.

The APU's first task was to look into how to monitor and control air pollution in Singapore. This included the setting up of laboratory facilities and ambient air monitoring stations to measure air pollutants, identifying and surveying air pollution sources, investigating complaints, drafting legislation on air pollution control, and working with other government planning agencies to ensure that new urban and industrial developments did not compromise air quality. Realizing that Singapore had much to learn from other cities, Lee Ek Tieng, the first Head of APU, spent five months in New Zealand and Australia to study their air pollution control measures and how they could be applied to Singapore.

AIR QUALITY MONITORING

Ambient air monitoring involves identifying and measuring levels of pollutants in the air, allowing the nature and magnitude of air pollution problems to be assessed. Through highlighting trends in air quality and flagging out potential problem areas, the data collected also help the government to put in place informed air pollution control policies and measures, for instance, in formulating siting guidelines for the planned establishment of new industries. In addition, the comparison of air quality before and after an air pollution control programme is implemented helps the government to assess the effectiveness and adequacy of the programme.

Air quality monitoring also allows for a comparison of Singapore's ambient air quality against international standards, as well as the air quality in other cities. As the USEPA and WHO air quality guidelines are strongly backed by comprehensive health studies and widely adopted by many other countries, Singapore benchmarks itself against these standards.

The APU started its ambient air quality monitoring programme in 1971 with six stations covering the commercial, suburban, rural, and industrial areas of Singapore. An air pollution control laboratory was established to analyse the samples collected from the monitoring stations. Over the years, manual monitoring methods were replaced by continuous automatic analysers which tracked real-time concentrations of air pollutants. More stations were added to the air quality monitoring network to include new housing estates and assess the impact of new industrial developments on air quality. Today, Singapore's air quality is tracked by a telemetric network of fifteen air monitoring stations located throughout the main island (as shown in Map 1).

Singapore had little expertise in air quality monitoring in the early years. To build up capabilities, it learned from the experience of other countries. Engineers and chemists were sent overseas. Some were sent to attend specialized courses in countries such as Australia and Japan, some went on overseas attachments, while others pursued postgraduate degrees in countries such as the United Kingdom. These APU officers brought back with them invaluable expertise and experience about air pollution control measures implemented in various countries, as well as an understanding of the relative successes and failures of the different air pollution control regimes. This enabled them to make an assessment of what would work for Singapore.

At the outset, fairly primitive air pollutant measurement methods were used. This involved passing air samples into chemical absorbers over a period of time to trap the air pollutants. A team of officers was deployed daily to collect the air samples from the monitoring stations. The samples were then brought to the air pollution control laboratory which ran simple chemical tests to determine the levels of total acidity, smoke, and dust fallout. This manual collection and laboratory analysis of air samples was resource intensive, and only provided periodic measurements of the air quality over the period of time when the air samples were collected.

The government kept abreast of technological developments overseas that would allow its systems to be improved upon. New technologies developed in countries such as the United States in later years enabled the measurement of concentration levels of specific air pollutants such as sulphur dioxide and particulate matter. These technologies were adopted not only to measure more specific air pollutants, but also to refine air pollutant measurement methods. This increased both the frequency and accuracy of air quality monitoring, providing more information that allowed potential air pollution problems to be identified early and effective air pollution control measures to be implemented.

In January 1994, the monitoring system was upgraded to the fully automated telemetric air quality monitoring and management system (TAQMMS). Using the most up-to-date technology available at that point in time, the TAQMMS comprises remote air monitoring stations linked to a Central Control System via dial-up telephone lines, providing an efficient means of obtaining and tracking air quality data. The system, which has been upgraded over the years, such as by adding a feature to allow for Internet-based access in 2005, is able to provide continuous real-time information on air pollution levels in different parts of Singapore at the touch of a button.

The monitoring stations track both ambient and roadside air quality. Automatic analysers and equipment at the stations measure the concentrations of major pollutants such as sulphur dioxide, oxides of nitrogen, carbon monoxide, ozone, hydrocarbons, and particulate matter (PM10 and PM2.5). The TAQMMS collects, processes, and stores these air quality data from the remote air monitoring stations and is also equipped with air pollution dispersion modelling capability to assess the impact of new developments on Singapore's air quality. This technological capacity to measure air quality in a comprehensive way and model for future developments has been indispensable to Singapore's efforts to manage air quality. Neighbouring countries have also come to Singapore to study how to deploy and utilize this advanced air monitoring system effectively.

The APU had been publicly reporting the ambient levels of pollutants such as sulphur dioxide, ozone, and dust on a yearly basis since 1972. However, the absolute air pollution concentration figures meant little to the layman, as the figures were not translated into useful information on whether or not the concentration levels were unhealthy. In 1991, the Environment Ministry decided to adopt the "Pollutant Standards Index" (PSI) developed by the USEPA as a means to communicate more clearly to the public information on Singapore's air quality.

The PSI was adopted because it had a strong scientific basis and was backed by comprehensive health studies. It takes into account the ambient concentrations of the key air pollutants, such as sulphur dioxide, particulate matter (PM10), ozone, carbon monoxide, and nitrogen dioxide, and translates them into an overall index ranging from 0 to 500. Taking into consideration the resulting health impact of different concentration levels of the various air pollutants, the PSI then assigns an assessment of the air quality based on the index value. PSI levels of between 0 and 50 are considered to be good, and levels from 51 to 100 are moderate. Index levels above 100 are assessed to be unhealthy. In this way, the PSI translates technical information on complex air pollutant concentration levels into a simple indicator, informing the public of the general daily air pollution level.

AIR POLLUTION CONTROL FOR INDUSTRIAL EMISSIONS

Siting industrial facilities far from the city is a key measure of ensuring that residents enjoy clean air quality. However, Singapore, being a small island city state, does not have the option of relocating its industries outside the city. Its dense population and limited land often lead to competition for land between residences and industries and at times results in industrial facilities being located close to residential areas. Residents may then suffer from air pollution, noise or odour nuisance caused by the nearby industrial facilities.

To manage the issue of competing land uses for new industries, office space, housing, social spaces (for example, parks and recreational facilities), and shared infrastructure such as the land transport network, Singapore has adopted an integrated approach to strategic land-use planning from the outset. This means town planners manage the overall land-use planning process in consultation with other relevant government agencies. Such a coordinated approach among government agencies not only ensures optimal allocation of land for competing uses, but also allows any adverse impacts of developments on the environment to be minimized.

After its formation, the APU worked closely with the Planning Department (which was then in charge of overall land-use planning in Singapore) to ensure that environmental considerations were incorporated into Singapore's national land-use planning. To minimize the air pollution impact from industries on residential areas, major pollutive users were grouped together in their respective land-use zones and were sited as far away as possible from residential areas and population centres. For upcoming industrial developments, the APU worked with the Jurong Town Corporation (JTC), responsible for developing industrial estates in Singapore, to ensure that new industries were sited in the appropriate land-use zones.

Where necessary, industries were relocated. An example is that of sawmills. There were about 150 sawmills in Singapore in the early 1970s, of which about forty-five were in urban and suburban areas. Sawmill operations, such as the open burning of wood waste resulting in abundant smoke emissions, as well as dumping of this waste on open land and in waterways, created serious pollution problems. This was a concern especially for the sawmills that were close to residential areas. The option of completely disallowing these sawmills from operating in Singapore was considered but not adopted as it would have badly affected the 5,000 workers in this industry. Instead, the sawmills were relocated to the Sungei Kadut industrial estate. This provided an opportunity to integrate the sawmills into the larger, modern, integrated timber industries that were equipped with proper pollution control facilities, as well as to phase out sawmills that were inefficient. This relocation exercise was completed in 1980.

Persuading industries to relocate is often difficult. Take, for example, Keppel Shipyard which was located in Telok Blangah, where they had been operating for decades. In the 1980s, residential developments in the area were expanding rapidly and inching ever closer to the shipyard. Grit blasting activities carried out at Keppel Shipyard soon became a problem, both in terms of air quality and noise, to the residents. However, Keppel was unwilling to relocate unless a suitable alternative site was found. Meanwhile, to reduce the air and noise pollution in Telok Blangah, restrictions such as rescheduling grit blasting activities and limiting the number of blasting guns in use at any one time were imposed. At the same time, the demand for ship repair was increasing. Keppel started a shipyard in Tuas in the early 1980s, and another, also in Tuas, in 1990. In 1999 Keppel Shipyard ceased operating at Telok Blangah as operations were consolidated in Tuas, thereby eliminating noise and air pollution from their activities in Telok Blangah.

The APU also had to work closely with the Economic Development Board (EDB) to pre-empt pollution from new industries. In the late 1960s and 1970s, growing the economy was a priority for Singapore to ensure its survival as a nation. As the labour-intensive industries moved out of Singapore to neighbouring countries, the EDB brought in many more capital-intensive industries that would help accelerate economic development in Singapore.

However, these industries brought with them attendant air pollution problems that could be potentially serious. New monitoring stations were set up at the anticipated locations of new industrial developments to monitor their impact on air quality so that necessary pollution control measures could be implemented in a timely manner. The APU and EDB held extensive discussions and arrived at a common understanding of the need to balance economic development with maintaining clean air quality. The APU identified industries that could potentially lead to serious pollution problems which could not be mitigated cost-effectively, and that were, therefore, not encouraged. One example was the ore-smelting industry which extracted metals such as iron and tin from the ore. Others include the manufacture of charcoal, refining of lead, and manufacture of hazardous pesticides. Such industries not only generated considerable air pollution, but also produced a lot of waste, some of which were difficult to treat.

Proposals for new industries were sent to the APU for its assessment and recommendations on potential pollution problems. The hazards and pollution impact of the proposed industries were assessed to ensure that they did not pose unmanageable pollution and health ramifications. A factory was allowed to be set up only if it was sited in an appropriate industrial estate and could comply with pollution control requirements. It should also be compatible with surrounding land uses. This remains of utmost importance today, especially to land-scarce Singapore, where the location of industrial and residential areas needs to be handled with care and caution, especially for pollutive industries or industries storing and handling large quantities of hazardous substances. Through the proper siting of industries at the planning stage, the government seeks to prevent pollution problems from arising later downstream.

Upfront industrial and urban planning alone is insufficient for achieving clean air quality. Singapore also has to ensure that all its industries and vehicles adopt measures to meet certain emission standards. Legislation was therefore put in place to guarantee minimum performance standards. Legislation also enabled the government to take enforcement action against parties which failed to meet the standards.

However, due to the compulsory nature of legislation, care had to be taken when deciding the specific standards to be legislated. The government had to manage the trade-offs between striving to improve air quality standards and ensuring that the legislated standards could be met at a reasonable cost. This often meant waiting for other countries to impose similar standards, which would then prompt the producers of industrial equipment and vehicles to manufacture goods that met the standards. Otherwise, as Singapore had a small domestic market and was an importer of most of these goods, setting standards that were too high would render them impossible to be met, or lead to companies having to pay prohibitively high costs to meet the standards, thereby eroding Singapore's economic competitiveness.

Prior to December 1971, there was no appropriate legislation that dealt specifically with air pollution control. There were, however, provisions in the Local Government Integration Ordinance, 1963, forbidding the discharge of accumulated dust and effluvium, and of smoke or other unconsumed combustible matter in a manner that could be a nuisance or dangerous to health. These provisions were subsequently incorporated in the Environmental Public Health Act, 1968. However, the provisions were subjective as no quantifiable emission standards were established, and as a result, they could not be enforced effectively.

The promulgation of legislation to deal specifically with air pollution control was examined by the APU after it was formed in 1970. The Clean Air Act was subsequently passed in Parliament on 2 December 1971. This Act gave power to the Director of Air Pollution Control to specify emission standards to be met by industrial and trade premises. In determining the emission standards, factors such as available pollution control technology, and the emission limits adopted in other countries at that time, were taken into consideration. The Clean Air Act also empowered the Director of Air Pollution Control to take action against parties that failed to meet the emission standards. Examples include powers to inspect industrial premises, impose financial penalties, and require factories to install pollution control equipment. The Clean Air Act also gave the Environment Minister the power to close down recalcitrant factories which posed a health risk to the public. These provisions under the Clean Air Act, which has since been repealed, now reside within the Environmental Protection and Management Act.

The Clean Air (Standards) Regulations were passed on 11 January 1972. The Regulations specify the emission limits of various pollutants, including smoke, which all factories must comply with. Over time, in tandem with technological improvements that enabled industries to meet higher emission standards, these standards have been tightened and extended to cover more pollutants. For instance, in 1978, revisions were made to the regulations to tighten emission standards for air pollutants and to introduce a standard for carbon monoxide.

Air emission standards were further revised in 2001 and stipulated in a new legislation now known as the Environmental Protection and Management (Air Impurities) Regulations. The air emission standards were revised taking into consideration significant advances in air pollution control technology, as well as new air pollutants that had become important and relevant with the advent of new industries and manufacturing processes. The revised air emission standards were also in line with standards adopted in developed countries. For example, emission limits for eight new air pollutants which are harmful to human health[2] were added into the new regulations.

Besides air emission standards, there are other air pollution control requirements for industrial facilities. However, different types of industrial developments have differing pollution impacts, and hence the pollution control requirements to which they have to adhere vary accordingly. For example, industries are required to be sited in their respective designated areas and to incorporate suitable pollution control measures at the design stage.

To assist industrialists, architects, professional engineers, and consultants in ensuring that their development proposals and building plans could meet the respective environmental requirements, a Code of Practice on Pollution Control (COPPC) was published in 1994. The COPPC lays out the environmental requirements for different types of developments, ranging from clean and light industries to special industries, warehouses, and business parks. These environmental requirements include controls on air, water, and noise pollution, hazardous substances, toxic industrial wastes, land pollution, as well as the remediation of contaminated sites. Air pollution control requirements include emission standards, chimney height, and the installation of monitoring equipment.

The COPPC summarizes the environmental requirements in Singapore and interprets the relevant legislation in a manner that can be readily referred to by industry players. It acts as a transparent and business-friendly guidebook for companies planning new industrial developments in Singapore. Since its environmental requirements specify the outcomes to be met rather than the methods to achieve them, companies can exercise flexibility and creativity in the design of their developments and find it less onerous to meet the environmental requirements.

The COPPC is periodically reviewed to take into account revised environmental standards such as tightened air pollution control requirements. To ensure that it remains relevant and useful, the COPPC review committees include members from both government and private sectors. For example, the review committee for the 2000 Edition of the COPPC included representatives from the Environment Ministry's Pollution Control Department, Association of Consulting Engineers Singapore, Institute of Engineers Singapore, and Singapore Institute of Architects.[3]

Standards and regulations help to ensure that industries in Singapore meet a minimum standard in air pollutant emissions. However, they are only effective if they can be enforced and penalties are imposed for non-compliance.

Since the APU was established, inspectors have been conducting factory visits to identify factories that are causing air pollution. These visits also establish the causes of air pollution and recommend remedial measures that can be taken.

In fact, even before a factory begins operation, checks are conducted to ensure that the pollution control facilities proposed at the planning stage are properly installed and working well. After the factory starts operation, regular inspections are conducted as part of the enforcement programme to assess environmental performance and to check for compliance with regulations, such as ensuring that pollution control equipment are being operated and maintained properly, or that companies do not dispose of industrial wastes by open burning. Open burning was a common practice at construction sites until regulations were introduced to prohibit this and enforcement checks carried out to ensure compliance. Source emission tests are conducted regularly at the chimneys to check that air emissions comply with the legal limits. The quality of the fuel used is also checked for compliance with the stipulated limits.

For example, in 1972, soon after APU was formed, a ceramics factory located next to a residential estate was a source of many complaints. Fine dust from the grinding process was being discharged into the atmosphere, causing serious air pollution which affected the residents. APU inspected the factory and required the company to install two venturi scrubbers to reduce the dust emitted and conducted regular inspections to ensure compliance with emission standards.

In January 1997, the Environment Ministry introduced a scheme which requires industries to conduct source emission tests themselves. This ensures that industries monitor their exhaust emissions regularly and take remedial measures where necessary to comply with the air emission standards. Instead of sending enforcement officers to check regularly on the emissions of all industries, random sample checks are conducted. This not only reduces the manpower required for enforcement, but also instils a sense of commitment among factory operators to reduce their own air pollutant emissions.

Control of Sulphur Dioxide Emissions

Currently, a key air pollutant of concern from industries is sulphur dioxide (SO_2). As Singapore's economy grew, air monitoring stations detected increasing SO_2 levels in the Jurong area in the 1990s, with the number of "moderate" PSI days increasing from thirteen in 1991 to eighty in 1995. The government also foresaw that upcoming developments such as the introduction of new power plants would only worsen the situation and could bring PSI levels into the "unhealthy" range. To ensure that residents were not unduly affected by increasing SO_2 from the major emitters, that is, refineries and power stations, a decision was made to cap the total emissions of these facilities[4] to ensure that the ambient air quality remained within safe limits established by the USEPA. Industries located in designated industrial estates were also required to use fuel oil containing not more than 1 per cent sulphur by weight. These standards were proposed based on what was already practised in other countries such as South Korea, and were implemented after consultation with the affected industries.

Figure 2.1 shows that the levels of SO_2 in Singapore have fallen since the introduction of emission limits in the early 1970s, and the subsequent tightening of these limits over the years. It also illustrates the rising levels of SO_2 in the early 1990s. The SO_2 levels fell after the SO_2 cap and limits on sulphur content of fuel oil used were imposed.

However, Singapore cannot be complacent. While the actual SO_2 level is well within USEPA standards, other cities have also been achieving significant reductions in SO_2 levels as they take steps to improve their environment (a comparison across various cities is shown in Figure 2.2). Hence, this is a moving target and Singapore will have to be constantly on its toes to stay ahead and be prepared to review air pollution control measures where necessary, for instance, by reducing the SO_2 cap for major emitters. Another factor to consider for the longer term is that Singapore's daily SO_2

FIGURE 2.1

Annual Average Levels of Sulphur Dioxide (1974 to 2007)

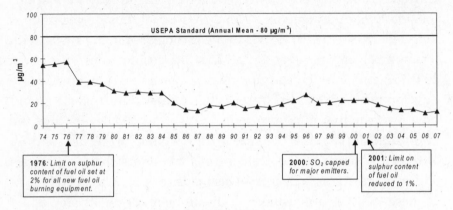

Note: Readings taken before 1989 are derived from total acidity in the ambient air.
Source: NEA.

FIGURE 2.2

Comparison of Sulphur Dioxide Levels

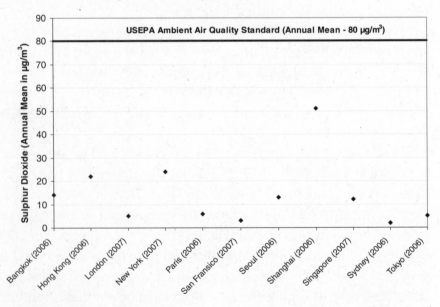

Note: Data collated from the environmental agencies of respective countries.
Source: NEA.

levels during certain times of the year do not meet the stringent guidelines set by the WHO,[5] and so even more reductions to SO_2 emissions would be required to address this issue.

Control of Particulate Matter Emissions

About 30 per cent of particulate matter (PM) in Singapore's ambient air is from industries, mainly power plants and factories. To control the level of PM emissions from industry, the Clean Air (Standards) Regulations enacted in 1972 imposed a PM emission limit of $400mg/Nm^3$. This was reduced to $200mg/Nm^3$ in 1978 and further tightened to $100mg/Nm^3$ in 2001, taking into consideration available pollution control technologies to limit PM emissions, and after consultation with industry players to confirm that the revised standards were realistic. Today most industries' PM emissions are well below this standard.

AIR POLLUTION CONTROL FOR VEHICULAR EMISSIONS

Industries are not the only source of air pollution. The motor vehicle population in Singapore has increased over the years with greater urbanization and a rising standard of living. Motor vehicles have been a major source of air pollution in Singapore, emitting pollutants such as SO_2, lead, and particulate matter into the ambient environment. To limit emissions from vehicles, the government controls the quality of automotive fuels and sets vehicular exhaust emission standards.

Control of Sulphur Dioxide Emissions

The control of fuel quality began with the control of sulphur content in diesel in 1976, as vehicles using diesel with high sulphur content were prone to excessive smoke emissions. In 1976, the maximum allowable sulphur content in diesel was limited to 0.5 per cent by weight. This was subsequently reduced to 0.3 per cent in 1996 and then to 0.05 per cent in 1999. The sulphur content in diesel was further reduced to 0.005 per cent by weight in 2005 with the introduction of ultra-low sulphur diesel or ULSD to pave the way for the implementation of Euro IV emission standards for new diesel vehicles in 2006. These revisions were made taking into consideration the greater availability of diesel with lower sulphur content, as well as similar standards being adopted in other countries.

For example, before reducing the permissible sulphur content in diesel from 0.5 per cent to 0.3 per cent in 1996, the government first confirmed with oil companies that they were able to supply such diesel if sufficient lead time was given for changes to existing refining processes and equipment to be made. The fact that the United States and European countries had already adopted this standard for sulphur content in diesel, and that Japan was in the process of adopting this standard, added to the confidence that it could be successfully implemented in Singapore.

Control of Lead Emissions

Besides the sulphur content in diesel, the amount of lead present in petrol was also a cause of concern. In the early years, air monitoring systems indicated a rising trend in lead concentration levels, and vehicles running on leaded petrol were identified as the key source of lead emissions. Subsequently, a 1991 study also showed the correlation between exposure to traffic and lead levels in blood.

To control the emission of lead from motor vehicles, lead in petrol was progressively reduced from an industry-set level of about 0.84 g/l to 0.8 g/l in 1980, to 0.6 g/l in 1981, 0.4 g/l in 1983, and finally to 0.15 g/l in 1987. Similar considerations as those involved in lowering the sulphur content of diesel were taken into account when reducing the lead content in petrol. In January 1991, unleaded petrol was introduced and sold side by side with leaded petrol at petrol stations. The use of unleaded petrol was promoted through a differential tax system which made unleaded petrol about 10 cents per litre cheaper than leaded petrol. As a result, the sale of unleaded petrol took off and soon the volume of unleaded petrol sold dwarfed that of leaded petrol. On 1 July 1998, oil companies stopped the sale of leaded petrol altogether as the demand for leaded petrol had dwindled significantly.

The mandated reduction in lead content and the introduction of unleaded petrol brought significant improvements to the air quality. From levels which exceeded the USEPA's recommended ambient air quality standard in 1981, the roadside lead level dropped to a virtually negligible level of less than $0.1\mu g/Nm^3$ in 2007. Ambient lead levels have similarly seen a sharp decline over the years, as shown in Figure 2.3.

The introduction of unleaded petrol also paved the way for the use of catalytic converters on vehicles to further reduce other pollutants such as oxides of nitrogen, hydrocarbons, and carbon monoxide. Catalytic converters, which were factory-fitted on the majority of new vehicles to comply with emission standards, could

FIGURE 2.3

Annual Average Levels of Lead (1981 to 2007)

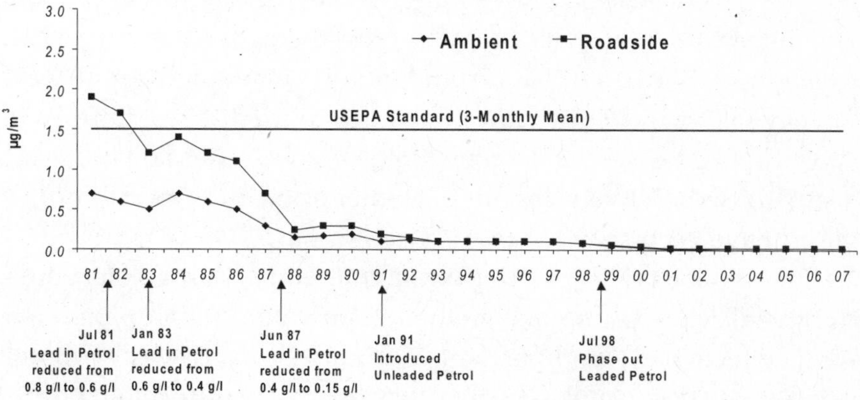

Source: NEA.

only be used with unleaded petrol as they could be rendered ineffective by lead.

Control of Particulate Matter Emissions

Currently, about 50 per cent of PM in the air is from diesel motor vehicles. Motor vehicles registered for use in Singapore are required to meet the air emission standards, including emissions of particulate matter, under the Environmental Protection and Management (Vehicular Emissions) Regulations. In-use vehicles are required to undergo mandatory inspections periodically to determine whether their exhaust emissions comply with stipulated emission standards. Vehicles which fail the inspections are not allowed to renew their road tax until they clear the inspection. These measures, together with the PM emission standards for industries, have ensured that Singapore's PM concentration levels are kept fairly constant (as illustrated in Figure 2.4) and are generally in line with other cities' (a comparison across various cities is shown in Figure 2.5) despite industrialization and vehicle population growth.

The first vehicular exhaust emission standards for diesel vehicles were introduced in 1991 with the implementation of UN/ECE Regulation No. 24.03. To help keep in check particulate matter emissions from diesel vehicles in Singapore, the emission standards for diesel vehicles have been progressively tightened in tandem with international standards and improvements in emission control technology. Euro I emission standards were adopted for all new diesel vehicles in 1997, followed by Euro II in 2001, and Euro IV in 2006. Table 2.1 gives an example of how the PM emission limits for heavy duty diesel vehicles, for example, prime movers and public buses, have been reduced from Euro I to Euro IV.

One obvious manifestation of the emission of particulate matter from vehicles is the smoke emitted from vehicles' tail pipes. The APU, which had been carrying out enforcement against motor vehicles emitting smoke, further increased its enforcement efforts with the assistance of the Registry of Vehicles (ROV) in 1981. In

FIGURE 2.4
Annual Average Levels of PM10 (1994 to 2007)

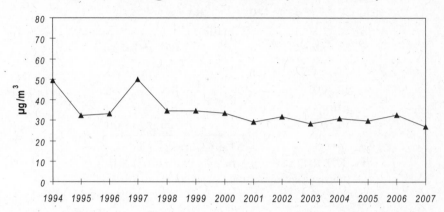

Note: Air quality was affected by transboundary smoke haze from the Indonesian land and forest fires in 1994, 1997, and 2006.
Source: NEA.

FIGURE 2.5
Comparison of PM10 Levels*

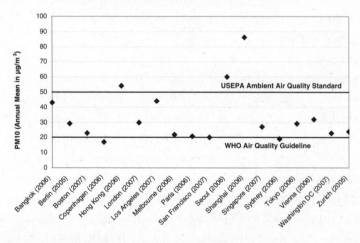

Notes: Data collated from the environmental agencies of respective countries.
*The USEPA has dropped its annual mean standard in December 2006 and now uses only the daily standard — the second highest daily average reading should not exceed 150 ug/m³. Such daily data is not widely available for comparison but Singapore is within the USEPA daily standard. In 2007, Singapore had 0 days with the daily PM10 levels exceeding 150 ug/m³.
Source: NEA.

TABLE 2.1
PM Emission Standards for
Heavy Duty Diesel Vehicles

Standard	PM emissions*
Euro I	360 mg/kWh
Euro II	150 mg/kWh
Euro III	100 mg/kWh
Euro IV	20 mg/kWh

Note: *PM limits for Euro I and II are specified as under the ECE R-49 test cycle while the limits for Euro III and IV are as tested under the European Stationary Cycle. *Source:* NEA.

1991, PCD worked with the Traffic Police and ROV to turn away recalcitrant smoky Malaysian vehicles. Smoky Singapore-registered vehicles were also stopped and tested for smoke emission. Drivers of vehicles found emitting smoke were fined. The power to take enforcement measures against smoky vehicles was vested with the Land Transport Authority (LTA), which took over the ROV in September 1995.

However, as the LTA and Traffic Police were predominantly concerned with vehicle and road safety respectively, enforcing regulations for smoky vehicles was not a priority. Hence, the law was amended to transfer the powers and responsibility for enforcement against smoky vehicles to the Environment Ministry, which augmented its enforcement operations in 1997 with the engagement of auxiliary police officers. Likely locations where smoky vehicles frequented were identified and enforcement officers were deployed daily to these locations. The officers would stop the smoky vehicles, escort them to the roadside, and test their exhaust emissions. Besides being issued fines, owners of the smoky vehicles were also requested to service and repair their vehicles prior to sending them for an exhaust emission test at an authorized vehicle inspection centre.

The process of stopping and testing smoky vehicles on the roads was very labour intensive. In 1999, after PCD's proposal to amend the law to accept video recordings as evidence in court was accepted, PCD began to conduct enforcement checks on the road using video cameras to capture the emissions from smoky vehicles so that action could be taken against offenders. The use of video cameras for vehicular emission enforcement allows enforcement officers to catch multiple smoky vehicles at a time, and this has proven to be an innovative and effective enforcement tool. Besides being efficient and cost-effective, the video camera also produces records that can be checked should disputes arise.

To step up enforcement further, NEA encouraged the public to report on smoky vehicles they see on the road, with details of the vehicle number, location, and time. To minimize abuse, the member of the public had to be prepared to go to court to testify against the vehicle owner if necessary, before a summons was issued. This method of enforcement was made possible by the simplicity of the regulation against smoky vehicles — any visible vehicle smoke was considered an offence. If more complicated criteria had been adopted, the public would have been discouraged from reporting on smoky vehicles. For example in some countries, smoky vehicles are deemed an offence only at certain times of the day, and if the degree of smoke visibility is higher (or the smoke is darker) than a certain opacity level.

On 1 September 2000, PCD introduced the Chassis Dynamometer Smoke Test (CDST), which replaced the conventional Free Acceleration Smoke Test (FAST) for diesel vehicles caught emitting smoke. Smoky diesel vehicles are subjected to the CDST at an authorized vehicle inspection centre. CDST is a more rigorous test method compared with FAST as it measures the smoke emission level of a diesel vehicle under simulated driving conditions. Since 1 January 2007, diesel-driven vehicles are required to undergo CDST in place of FAST as Singapore tightens the testing standard during mandatory periodic roadworthiness inspections.

In spite of efforts to control particulate matter emissions from vehicles, Singapore's fine particulate matter (PM2.5) concentration level is still above USEPA standards. Many other developed cities also have lower PM2.5 levels than Singapore. In addition, Singapore's PM2.5 level exceeds the guideline set by the WHO, although that is a standard not many cities are able to meet at the moment. Hence, in continuing to control particulate matter emissions, Singapore may need to consider new air pollution control measures where necessary. Possible measures include introducing the Euro V emission standards for diesel vehicles, as well as tightening emission standards for industries, the other major source of particulate matter.

Land Transport Planning

Complementing the efforts to control vehicular emissions is the land transport planning undertaken by LTA. Although the primary consideration in these measures is to abate congestion through managing demand, these measures also have the added benefit of helping to control vehicular emissions.

One key measure is congestion charging. First introduced in 1973 as the Area Licensing Scheme (ALS), this was implemented as part of an overall package of road pricing measures and public transportation improvements based on public feedback. Motorists entering a restricted zone (including areas such as the Central Business District and Orchard Road) had to purchase and display a licence on the car windshield or on the handle bars of motorcycles during peak hours. Overhead gantries were set up along the boundaries of this restricted zone for auxiliary police officers to carry out visual checks. The ALS also helped to reduce air pollution in the restricted zones. The WHO worked with the APU to monitor carbon monoxide levels in the restricted zones before and after implementation of the ALS and found that carbon monoxide levels had been reduced by 60 per cent.

After ten years of planning and testing, the ALS was replaced by the current Electronic Road Pricing (ERP) system in September

1998. Charges are automatically deducted from a pre-paid card as the vehicle drives past the gantry. This way, the levy can be varied according to the congestion levels on each road and at different times of the day. LTA reviews the traffic conditions on the expressways and roads where the ERP system is in operation on a quarterly basis. After the review, the ERP rates would be adjusted where necessary to minimize congestion on the roads. ERP has been effective in maintaining an optimal speed range of 45 to 65 km/h for expressways, and 20 to 30 km/h for arterial roads.[6]

In maintaining optimal traffic flow, the LTA has also implemented the Vehicle Quota System since 1 May 1990 to manage the growth of the vehicle population. The number of new vehicles allowed (that is, the quota) is pre-determined every year, taking into account the prevailing traffic conditions and the number of vehicles taken off the roads permanently. The quota for a given year is administered through the monthly release of Certificates of Entitlement (COEs). An aspiring vehicle owner would need to bid for and acquire a COE before he can buy a vehicle. This system has capped the growth rate of the vehicle population at 3 per cent per annum, compared with an average of 6.8 per cent per annum in the few years prior to its implementation.[7]

Public transport was also improved to encourage commuters to use public instead of private transport. With limited road space available, the heavy traffic during the morning and evening peak hours led to longer waiting and travel times for passengers on public buses, especially as public buses needed to make stops to pick up and drop off passengers. In order to meet the transport needs of commuters better and to offer an attractive alternative to cars, bus lanes were instituted to give scheduled public buses a dedicated right of way during the morning and evening peak hours. Full-day bus lanes have also been instituted for selected roads in the central business district to further improve the commuting times for bus passengers. The Mass Rapid Transit (MRT) routes were also progressively extended to improve its accessibility. The MRT system, which has reduced reliance on cars and buses, efficiently transports large numbers of commuters to various parts of the island each day.

In Singapore, transport planning is very closely integrated with land use planning. The planning and development of a high density and compact city, as well as the strategy of providing jobs close to homes and community amenities in each residential town, has reduced the need for commuting, thereby reducing vehicular emissions, especially during peak hours.

The new Land Transport Masterplan launched on 30 March 2008 also includes initiatives that will further enhance the public transport system and reduce congestion on the roads. Measures such as further extending the MRT routes, increasing ERP charges, reducing the annual vehicle population growth rate from 3 to 1.5 per cent, and promoting cycling as an alternative mode of transport,[8] not only ensure a more efficient land transport system in Singapore, but also help to reduce air pollution from vehicles.

ENVIRONMENTAL NOISE

Singapore's dense urban landscape has contributed to the problem of environmental noise, with noisy activities such as construction and traffic being close to residences. This is further exacerbated as increasing affluence leads to higher expectations of peace and quiet.

The approach taken towards environmental noise has been one of compromise. It is recognized that a certain amount of noise is inevitable, but measures have been taken to ensure that noise levels remain acceptable. These include standards and guidelines developed in consultation with the industry and benchmarked to international ones.

For example, construction sites, which are a major source of noise in Singapore due to their proximity to residences, have their noise emissions governed by the Environmental Protection and Management (Control of Noise at Construction Sites) Regulations. Maximum permissible noise levels covering both continuous and intermittent noisy activities are set under these Regulations. Recognizing that residents would be affected more by noise at night and on Sundays and public holidays, the standards for these times are tighter. This gives the industry flexibility to schedule their activities appropriately, compared with the practice in some other countries where construction work at night is banned. The standards are also tighter for construction sites close to hospitals, schools, institutions of higher learning, and homes for the aged.

Another source of noise is traffic. The impact of traffic noise has been reduced through the use of planning guidelines that require setback distances for residential premises adjacent to major roads and MRT tracks. As an example, the setback distances for MRT tracks are 35 metres for buildings fronting the MRT track, and 25 metres for buildings with the end-wall facing the track. For individual motor vehicles, limits are also set on noise measured from the exhaust.

However, as public expectations increase and Singaporeans aspire towards a higher quality of life, the government may need to review these measures as well as consider new ones, such as possibly tightening construction noise limits and using sound barriers to reduce the effect of traffic noise on nearby residences.

TRANSBOUNDARY AIR POLLUTION

Through the government's efforts, local sources of air pollution have been brought under control. The PSI is in the "good" range for most of the year and the concentration of major air pollutants is largely within USEPA standards. However, Singapore cannot ensure that the PSI is always in the good range because pollution is partly transboundary in nature. During the two periods of dry season a year, southern ASEAN countries, including Singapore, suffer from haze caused by forest fires in Indonesia. ASEAN recognizes the severity of the problem and has been working to resolve the matter since 1997. The indiscriminate burning of Indonesian forest not only pollutes the air of neighbouring ASEAN countries, but also poses a serious global problem as it aggravates global warming with Indonesia being the third largest emitter of carbon dioxide after the United States and China. While the issue needs to be tackled at the global level, Singapore at the same time continues to work with the Indonesian authorities, at both the national and the provincial levels, to try to bring about sustainable forest management.[9]

CONCLUSION

Singapore today enjoys a high standard of air quality comparable with that in many major cities around the world. Air quality monitoring, together with integrated urban and industrial planning and development control, have enabled the government to put in place preventive air pollution control measures during the planning stage. Beyond this, practical legislation and enforcement measures have helped to ensure that air quality standards are maintained in the long run.

Nevertheless, with increasing scientific evidence suggesting the need for more stringent air quality standards, Singapore may need to undertake measures to improve its air quality further to safeguard public health. As other cities continuously improve their air quality, Singapore will similarly have to ensure that its air quality improves in tandem so that it stays ahead or, at least, has comparable air quality and remains an attractive city in which to live, work, and play. Reducing the levels of air pollutants such as sulphur dioxide and fine particulate matter (PM2.5) will be the key challenge moving forward since many major cities today already have lower levels of such air pollutants compared with Singapore.

Possible initiatives for the future include moving towards cleaner fuels for industry and transport, tightening emission standards, improving energy efficiency, as well as improving the coverage of the air quality monitoring system and implementing remote-sensing of air pollutant emissions. Remote-sensing can also ensure that the growing number of factories comply with emission standards without the need for any substantial increase in enforcement manpower.

In addition, Singapore will implement a mandatory Fuel Economy Labelling Scheme for passenger vehicles in 2009. This will allow car buyers to take into account fuel consumption when making car purchase decisions. Singapore has also implemented the Green Vehicle Rebate scheme to encourage car owners to choose cleaner vehicles such as hybrids, compressed natural gas, and electric vehicles, over conventional petrol and diesel vehicles. The lower emissions from these green vehicles, as well as vehicles that are more fuel efficient, will contribute to further improvements in air quality.

These initiatives notwithstanding, factors such as the fast pace of industrialization, as well as transboundary pollution, will continue to pose challenges to maintaining the current level of air quality. As the economy continues to grow, new industries will be brought in, and these could potentially introduce new air pollutants currently not present in Singapore. This is particularly so for the chemicals and petrochemicals industries. Singapore will, therefore, have to continue to improve air monitoring and air pollution control measures.

On 2 December 1971, the rationale for the Clean Air Act was stated in Parliament:

> The ill effects of air pollution on human beings are numerous… they are impairment of general health, irritation of the eyes and throat, and chronic bronchitis… it can also cause economic loss through high maintenance costs and loss in man-hours, and can also contribute to the physical deterioration of the cities.[10]

These repercussions remain valid today. The government will have to make careful choices and implement measures that are applicable to Singapore's circumstances as these evolve, so that air quality can improve even as the country continues to achieve sound economic growth.

3

CLEANING THE LAND AND RIVERS

We can make Singapore cleaner by placing community before self. Showing concern for the well-being and cleanliness of the environment is the mark of a mature, refined society. In short, the environment is everybody's responsibility. Everyone has a stake in it. In a society like Switzerland, those who litter are deeply frowned upon. There is great social pressure to conform to good environmental habits. I think there should be more such peer pressure in Singapore. Many litterbugs still do not feel the shame for what they do.

Prime Minister Goh Chok Tong, at the Model Environmental
Workers Award Ceremony, 9 November 1997

The warm and humid equatorial climate in Singapore is highly conducive to the rapid decomposition of refuse and the breeding of vectors or disease-bearing insects such as mosquitoes and flies. In the 1960s, against the backdrop of a high population density of more than 3,000 persons per sq. kilometre (rising to about 15,000 per sq. kilometre in the urban areas), improper disposal of refuse and indiscriminate littering would inevitably create health hazards to the population, and could result in rapid infectious disease transmission.

Keeping Singapore clean was thus one of the foremost challenges that the government had to tackle after the island state gained independence in 1965. It was a challenge born out of necessity.[1] Moreover, during the early days of nationhood, a clean living environment was seen as a boost to the national morale and civic pride of a nascent state, helping to motivate the people to strive for higher standards of performance.

Removing litter is expensive as it involves the labour-intensive task of sweeping roads and drains, as well as subsequently collecting and disposing the litter. With the cost of litter removal many times that of domestic refuse removal, cost considerations alone would underscore the need to stop or minimize littering.

The government also recognized that improving public cleanliness was a crucial step towards achieving a good standard of public health, which in turn would contribute to a higher quality of life for Singaporeans. In addition to providing a more comfortable living environment for residents, a clean and litter-free Singapore also presents a significant competitive advantage in terms of attracting tourists to visit, foreign talents to work, and businessmen and industrialists to invest in Singapore.

CLEANING THE LAND

With these motivations, an ambitious plan of action was worked out to transform Singapore into one of the cleanest cities in the world. The formula that has proven to work for Singapore has four components — providing good and reliable public cleansing services and collecting refuse daily (elaborated on in Chapter 4); educating the public on the need to keep the environment clean; strict law enforcement; and investing in infrastructural improvements.

Providing Good and Reliable Public Cleansing Services

Since 1961, the Environmental Health Branch, which was then under the Ministry of Health, has been tasked with the responsibility of cleansing the streets. While it may sound straightforward, cleansing the streets was an enormous and highly laborious task in those days. The street cleaners had to make do with primitive and cumbersome methods and tools, pushing large and bulky wooden handcarts to bring their sweepings to the bin points. This was not helped by the prevalence of spitting, indiscriminate littering, and rampant illegal dumping. Although refuse bins were placed in designated open areas in the backlanes and vacant lands, these areas more often than not ended up as public dump sites due to the bad habits of the people. This made the cleansing work all the more difficult.[2]

The street cleaners, also referred to as the "broom brigade", were daily-rated employees (DREs) and were paid a wage for each day of work performed. To this day, every DRE is assigned a "beat", or a length of street that could range from two to five kilometres, and is responsible for ensuring that his assigned beat is free of public health nuisances. Thus, apart from sweeping the streets, he also goes into drains to clear chokages.

Wanting to put in place a reliable system with no lapses in cleansing work, the government amended the labour laws to allow cleaners who worked on a Sunday or public holiday to be given a day off on any other day, in lieu of additional pay. This paved the way for the introduction of a daily public cleansing regime by 1968. Henceforth, the streets were swept and refuse removed every day of the week including Sundays and public holidays. Following the formation of the Ministry of the Environment (ENV), the Environmental Health Branch was transferred to a newly created Environmental Public Health Division (EPHD) in the new Ministry.

Even after the daily cleansing regime was introduced, the government continued to pursue innovative ways to achieve greater operational efficiency. One measure was to decentralize the management of public cleansing services to the district offices under the Environmental Health Department, through integrating the supervision of public cleansing work into the duties of the public health inspectors based in these offices. Because the inspectors were familiar with every nook and cranny of the areas under their charge, they were able to schedule the cleaning work to achieve a high level of performance.

Despite decentralizing the management of public cleansing services, a more fundamental problem remained — the difficulty in recruiting DREs as cleaners. The abundance of employment opportunities in the rapidly growing economy meant that many people shunned a cleaner's job, which was seen as a low-grade, menial occupation. As a result, it became necessary to turn to mechanical sweepers.

First brought into Singapore in 1972, mechanical sweepers quickly proved to be an effective substitute for manual labour. Each sweeper is able to take on the work ordinarily performed by thirty to forty workmen. As a result, more of such vehicles were progressively deployed to clean the roads, while ENV continued to source for other labour-saving tools that were lighter and better designed to perform specific tasks such as litter picking.

Although the introduction of mechanical sweepers went a long way towards easing the labour crunch, the ageing DRE workforce soon emerged as a new challenge. By the end of the 1990s, some of the longest serving DREs had worked for more than half a century. The prospect of finding younger workers to replace the retiring DREs was a daunting one. Certainly, judging from the retiring DREs who were still cleaning the same streets decades after their initial employment, the career prospects for their replacements were not rosy.

With this consideration, as well as with the aim of improving operational efficiency, ENV found that it was necessary to deploy mechanical road and pavement sweepers to carry out the cleansing work, as far as the physical conditions of the roads and pavements allowed these machines to be used. This reduced further the number of workmen who had to be recruited. However, the route to mechanization was not plain sailing. Street fixtures such as lamp posts, signs, and benches obstructed the movement of the mechanical vehicles, particularly the pavement sweepers, such that these areas ended up having to be cleansed manually. To overcome this problem, the relevant government agencies were roped in to ensure that street fixtures and furniture were sited in a way that would minimize obstruction. This facilitated the wider deployment of pavement sweepers. An unexpected positive spin-off engendered by this exercise was that the pavements were also made more user-friendly for the elderly and handicapped on wheelchairs.

The government also decided to outsource the provision of public cleansing services to private contractors to allow private sector involvement and reap the efficiency gains from competition. Today, public cleansing services in two-thirds of the island are provided by private contractors, and there are plans to outsource progressively the remaining part over time.

Educating the Public on the Need to Keep the Environment Clean

In spite of the efficient public cleansing service that has been put in place over the last three decades, the government recognized from the early days that public cleansing alone would not be sufficient to keep the streets clean. While public cooperation and participation are critical to controlling the littering problem, these were also the most difficult to achieve as they required the public to develop a sense of civic consciousness, social responsibility, and discipline. Hence, a two-pronged approach was adopted to cultivate civic consciousness — national public education and law enforcement.[3]

The first national public education effort was a month-long "Keep Singapore Clean" campaign that was launched in October 1968. The campaign sought to educate each individual on the importance of not littering the streets, drains, and public places.

This campaign was planned and run by an intersectoral committee headed by the then Minister for Health. The committee comprised representatives from organizations with a broad mass base or those that provided specialized services. These included the chambers of commerce, employers' and trade unions, government ministries (Education, Interior and Defence, and Culture), the Police and the Public Works Department, as well as statutory boards such as the Housing and Development Board, the Public Utilities Board, the Tourist Promotion Board, and the Jurong Town Corporation. It was probably one of the earliest examples of inter-agency collaboration within the government.

The national campaign was a month-long intensive programme of activities, with sustained and extensive coverage by the mass media since this was the most effective channel in reaching out to individuals. Jingles, newsreels, documentaries, filmlets, and slides were broadcast daily over TV and radio, while a roving exhibition was held to reach out to the rural population. Social pressure was subtly used in the campaign, with "candid camera" style films and photographs of places and establishments found in a bad state of cleanliness, and errant members of the public caught littering the streets.

Children in schools were a key target audience. As they were at an impressionable age, it was hoped that they would internalize the message and form desired habits. Poster design and essay competitions exclusively for school children were organized. Special talks on cleanliness by health officers, inspectors of schools, and principals were made at least twice in each school during the campaign month. Teachers also gave daily reminders against littering and the importance of keeping the premises clean.

To promote mass participation, public and private entities were encouraged to organize their own Keep Singapore Clean activities over and above those at the national level. The most significant were competitions held to select the cleanest offices, shops, restaurants, markets, factories, government buildings, schools, and public vehicles, in which the judges not only picked the ten cleanest premises, but also the ten dirtiest premises. The political leadership provided much support for the campaign. Members of Parliament, together with community leaders, organized activities at the constituency level to get as many of their constituents involved as possible.

While the national public education campaign received resounding responses from all sectors of society, its momentum would be lost unless it was followed up with some concrete action after the campaign. This follow-up action had to be the strict enforcement of the anti-litter laws. However, to provide time for the public to become accustomed to the enforcement, those who were caught littering and indiscriminately disposing refuse during the campaign month were not penalized, but were warned of the possible penalties. The intent was that when the enforcement kicked in after the campaign, there should be no complaints that no adequate warning had been given.

While the majority of the public became aware of the need not to litter and also supported enforcement against litterbugs, there was inevitably a minority who persisted in their bad habits, and on whom the law had to be brought to bear. The government took the unpopular decision to prosecute recalcitrant adult offenders strictly and even published their names in the media. School children offenders were reported to their school principals, who would then discipline them by making them sweep their classrooms or school compounds.

The national public education campaign successfully imprinted indiscriminate littering and dumping in the minds of the public as anti-social acts that would not be condoned.

Riding on this initial success, annual campaigns in the ensuing years were conducted along similar lines, with each focusing on a specific theme in addition to the underlying one of keeping Singapore clean. The theme in 1969, for instance, was "Keep Singapore Clean and Mosquito-Free" to generate public interest and participation in the prevention and control of mosquito breeding so as to contain the mosquito population at a low level.

The "Keep Singapore Clean" campaign took on an additional dimension in 1971 with the launch of the "Tree Planting Day" by then Deputy Prime Minister Dr Goh Keng Swee on Sunday, 7 November at the summit of Mount Faber. It marked the beginning of a tradition that spanned the next two decades, during which Tree Planting Days were held on the first Sunday of each November. The Tree Planting Day was a hallmark event supporting the tropical garden city initiative, which aimed to transform Singapore into a clean as well as green city. In his book, *From Third World to First*, the first Prime Minister Lee Kuan Yew wrote about the drive to make Singapore a tropical garden city. He said that greenery not only raised morale and made people proud, but also demonstrated the efforts put into maintenance. The Tree Planting Day was deliberately set at the beginning of the rainy season in November to minimize watering.

The annual campaigns were significant in many ways. First and foremost, they made Singaporeans aware of the need to be socially responsible and disciplined, and provided an excellent platform to address a number of important public health issues, ranging from communicable diseases and poor food hygiene to mosquito control and pollution. Through the campaigns, the public was informed of public health issues to look out for and changes that were taking place, such as the commencement of daily refuse collection, and the availability of public cleansing services. The campaigns also created avenues of communication between the people and the authorities, and served as a gauge for the public's response to new services and regulations that were introduced.

By the 1980s, the series of annual campaigns had enabled the government to make significant advances in several other aspects of environmental health such as managing the mosquito problem, raising standards of personal hygiene, and controlling air and water pollution. With increasing urbanization that also improved the physical environment, the focus of the national public education campaign accordingly shifted from broad-based issues to more targeted ones, such as proper disposal of refuse in plastic bags, cleanliness of public toilets, and anti-spitting.

In 1990, the Ministry of the Environment launched the first Clean and Green Week (CGW) as a new approach to environmental education. The CGW incorporated the Tree Planting Day, with tree planting activities still held in every Clean and Green Week.

The CGW was a week-long campaign that occurred in November each year. Apart from continuing to promote an appreciation for a clean and green environment in Singapore, it also sought to increase community awareness for global environmental concerns, as well as encourage their participation in caring for the environment. Consequently, themes such as "Commitment and Responsibility", "Awareness and Action", and "A Better Living Environment" were adopted in different years to make Singaporeans realize that caring for the environment was one aspect of social responsibility.[4]

One particular CGW programme is the Cleanest Estate Competition, which ran from 1995 to 2002. The competition pitted HDB estates against one another in a race to clinch the title of the cleanest estate, thereby encouraging their residents to stop littering and do their part in keeping their surroundings clean. The assessment covered both the physical appearance of the estate, such as the presence of litter in common areas, as well as the social behaviour demonstrated by the residents. Points were deducted for irresponsible acts such as killer litter,[5] vandalism to common property, and the illegal dumping of bulky refuse and other obstructions in common areas.

While the competition was largely successful in the beginning, it became increasingly seen as a battle between town councils managing the estates (including their cleaners) rather than as a healthy competition among the residents. Instead of encouraging the residents to take ownership of keeping their living environment clean, the competition led to town councils competing on the strength of their cleaners. In 2007, the Islandwide Cleanest Estate Competition (ICEC) was introduced, with an emphasis on raising community awareness and promoting social responsibility in keeping the living environment clean, and promoting the residents' sense of ownership over the common areas in the estates. The judging criteria of the ICEC give greater weight to community efforts in promoting social responsibility among residents than to efforts by the cleaners.

Strict Law Enforcement

Although public education has played a significant part in helping Singapore achieve its reputation as a clean and green city, it would be too simplistic to conclude that education alone has had such a transforming effect. No matter how successful public education initiatives may be, there will invariably be a small group of individuals who remain recalcitrant.

Prior to 1968, health officials had been working with legislation that was formulated for a colonial era. However, this would not be adequate in addressing future public health problems since past legislation focused mainly on preventing the spread of infectious diseases and the control of epidemics, while other challenges such as the cleanliness of the environment were not sufficiently covered. Therefore, a thorough and complete revision of all principal and subsidiary legislation governing matters of public health was necessary.[6]

The revision took into account the prevailing political and social conditions as well as the behaviour and attitudes of the population. It also included a reappraisal of what constituted acceptable health standards or requirements. This culminated in the birth of a new piece of legislation in 1968 that equipped the then Ministry of Health to carry out its battle against litterbugs — the Environmental Public Health Act (EPHA). The EPHA replaced Part IV of the Local Government Integration Ordinance, 1963, which had previously governed the maintenance of public health.

The Act in its fourteen parts covers all fields of environmental health. In particular, Part III (Public Cleansing) deals with the cleansing of streets, the collection and removal of refuse, and the cleanliness of "public places". Comprehensive provisions against littering and the disposal of refuse in public places were introduced. Under the Act, it is an offence to throw or leave behind bottles, paper, food containers, food, and cigarette butts. The spilling of noxious and offensive matter and the dropping or spilling of earth in public is also considered an offence.

The Act further requires the owners and/or developers of flats and industrial complexes to provide at their own expense proper facilities for refuse collection and disposal. Bin centres are now a requirement for building complexes as they provide a convenient point from which refuse can be removed by refuse collection vehicles. Compactors have also been introduced to maximize the storage space in bin centres, as well as improve on the efficiency of transporting the refuse to the incineration plants.

Among the new provisions introduced was a fairly controversial presumption clause, which provided that any litter or refuse found on the frontages of premises would be presumed to be deposited by the occupiers of the premises until proven otherwise. As the burden of proof is on the individuals committing the act, it provided a form of deterrence, and is likely to have also resulted in social pressure against littering.

Most of the offences under the Act carried a fine not exceeding S$500 for the first conviction, and a fine not exceeding S$2,000 for the second and subsequent convictions, which was a hefty sum in the 1960s and 1970s. A more severe penalty was imposed on builders, developers, and contractors who, during the course of their work, left building materials in public places, or failed to take reasonable precautions to prevent people in public places from being injured by falling dust or building fragments.

To achieve the desired outcome of improving public cleanliness, strict legislative provisions had to be accompanied by equally serious enforcement. Much thought was put into how the legislation should be enforced. The first consideration was that the public should be provided with sufficient means and opportunity to comply with the law, without being overly inconvenienced in their daily routine. For instance, provisions were made for people to have adequate and conveniently sited bins that were emptied and cleaned regularly, to throw their litter.

Second, the new laws were publicized and explained to raise awareness and gain the public's acceptance of the changes in behaviour that were expected of them.

Third, great care was taken to ensure that the legislation was properly spelt out so that the implementation would be uniform and not subject to bargaining. Enforcement officers were expected to be firm, but fair, in enforcing the laws. For instance, if a person unconsciously drops litter and regrets his action, he would be given an opportunity to pick the litter up for proper disposal. However, if the act was deliberate, the person would be penalized. Also, while the maximum penalty or fine for each offence may seem harsh, they are only applied to recalcitrant offenders. For others, lighter penalties, such as the offer of composition, would apply.

Finally, swift action must be taken against recalcitrant offenders who fail to abide by the laws. This is important as environmental offences are often viewed as being negligible when compared with statutory offences. The offender is given an immediate punishment after committing the offence so the deterrent effects of punishment are not lost.

To this end, enforcement procedures for certain offences under the EPHA are designed to be dealt with expeditiously, with minimal paper work. Under this procedure, a littering offender is served a ticket on the spot requiring him to attend a designated Court on a prescribed day. The offender is dealt with summarily if he pleads guilty; the offence is compounded by levying a fine not exceeding S$500. If the fine is paid, no further action will be taken. If the offender claims trial, a date will be fixed for the hearing. Any offender who fails to turn up in court will be arrested on a warrant.

Over the years, the combination of anti-littering laws with fines as penalties and the series of annual "Keep Singapore Clean" campaigns, have helped reduce the littering problem to a large extent. Nonetheless, litter has never been totally eradicated due to the thoughtlessness of litterbugs, especially the "diehards". A Littering Behaviour Survey conducted by the National Environment Agency (NEA) in 2006 found that about 14 per cent of the people interviewed felt that it was acceptable to litter.

The Corrective Work Order (CWO) introduced in 1992, in place of a hefty fine, sets the offender to work in cleaning up the community for periods of up to three hours, subject to a total of twelve hours. This applies to those who are above sixteen years old, are repeat offenders, and/or have committed serious littering offences. The first CWO was performed in 1993 in public places such as parks and beaches, and was subsequently extended to housing estates. Other than being punitive, the CWO regime also had a reparative element as cleaning up housing estates was a means to increase the offenders' awareness of the impact of littering, and to experience the difficulties faced by the cleaners.

Not surprisingly, the CWO regime attracted its fair share of controversy, with many seeing it as a shaming tool. While the majority accepted the CWO as an additional punitive option, there were some who felt that the initiative was introduced ahead of its time, with the public in Singapore still relatively unreceptive to the idea of performing work in lieu of a financial penalty, unlike in developed countries where such punishment was more common. Notwithstanding this, the government stood its ground.

This was not an altogether easy decision. However, to realize the vision of a clean Singapore, the government was prepared to make the unpopular choice by adhering to strict enforcement against littering. This would be borne out in the longer term, when there are clean streets and public places for all to enjoy.

INVESTING IN INFRASTRUCTURAL IMPROVEMENTS — RE-SETTLING HAWKERS

Investing in infrastructural improvements has gone a long way in helping Singapore to address a major public health challenge — the unsanitary and hygiene problems posed by itinerant hawkers.

In the post-World War II period, unemployment was a widespread problem. Many unemployed people took to the streets, literally. Street hawking became a thriving trade because the entry barrier was low. The good income attracted many poorly educated individuals with little capital and skills.

The number of street hawkers soon grew, with many congregating in convenient open areas within housing estates, and along major traffic routes. Although they were unsightly, the government then adopted a liberal attitude towards street hawking as it not only encouraged entrepreneurship, but was also a means for the unemployed to earn an honest living.

By the late 1960s, rapid industrial and economic development followed Singapore's independence. The abundance of employment opportunities saw more family members going to work and taking their meals outside. The demand for cheap and convenient hawker food grew, and consequently, many more people were drawn to the lucrative hawking trade. It was estimated that at one stage, hawkers numbered close to 25,000, or nearly one in 100 of Singapore's population.

The rapid proliferation of street hawkers soon posed a major public health problem. Street hawkers lacked proper equipment and amenities (such as refrigeration and clean tap water) and many did not observe good personal and food hygiene. The food was mainly prepared in makeshift stalls, with no direct access to clean water for cooking and washing of utensils. Consuming hawker food was often associated with food-borne disease outbreaks such as cholera and typhoid. Those peddling perishable food items such as cut fruits, cold drinks, and ice-cream were particularly culpable, as they often used contaminated water and ice.

Without a refuse management system in place, food waste generated from street hawkers was indiscriminately dumped onto streets, or thrown into drains and waterways, giving rise to severe chokages and water pollution. The market produce hawkers were also a problem, as they left behind vegetable waste, poultry droppings, fish cuttings, and other litter on the roads. These invariably found their way into the waterways and streams.

The accumulation of waste gave rise to the proliferation of vectors such as rats, flies, and mosquitoes. Street cleansing works were practically impossible to carry out because roads and drains were obstructed by the makeshift structures of the vendors and their paraphernalia. The noise generated by hawkers hawking their fare was also a distraction to nearby schools and public institutions.

It did not take long before the appearance of the city deteriorated. The presence of hawkers in almost every street, footway, and backlane was a blight to the cityscape. The dilapidated makeshift structures put up by the hawkers caused many parts of the city to resemble slums. The negative externalities went beyond just public health, with many able-bodied adults preferring street hawking, which was perceived to be a lucrative trade, to joining the workforce to serve in more economically efficient sectors.

It soon became imperative that effective policies and measures be put in place to curb the uncontrolled proliferation of street hawking. As a step towards achieving this, an island-wide census of street hawkers was carried out between December 1968 and February 1969. The government then decided on two courses of action — a short-term and a long-term solution.

The short-term solution involved the licensing of street hawkers and relocating them to temporary sites. This effectively limited the number of street hawkers so that their activities could be properly circumscribed. As this move was not popular with street hawkers, the licensing exercise was carried out in close consultation with the Citizens Consultative Committee members. Because of the political repercussions, a committee was set up to decide on the policies governing licences and to consider complaints and appeals.

A total of 24,000 hawkers were licensed in the exercise. Of these, 6,000 were operating in markets while the remaining 18,000 were operating on the streets. These hawkers were issued with temporary street-hawking licences and resited to side streets, back lanes, side lanes, and car parks, where washing areas connected to the sewers were provided wherever possible. New licences were issued only to those who were genuinely suffering financial hardship. The Environmental Public Health (Hawkers) Regulation and relevant sections of the Environmental Health Act regulating the activities of the hawkers were strictly enforced to ensure that stall sites and their surroundings were kept clean at all times.

The licensing exercise was to pave the way for identifying *bona fide* hawkers who would ultimately be relocated into permanent premises. This represented the long-term solution — to house all street hawkers in purpose-built buildings within five years. This was kickstarted with an initial provision of S$5 million to the Housing and Development Board in 1971 for the construction of permanent hawker centres and markets, which served the dual objectives of resiting street hawkers and providing amenities for residents of new towns.

Each market cum hawker centre comprised a market section and a cooked food section. The centres were provided with essential amenities such as proper sewage connections, piped water and electricity, and bulk bin centres for the disposal of refuse. The cooked food stalls were also compartmentalized, and lined with glazed tiles. Fixed tables and stools for customers became a common feature in all hawker centres. Ceiling fans and toilet facilities were also available for the comfort and convenience of the patrons.

Riding on the initial success, the government embarked on a massive programme to build markets and hawker centres outside the new towns. To accelerate the pace of building such centres, a policy was introduced in which the permission for land redevelopment use was granted to a developer, on the condition that a hawker centre was built to house the street hawkers affected by the redevelopment.

The resettlement of the street hawkers was not without its problems. First, all hawkers along the same street would need to be resettled *en masse* to a nearby location, while ensuring that no new unlicensed hawkers reoccupy the vacated street. This necessitated working closely with the Police. In spite of the better environment, many street hawkers were reluctant to move into the centres as business was deemed to be better on the main streets where there was more human traffic. To encourage street hawkers to relocate into the newly built centres, the rent for stalls was deliberately kept at the same level as that levied on street hawkers. At that time, the need to recover the costs of building and maintaining these hawker centres from the hawkers was the least of the government's considerations when deciding on the rental to be levied. The hawkers also had to be convinced of the benefits of operating in a hawker centre, such as the availability of utilities, and not being subjected to the vagaries of the weather.

To clear the entire nation of street hawkers, the government worked closely with Members of Parliament, grassroots leaders, and the hawkers themselves. In many cases, Members of Parliament themselves presided over the balloting of stalls, to ensure that this was perceived as a fair and transparent way of stall allocation. The entire resiting programme was successfully completed after about fifteen years in 1985. Today, there are 111 government markets cum hawker centres, housing about 15,000 stalls.

The earlier generations of markets and hawker centres were constructed with the main purpose of providing a permanent site for the resettlement of street hawkers. Practicality was the key consideration, with little attention paid to their façade. By the late 1990s, most of these centres were at least twenty years old. Many of them were in poor physical condition, which made maintenance a big challenge. Visually, these centres had also not kept up with the rejuvenation that had been taking place in the housing estates where they were located.

In 2001, the Environment Ministry, therefore, decided to embark on the Hawker Centres Upgrading Programme (HUP), committing more than S$420 million over ten years. The upgrading works range from complete demolition and rebuilding of the centre to retrofitting such as re-tiling, installation of new tables and stools, widening of passageways, replacement of utility infrastructure such as sewer pipes, rewiring, improvement to the ventilation, bin centres, and toilets, provision of improved lighting, and optimizing the space utilization with better layout.

The newly upgraded centres boast features such as better ventilation and lighting, open courtyards, and outdoor dining areas. They also have a more visually pleasant building façade and finishings, as well as flexible seating arrangements. The toilets have been refurbished, not only to improve them, but to make maintenance easier. The upgrading has not only benefited the stallholders, but the patrons as well, who now have a more pleasant and congenial ambience to enjoy their meals. As of 2008, 63 out of a total of 110 eligible centres have been upgraded under the programme.

Hawker centres may have been born out of necessity. But today, many say they provide the best eating experience in Singapore. In fact, dining in a hawker centre has achieved international acclaim, and was featured in Patricia Schultz's book in 2003 — *1,000 Places to See before You Die*.[7]

THE SINGAPORE RIVER AND KALLANG BASIN CLEAN-UP

Much of what pollutes the land will eventually pollute the rivers. Any rubbish on the road, if not cleared, will be washed by rain into the drains, and from there to the culverts, then on to the canals, and eventually into the rivers. The cleaning up of the Singapore River and Kallang Basin serves to highlight the importance of keeping the land clean. By doing so, the high-quality living environment on land can extend to the waters as well.

The Singapore River, the disembarkation point for many early settlers and the birthplace of Singapore's commercial hub, has been associated with the traditional trading and business activities of Singapore for more than a century. Over the years, the Singapore River, together with the Kallang River, which are both waterways with urban catchments, became highly polluted due to population growth, urbanization, industrial expansion, and the uncontrolled discharge of all forms of waste and pollution.

From the early 1800s, as more and more settlers arrived on Singapore's shores, many of them found accommodation along the quays and riverbanks. Some of their activities, such as dumping garbage into the water and using the rivers for sewage disposal, probably marked the beginnings of a river that was soon to become extremely polluted. Early industries that were sited along the banks of the Singapore River, such as processing of gambier, sago, and seaweed, also contributed to the pollution.[8]

By the second half of the century, the importance of these industries had diminished, but the escalating problems of pollution did not end. Port-related activities along the Singapore and Kallang Rivers, including warehouses and bumboats that carried goods from the large ships in the harbour, flourished. Ship building and repairs were also carried out at the Kallang Basin. The by-products of these activities, namely oil, sullage water, and solid waste, were either disposed of directly into the rivers, or eventually found their way to the rivers via the drains.[9]

Markets sprang up in the riverside community, where perishables were sold. As they were adjacent to the river, any leftovers were conveniently discarded into the water. Street hawkers also set up shop right by the river, often dumping used water and food into the drains or even directly into the river. Squatters set up homes along the river without sewage facilities. Some had overhanging latrines that would discharge waste directly into streams. Backyard trades and cottage industries in these unsewered premises aggravated the problem. Their trade effluent was also discharged into drains. Pig and duck farms proliferated, adding animal waste to the cocktail of pollution in the rivers.[10]

These rivers were essentially open sewers and became extremely polluted by the 1960s. With office towers and hotels being built along a newly created central business district, there was a pressing need to clean up the rivers.

At the same time, water reserves grew insufficient. The few reservoirs could not hold sufficient water to serve the needs of the expanding population which had reached one million by the 1950s. Water supply for the island had to be imported mainly from the Tebrau River in Johor, as local water sources were inadequate. A drought in 1963 demonstrated the severity of the situation, with local reservoirs drying up and the volume of water in the Tebrau River dropping dramatically. Water rationing had to be imposed on the people in Singapore. With high density housing projects springing up to accommodate an exploding population, efforts to ensure the provision of a good water supply and maintain cleanliness were strained to the limit. Hence, a programme to build more local reservoirs and maintain the cleanliness of the water supply at all costs became a matter of utmost importance for the future of Singapore.[11]

It was apt that in declaring the Upper Peirce Reservoir open on 27 February 1977, then Prime Minister Lee Kuan Yew said, "It should be a way of life to keep the water clean, to keep every stream, every culvert, every rivulet free from unnecessary pollution. In ten years, let us have fishing in the Singapore River and fishing in the Kallang River. It can be done."[12]

What was involved was no less than unclogging the way Singapore worked. Engineering solutions to remove pollution could not adequately address the pollution. Rather, the very causes and sources of pollution needed to be tackled. The river was a workplace and a home for the many hawkers and squatters lining its banks. It was not enough simply to prevent them from dirtying the river. They had to be given an alternative way of life where possible.[13]

Since livelihoods were at stake, cleaning up the river meant giving people a different lifeline to the future. Squatters and farmers had to be resttled. Backyard trades and industries had to be relocated. Street hawkers had to be resited. These meant building houses, industrial workshops, and food centres, in addition to developing proper sewage infrastructure. To free the river from pollution meant, in many ways, constructing a new Singapore through which a rescued river could flow. The physical task was gigantic, but it was only one aspect of a larger human drama.[14]

A Master Plan for the cleaning up of the Singapore River and Kallang Basin was drawn up for the purpose. The draft plan indicated that the Singapore River and Kallang Basin were the two most badly polluted catchments in the city. The Kallang Basin was drained by the Kallang River, Bukit Timah-Rochor Canal, Whampoa River, Geylang River and Pelton Canal. The plan also noted the scope of the challenge:

> In general, the pollution problem is three-fold. In areas where pollution control facilities have been provided, we have to ensure that these facilities are used and efficiently operated. In some areas where such facilities have not been provided, but are possible with redevelopment, we need to know what plans there are for redevelopment and if need be, to spur them on and set targets. In the remaining areas where it is either impossible or economically not feasible to provide such facilities (e.g. for roadside hawkers, boat colonies, etc.), we need to have a plan of action to control, minimise or eliminate these sources. The main objective is to restore the Kallang Basin and Singapore River to the extent that marine life can thrive in the water. Organic and inorganic pollution in the form of solid and liquid waste should be prevented or minimised.[15]

As the catchments made up some 30 per cent of Singapore's area, it was a challenge for the planners, who had to piece together an overview of the entire range of pollutive activities in the catchments. These included pig and duck farms, squatter huts, backyard industries, and hawkers, some of which were actually located quite a distance from the rivers.[16]

The draft plan revealed the enormity of the task, the undertaking of which would not be restricted to the departments under the Ministry of the Environment, such as environmental health, sewerage, drainage, and hawkers, but also involved departments and agencies under the Ministry of National Development (MND), Ministry of Trade and Industry (MTI), Ministry of Communications & Information (MICA) and Ministry of Law (MinLaw). These agencies included the Housing and Development Board (HDB), Urban Redevelopment Authority (URA), Jurong Town Corporation (JTC), Primary Production Department (PPD), Port of Singapore Authority (PSA), Public Works Department (PWD) and Parks and Recreation Department.[17]

Approximately 46,000 unsewered squatters were affected by the clean-up exercise. The Kallang Basin was very heavily squattered with about 42,000 squatters in its five catchments, while the Singapore River Catchment had about 4,000 squatters. This included about 26,000 residential families, 610 pig farmers, and 2,800 backyard trades and industries.[18]

The squatters were resettled under a Resettlement Policy, which was introduced in the 1960s. Under the policy, all persons and business establishments affected by resettlement were to be offered rehousing and compensation. However, the benefits only applied to Singaporeans. Some of the squatters were not Singaporeans and hence were not entitled to resettlement benefits. If they were forcibly evicted, they could become destitute vagabonds sleeping on the sidewalks. These were sensitive issues which had to be resolved in a way that would not make the government appear uncaring and callous. Whenever possible, non-Singaporean squatters were allowed to rent flats. Another problem arising from the resettlement process was the question of whether the squatters were on private land or State Land. If they were on State Land, the government could readily resettle them and then spruce up the vacant land. However, if they were on private land, the government had to acquire it, which was not a popular move. The resettlement of squatters was thus a slow process.[19]

The 610 pig farms, as well as 500 duck farms located within the Kallang Basin, were initially relocated to Punggol. However, by the mid-1980s, to eradicate such pollutive and unhygienic activities, as well as conserve Singapore's limited land and water resources for housing and industry, the decision was made to phase these activities out completely.[20]

In 1971, for reasons of hygiene, the hawker resettlement programme was introduced, in which street hawkers were moved to purpose-built hawker centres and markets. The river clean-up project accelerated the programme. Close to 5,000 street hawkers within the catchments were relocated to markets and hawker centres, such as those at Boat Quay, Empress Place, and Chinatown. So that the hawkers would not lose their clientele, the new food centres were built very near the streets where the hawkers were operating. Vegetable wholesalers who had been traditionally operating on the five-foot ways, streets, and vacant land without proper facilities were also relocated to the Pasir Panjang Wholesale Market.[21]

To prevent human waste, sullage water, and other forms of waste from being discharged into the rivers by bumboat operators and their families staying on board the vessels, cargo handling, storage, and mooring facilities were established at Pasir Panjang for the purpose of relocating the lighters there. By 1983, the lighters were completely relocated. The decision to do so was carefully weighed, given its potential impact on Singapore's entrepôt trade. The conclusion was that the phasing out of lighter transport was not undesirable as it would mean moving from a two-transfer system to a one-transfer system where vessels worked alongside wharves, simplifying the process. Initially, there were many complaints about the lighter anchorage at Pasir Panjang, with claims that the waves were stronger there than in the sheltered water of the rivers, and that it was too far away, as most lighter operators lived in the Chinatown area. To make the move less painful, a breakwater was built to buffer the lighters from the waves, and a canteen set up to provide food. The canteen also served to reduce the practice of cooking on the boats and throwing the resulting waste into the water. Four years later, the lightermen were quite happy to be in Pasir Panjang despite their initial complaints.[22]

There were also some sixty-six boatbuilders and repairers in the Kallang Basin catchment. To remove them in one fell swoop would have been too harsh. To let them vanish through attrition would have taken too long. Thus, a compromise was struck. The larger boatyards were required to upgrade their operations to comply with anti-pollution requirements. Where possible, neighbouring boatyards were also advised to join these larger yards so that pollution control facilities could be provided in a more economical and technically feasible manner. Small boatyards which were unable to upgrade their operations and comply with pollution control requirements but were otherwise viable, were offered alternative sites in Jurong.[23]

Rubbish and flotsam that had accumulated in the rivers and along their banks were dredged and removed after these primary sources of pollution had been addressed. During the month-long removal operation, more than 260 tonnes of rubbish were collected and disposed of. In 1986, the PWD improved and tiled the riverside walkway along the Singapore River, while the Parks and Recreation Department carried out landscaping along the riverbanks. In the same year, the Environment Ministry commenced physical improvement works at the Kallang Basin. The river bed was dredged to remove the mud at the bottom and 1 metre of sand was put in. Certain sections of the Kallang Basin were also covered with sand to create aesthetically pleasing sandy banks.[24]

The clean-up cost the government nearly S$300 million, excluding resettlement compensation. In addition to addressing the sources of pollution, engineering measures were also used to prevent the entry of further pollution into the river. For instance, drains in litter-prone areas were covered with slabs, vertical gratings were installed at selected outlet drains leading to main canals and rivers, and float booms were installed across rivers and canals to trap inorganic litter, such as plastic bags and bottles.[25]

The entire nation rejoiced when the programme was completed in September 1987. The river could flow freely. Its banks, once cluttered with boatyards, backyard trades and squatters, were transformed, almost unbelievably, into attractive riverside walkways and landscaped parks. Fish and other forms of aquatic life returned to the river. So did the people, to relax along the shores or play in the waters of a riverine stretch that Singapore had reclaimed as its own.[26]

The team behind the clean-up was led by the Permanent Secretary of Environment, Lee Ek Tieng, who would go on to become Head of the Civil Service. He and nine others were each awarded a gold medal by the Prime Minister for their efforts in cleaning up the Singapore River.[27]

On completion of the clean-up in 1987, the Environment Ministry launched the Clean Rivers Education Programme to educate the public on the massive efforts taken to clean up Singapore's waterways, and urge them to act responsibly and do their part in contributing to this effort.[28]

In a television interview shortly after the clean-up, then Prime Minister Lee Kuan Yew said:

> In 20 years, it is possible that there could be breakthroughs in technology, both anti-pollution and filtration, and then we dam up or put a barrage at the mouth of the Marina — the neck that joins the sea — and we will have a huge freshwater lake. The advantages are obvious. One: a large strategic reserve of water — fresh water — for use in emergency: a drought, or some such period. Second, it will help flood control because at high tides — exceptional high tides — which happens about two periods a year, if they coincide with heavy rain, the three rivers and canals

will flood parts of the city. Now with the barrage, we can control the flooding. And with the barrage, the water level can be held steady. We need never [sic] have low tides. So the recreational use and scenic effect would be greatly improved. And it is possible in another 20 years, and therefore, we should keep on improving the quality of the water.[29]

The clean-up of the Singapore River and the rivers in the Kallang Basin had become a model for other rivers and set in motion a process to realize the vision of creating a reservoir in the city. Today, that vision has become reality. With the construction of the Marina Barrage, Singapore will have a new source of freshwater, an ability to alleviate flooding in the city, as well as a new venue for recreation and revitalization. As it was said, "It can be done."

CONSERVING SINGAPORE'S NATURAL HERITAGE[30]

Keeping the land and rivers clean not only has benefits for public health and results in a higher quality living environment, but also supports efforts to conserve Singapore's natural heritage through preventing its natural ecosystems from being polluted.

Singapore's conservation model is one that enables environmental sustainability in a small urban setting, balancing growth with conservation. Areas which are representative of key indigenous ecosystems are legally protected by the government as gazetted nature reserves. There are four nature reserves in Singapore, namely the Bukit Timah Nature Reserve and the Central Catchment Nature Reserve which is made up of primary and mature secondary forests and a fresh water swamp; the Sungei Buloh Wetland Reserve which conserves a mangrove forest and is also a bird sanctuary; and the Labrador Nature Reserve which comprises coastal secondary vegetation and a rocky shore. Together, these cover more than 3,000 hectares or about 4.5 per cent of Singapore's land area. Outside of the nature reserves, Singapore's network of green spaces, park connectors, and water bodies cover a further 4.5 per cent of its land area. Through careful management, these areas are also optimized to enhance urban biodiversity. Even Singapore's offshore landfill, Pulau Semakau (see also Chapters 4 and 11), defying the common stereotype of a landfill as a dirty, unpleasant dump, is a green natural environment thriving with rich biodiversity. The island is home to over 13 hectares of mangroves, which shelter a thriving community of flora and fauna. A coral nursery has also been established off Semakau to maximize the survival of naturally occurring corals, in which coral fragments are grown for transplanting to existing coral reef habitats.

Through these conservation efforts, Singapore can count itself a city which is rich in biodiversity despite being a small, island city state. For instance, Singapore has some 360 species of birds, which is slightly more than 60 per cent of the 568 species in the United Kingdom. It has eleven out of twenty-three seagrass species found in the Indo-Pacific region. Singapore also has over 250 species of reef-forming hard corals that account for about 30 per cent of the world's hard coral species — there are more coral species per hectare of reef in Singapore waters than there are in the Great Barrier Reef.

VECTOR-BORNE DISEASES

The systems and processes that the government had put in place in cleaning up the land and waterways also greatly benefited Singapore's environmental public health, particularly in the control of infectious disease transmission. First, the resettlement of street hawkers into purpose-built food centres has minimized the likelihood of food being prepared in unsanitary conditions, thus contributing to a low incidence of food-borne diseases and food poisoning. Second, the rodent population has been kept under control with improvements in refuse management practices that deprived these vectors of food sources. This has helped to keep the incidence of rodent-borne diseases low all these years.

Perhaps the most significant impact that a high standard of public cleanliness has made is in helping Singapore tackle the threat of mosquito-borne diseases, since mosquito breeding is often closely associated with poor sanitary conditions. Malaria, in particular, was the most threatening vector-borne disease in Singapore before World War I, and again during and soon after World War II. Fortunately, the rapid urbanization that took place in the 1970s saw the progressive displacement of hilly and swampy areas that were once conducive to the breeding of the *Anopheles* mosquitoes, the vectors for malaria.

While this had, to a large extent, reduced the availability of breeding sources for the vector, it would not have been possible to bring the disease well under control if not for the intensified integrated disease control programme. This was backed by a well-established epidemiological surveillance regime that was capable of detecting and eliminating the focus of transmission quickly, thus preventing the re-establishment of endemicity. Through these relentless efforts, Singapore's malaria control programme finally achieved success on 22 November 1982, when the name of "Singapore" was entered in the World Health Organization (WHO) Official Register of areas where malaria has been eradicated.[31]

This "malaria-free" status has remained till this very day, even though Singapore is situated in a region that is still endemic for the disease. Today, although Singapore has continued to maintain a low incidence rate for malaria, with a majority of the cases imported, the government still maintains a close vigilance on the disease and the vectors that are present in some poorly-drained areas so as to ensure that the disease has no chance of staging a comeback.

The threats from mosquito-borne diseases were, however, far from over. After indigenous malaria was eradicated, Singapore was soon confronted by a different mosquito-borne disease — dengue, whose vectors, the *Aedes* mosquitoes, are highly adaptable and habituated to an urbanized, domestic environment. They commonly breed in stagnant water found in places such as roof gutters, ornamental flower pot plates, and domestic water containers in houses. The close proximity of their breeding habitats to human hosts and the presence of the virus in the country and the region also means that people are always at risk of becoming infected. Since the *Aedes* mosquitoes breed in relatively clean water, dengue will continue to be around in the foreseeable future.

Being located in dengue-endemic Southeast Asia, Singapore is not spared from this public health threat. By the mid-1960s, dengue had replaced malaria as the most menacing mosquito-borne disease in Singapore. A Vector Control Unit (VCU) was set up in 1966 under the then Ministry of Health to develop a comprehensive system of dengue control, with source reduction as the mainstay of control. The government also realized that to maintain adequate control after the initial reduction, it was necessary to involve the people and this could only be achieved through public education supported by law enforcement.[32]

Thus, in 1968, the DDBIA (Destruction of Disease Bearing Insects Act) was introduced to replace the outmoded Mosquito Ordinance that was enacted during the rule of the British colonial government. The DDBIA gave the government more teeth for tighter and more effective control over persons who intentionally or unintentionally propagated disease-bearing insects. Following its enactment, the DDBIA was enforced on a limited scale against persons who bred mosquitoes. In the following year, a countrywide, month-long "Keep Singapore Clean and Mosquito Free" Campaign was launched to educate the public and elicit the widest possible community participation in mosquito control. For the first time, the public was made aware of the seriousness of vector-borne diseases, and that they had a responsibility to act in order to curb its propagation. With the implementation of an integrated system of *Aedes* mosquito control encompassing public education, law enforcement, and source reduction, Singapore was able to achieve long-term suppression of the mosquito vector population, with a concomitant improvement in the disease situation from the mid-1970s.[33]

In 1998, the DDBIA was replaced by the Control of Vectors and Pesticides Act, which strengthened the powers of the government in the destruction of vectors and the control of vector-borne diseases. The Act also provided for the control of the sale and use of pesticides and vector repellents, as well as the registration, licensing, and certification of persons engaged in vector control work, to raise the professional standards of these personnel.

Since the start of the 1990s, Singapore, like many countries worldwide, has been experiencing a resurgence of dengue. In the local context, the interplay of the following factors could have fuelled this trend. First, rapid urbanization taking place in the country and region has favoured the breeding and propagation of the mosquito vectors, contributing to a global resurgence of dengue. Next, increased global travel has greatly accelerated the rate of importation of dengue virus. Furthermore, while the decades of intensive vector control operations had successfully suppressed the mosquito population, it has paradoxically also resulted in a lower immunity among the local population. This means that the population has become more susceptible to infection, and transmission can be easily sustained, despite a relatively low *Aedes* mosquito population here. The problem is further compounded by the presence of four different dengue virus serotypes.

Although the odds were clearly stacked against Singapore, NEA pressed on relentlessly with the integrated approach to dengue control. Source reduction continued to be the primary focus of NEA's mosquito control strategy as it is only through removing the source of breeding in outbreaks and, more importantly, during the inter-epidemic months (through the intensive source reduction exercises) that there is a better chance of breaking and preventing disease transmission, given that a dengue vaccine was unlikely to be available any time soon.

Dengue surveillance in Singapore evolved into an integrated approach that includes both passive and active case surveillance from the medical community, entomological surveillance in the field, and virological surveillance in the laboratory. First, accurate and timely "ground intelligence" is gathered. While some 500 field officers collect field entomological data, perform source reduction, and enforce against mosquito breeding in premises to reduce the incidence of *Aedes* breedings, the Environmental Health Institute (EHI) provides virological surveillance and identification of mosquito species collected. This information is fed into a Geographical Information System (GIS) that tracks the spatial and temporal distribution of reported dengue cases obtained from the Ministry of Health. The GIS promptly detects any unusual clustering of cases, which then triggers off epidemiological investigation to determine the source of infection, and concurrently, the ramping up of intensive search-and-destroy operations to eliminate these sources, thus abating disease transmission.

Second, proactive surveillance and source reduction is practised. Source reduction is no longer confined to just the locality or period with a clustering of reported cases. A pre-emptive approach is adopted instead, utilizing information about the spatial and temporal distribution of the mosquito population, the geographical distribution of the predominant dengue virus serotype that is circulating in the local population, as well as the ambient temperature and the susceptibility of the population in a particular locality. This allows for the stratification of different localities based on their potential for outbreak into focus areas thereby allowing prioritization in the deployment of manpower to carry out pre-emptive source reduction, according to the assessed risk level. Such proactive surveillance allows the problem to be nipped in the bud before it has a chance to escalate into an outbreak situation.

Third, NEA focuses on improving operational effectiveness. NEA's environmental health officers, having operated on the ground for years, are highly attuned to seeking out mosquito breeding habitats. In fact, many of them have also acquired the knack for picking out unusual breeding habitats, and this has continuously allowed transmission to be interrupted quickly in most clusters. Last, but not least, NEA adopts a system of continuous follow-up and assessment. Following the successful abatement of transmission in each cluster, NEA continues to survey the cluster area for mosquito activity for up to two weeks, to ensure that the sources of infection are completely eliminated and transmission has abated.

Recognizing that tackling the mosquito problem cannot be accomplished by the government alone, NEA has actively continued to encourage the participation of the community and other stakeholders through a combination of intensive public education and community outreach campaigns. Over the years, NEA has built a network of grassroots volunteers who help to disseminate dengue prevention messages to residents in the locality of an outbreak, so as to ensure that transmission is curbed in the shortest possible time. Through the Inter-Agency Dengue Taskforce, the other government land agencies come together to strengthen and intensify mosquito control efforts.

Despite being held up by WHO[34] as having one of the most successful dengue control programmes in the world, it is not possible to eradicate completely the mosquitoes that transmit dengue. Moreover, because Singapore has succeeded in keeping the mosquito vector population low, more intensive vector control efforts are likely to yield only marginal improvements in the disease situation. Consequently, new approaches that are based on scientific understanding of both the vectors and the viruses are needed to achieve a further breakthrough.

Leveraging Scientific Research to Control Diseases

The VCU that was set up in 1966 had functioned as an advisory and research body, providing laboratory support services for Singapore's vector control operations. The Unit was later renamed the Vector Control and Research Department (VCRD), and in

February 1992, took over vector control operations to streamline the coordination and lines of commands between planning, research, and operations. However, scientific research on vector-borne diseases was mostly carried out on an *"ad hoc* need-to" basis, with studies commissioned from research institutions, universities as well as hospital laboratories. Apart from these studies, some laboratory studies on vector biology and behaviour were conducted in an in-house laboratory under the VCRD. Other than this, research on vector-borne diseases in Singapore was relatively unstructured, as it was felt that outsourcing such research to the private sector was more cost-effective than building up in-house research capability.

The highly competitive biomedical research landscape meant that individual research institutions had their own research focuses and priorities. These were often not aligned with the research priorities of the government agencies concerned with public health. Yet, from the government's perspective, building up capabilities in public health research was necessary to fulfil a national need. Having such capability would enable the government to be better prepared to react to and handle outbreaks as well as the emergence of new viruses, and more importantly, to detect the introduction of these diseases into Singapore, without relying on laboratories overseas.

The development of this capability was made possible with the establishment of the Environmental Health Institute (EHI) in April 2002 as a department under the Environmental Public Health Division of NEA. The mandate for EHI was clear — to support the division's role as the national authority responsible for vector control, through carrying out research on vectors, vector-borne pathogens, and their control. The Institute carries the mission of ensuring that Singapore's environmental public health standards are not compromised in the face of a growing population, increased urbanization, and emerging infectious diseases of environmental health concern.

The vision is for EHI to leverage scientific research and the latest biomedical technologies to understand better the vectors and the diseases they transmit, with a special focus on the *Aedes* mosquitoes and dengue. The Institute also conducts risk assessments of the vulnerability of the local population to vector-borne diseases, and applied research to develop new, innovative, and cost-effective disease prevention strategies.

Attracting the right talent to join the Institute was an important first step. With the rapidly growing biomedical industry, there was no lack of employment opportunities for biomedical researchers. However, it was critical to attract talented individuals who were interested in carving out a career in public health research and prepared to cast their lot with a nascent set-up that had no track record, and hence no efforts were spared in recruitment. From a humble beginning of fewer than twenty employees, the Institute has grown to a staff strength of forty in 2008, with nine researchers holding postgraduate qualifications, and twenty-five with tertiary qualifications.

Over time, research at the Institute has also shifted from an initial focus on vector-borne diseases, centring on dengue fever and Japanese encephalitis, to becoming organized into five programmes, namely Surveillance, Vector Research, Epidemiology, Diagnostics, and Pathogenicity, as well as Indoor Air Quality, each staffed by specialists trained in the relevant disciplines. Far from being just a speciation of research programmes, this move signified the adoption of an integrated approach to environmental public health research that amalgamates clinical and laboratory surveillance with field vector control operation.

EHI and the SARS outbreak in 2003

Although the EHI was set up primarily to carry out research work on vector-borne diseases, it contributed its expertise readily during the SARS outbreak of 2003 by agreeing to cultivate the live SARS virus in its laboratory. The live virus was required for the study of the SARS coronavirus and the development of diagnostic kits.

Unfortunately, a student contracted SARS while working in the laboratory. The government took prompt remedial action. All activities within the Institute were suspended and a Review Panel, comprising international and local experts, was invited to audit the laboratory's biosafety procedures and recommend measures to strengthen the work processes at the Institute. Through interviews and laboratory investigations of samples from the laboratory, the panel found that the infection was caused by inappropriate laboratory practices and cross-contamination of West Nile Virus samples with the SARS coronavirus. The Biosafety Level 3 (BSL-3) laboratory was disinfected and downgraded to Biosafety Level 2 (BSL-2).

It was an eye-opening lesson for EHI and Singapore as it highlighted the need to manage inherent risks associated with the operation of a high-containment laboratory, and the need for a robust biosafety framework to govern the conduct of research activities. Since then, biosafety procedures have been put in place, and research staff given refresher training on biosafety.

In 2005, EHI began a new lease of life when it moved into a new facility at Biopolis, the hub of Life Sciences research in Singapore. Apart from the High Containment Laboratory at BSL-3, the facility is also equipped with an Arthropod Containment Laboratory (ACL) Level 3, that allowed the Institute to expand its scope of research to address more vector-borne diseases of public health importance. More importantly, the various biosafety procedures that the Institute has put in place allows it to comply with the requirements prescribed by the Biological Agents and Toxins Act, a legislation which was enacted in 2006 to, among other things, provide for safe practices in the handling of such biological agents and toxins at BSL-3.

The BSL-3 laboratory provides an appropriate setting for surveillance and research of high risk vector-borne viruses, including West Nile virus, Japanese encephalitis virus, Chikungunya virus, and Hanta viruses, while the ACL allows research on infected mosquitoes to be conducted. Until then, most of the research was centred on the vectors that spread the disease. The complexity of vector-borne diseases due to the interplay of many factors, however, means that a holistic understanding of the role played by the viruses, host, and environmental factors in disease transmission is necessary. To this end, the Institute, with the availability of the new facilities, has become better positioned to study the viruses directly responsible for the diseases in order to obtain a fuller picture of the problems, as well as possible solutions.

Contributing to Dengue Prevention Efforts

EHI's capability was put to the test during the dengue resurgence in 2005. The Institute had at the time just completed the development of a PCR (polymerase chain reaction)-based diagnostic assay that could accurately detect the dengue virus and its serotype in an infected blood sample, as early as the first day of disease onset. The new capability shortened the diagnostic and serotyping time from weeks, using the current gold standard of virus isolation, to less than an hour.

Accurate and rapid diagnosis is essential in the fight against dengue. It is needed for patient management and directing vector control response to miminize further transmission and spread of the disease. In the dengue epidemic of 2005, the test contributed to an improvement in the rate of the clinicians' diagnosis. Riding on this success, the EHI went on to develop a test kit that is able to detect anti-dengue antibodies in the saliva. This non-invasive approach holds the potential for early post-infection detection of the disease and is currently undergoing field trial.

Apart from improving the diagnostic capability for dengue, the EHI has also enhanced its surveillance system for early detection of the emergence of any new predominant serotype circulating in the population. The system leverages a close network of medical practitioners who collect blood samples from patients displaying symptoms of dengue, and send them for laboratory diagnosis by the Institute. The early detection of a switch from Dengue 1 to Dengue 2 in 2007 enabled the vector control response to be initiated more promptly to mitigate the effects of an ensuing outbreak. The detection of an emergence of the uncommon Dengue 3 serotype in 2005 and 2007 (in several areas in Tampines) also triggered an enhanced effort in these areas to prevent the spread of the serotype to other parts of Singapore. Since 2006, the Institute has further extended this surveillance system to include the Chikungunya virus, West Nile virus, and Hanta virus.

EHI's research has also contributed to a better understanding of mosquito vector biology. In a study of the dispersal range for dengue vector mosquitoes, *Aedes aegypti* and *Aedes albopictus*, the Institute has found that the mosquitoes could disperse easily and quickly throughout areas of radius 320 metres in search of egg-laying sites. This contrasts with the general belief that the *Aedes* mosquito seldom flies more than 50 metres in its lifetime. In the same study, it was also found that with releases on the twelfth storey of a twenty-one-storey apartment block, the mosquitoes showed a similarly easy and rapid dispersal to the top and bottom of the block. The work, published in an international journal in 2004, won the Royal Entomological Society Award for best publication in Medical and Veterinary Entomology during 2004–2005. These findings provided a firm scientific basis to refine existing vector control practices such as expanding the geographical range of source reduction to ensure better effectiveness.

The research at EHI has also shaped the way mosquito vectors are controlled. For instance, trials conducted by the Institute have found the use of *Bacillus thuringiensis* strain *israelensis* (Bti) to be effective in controlling mosquito breeding at construction sites. *Bti*, a biological vector control agent, eliminates mosquito larvae through degradation of their digestive tract, but is environmentally friendly since it is non-toxic to human and other animals, compared with chemical pesticides. The finding has led to the successful and widespread usage of *Bti* as a mosquito control method, particularly in Singapore's many construction sites. The Institute also conducts other trials, including the use of residual spray, traditionally used for malaria control, for dengue control.

With EHI's research capability gaining better recognition, the Institute has gradually moved beyond the role of supporting the national vector-borne disease control programme, to collaborating with, and supporting other aspects of public health research in Singapore also. EHI's team of researchers has collaborated with various local and international academic bodies, research institutes, and organizations, constantly identifying working partners with relevant expertise for mutual exchange of knowledge and expertise. As a member of the Dengue Consortium and the Malaria Consortium, EHI has worked closely with other major research institutions in Singapore on projects, including the surveillance of rodent-borne diseases. EHI also supports local and overseas pharmaceutical companies in the development of anti-dengue drugs through the provision of supporting services such as viral testing for drug companies that are carrying out trials, as well as sharing of knowledge about the local vector-borne disease situation.

Even though EHI has developed considerable research capability, the Institute is acutely aware of the need to further its understanding of the disease so as to enhance Singapore's own vector-borne disease control efforts. The Institute has, therefore, been actively exchanging notes with other research institutes. In 2007, NEA entered into a Memorandum of Understanding with the Instituto de Medicina Tropical "Pedro Kouri", in Cuba, a country that is also well known for its dengue control programme, to collaborate on various projects in dengue surveillance, control, and research.

Diseases such as dengue or Chikungunya fever do not recognize geographical boundaries or socio-economic status. Singapore cannot fight the battle against dengue alone. To this end, EHI has started to assist in capacity building in less developed countries, through helping to strengthen their disease surveillance capability, and thereby reducing their disease burden. As a way for Singapore to reciprocate the help that international organizations such as WHO rendered it during its early developing years, the Institute has contributed to the WHO WPRO's (Western Pacific Regional Office) efforts in developing research plans on communicable diseases, as well as the Asia-Pacific dengue control strategic plans.

Besides vector and vector-borne viruses research, the EHI's other focus is on gathering scientific evidence to support the formulation of environmental public health policies. This was particularly evident in the assessment of the indoor air quality in entertainment outlets in 2006 in preparation for the introduction of smoking prohibition in these places. Parameters, including the indoor and outdoor levels of respirable suspended particles and carbon monoxide, were measured in these outlets. A comparison of the air quality measurements taken one month before and after the introduction of the smoking prohibition showed a significant reduction in the levels of key indoor air pollutants, thus affirming the value of indoor smoking bans. The Institute has also undertaken surveys to assess the risk of *Legionella* infection in spa pool water as part of the evaluation of the need to regulate spa pool water quality to protect the health of spa users.

CONCLUSION

Singapore's experience in cleaning up the land and rivers is a unique one. It began with a clear vision by the government, who appreciated that economic development need not progress at the expense of the environment, and more importantly, a high standard of living for the people could not be achieved without a clean and healthy environment.

In translating this vision into reality, the government understood the need to adopt a long-term perspective in planning and executing the various programmes to support the realization of the vision. For example, to tackle the problem of illegal street hawking permanently, the government was prepared to invest heavily in infrastructure, i.e. purpose-built food centres and markets.

Realizing the vision of a clean Singapore could not have been achieved within such a short span of time, if not for the practical and effective implementation of policies and programmes. In solving the pollution problem of the Singapore River, for instance, the government had decided that controlling the sources of pollution was the most practical and effective approach, rather than implementing direct engineering solutions to remove pollution from the river. Other than emphasizing practicality, continuous innovation has also been a hallmark of many environmental policies and programmes. The evolution of the "Keep Singapore Clean" campaign in the early years to the "Clean and Green Week" of the 1990s shows how the government explored new approaches of engaging the population to sustain a clean and healthy environment, in response to changing socio-economic trends as well as public expectations.

Today, Singapore can pride itself on being among the few cities in the world where residents can regard a clean environment as a matter of fact. Some may even take this quality living environment for granted, forgetting that not so long ago, the environment in Singapore left much to be desired. Indeed, in spite of the four decades of efforts spent exalting the benefits of a clean living environment, and encouraging all residents to play their part in keeping the country clean, the current state of cleanliness is still far from ideal, and to some extent, still very much dependent on the efforts of the cleaners.

The behaviour and psyche of persistent litterbugs are still poorly understood. This is an area where perhaps socio-psychology experts may provide some insights.

Beyond a better understanding of the motivations of the litterbugs, there is also a need to develop the cleaning industry through raising the professional standards of the workforce, as a skilled and well-trained workforce would be better equipped to meet the rising expectations of the public, and at the same time, address the inferior image that has long been associated with the industry. Moving forward, the government should also be prepared to leverage technological advancements in materials research that could lead to the design of buildings and other structures that facilitate more efficient cleansing.

But most importantly, the people in Singapore must come to the realization that the cost of keeping the country clean would ultimately be borne by them, in one form or another. Apart from paying directly for the cost of cleaning up public places, the people must recognize that the indirect cost of an environment with poor sanitation would be many times more — the higher likelihood of infectious disease transmission, or tourists and investors staying away.

As the transformation of Singapore's living environment in the last four decades was an achievement made possible only through the dedicated efforts of both the government and the people, this partnership must continue. Sustaining the cleanliness of the land and waterways will need to be a perpetual commitment, one to be carried through to future generations.

4

INTEGRATED SOLID WASTE MANAGEMENT

As urbanisation and economic development increases in Asia, nowhere is the impact more obvious than in society's "detritus," or solid waste. Today, the urban areas of Asia produce about 760,000 tonnes of municipal solid waste per day, or approximately 2.7 million m³ per day. In 2025, this figure will increase to 1.8 million tonnes of waste per day, or 5.2 million m³ per day. Local governments in Asia currently spend about US$25 billion per year on urban solid waste management. In 2025, this amount will be doubled.

What a Waste: Solid Waste Management in Asia,
World Bank, 1999

Every community produces solid waste. Rapid urbanization and population growth in many cities will lead to an ever increasing amount of solid waste being generated. If there were no systematic means of waste collection and disposal, piles of rubbish would accumulate, with their associated stench, and create potential breeding grounds for pests and vectors. This will add stress to existing waste management infrastructure and pose potential threats to public health.

The effective management of solid waste is thus a priority that every city needs to address as it is an integral aspect of people's daily lives, and affects their quality of life. However, as many developing cities have found, putting in place an effective waste management system is not a straightforward matter.

It was no different in Singapore. Managing solid waste was one of the key environmental challenges that had to be tackled in the early days of Singapore's development and industrialization. The government had to cope with an increasing amount of waste by continually improving the system and learning from best practices in other cities. This has resulted in a solid waste management system that best suits local circumstances and caters to Singapore's needs.

LOCAL CIRCUMSTANCES

Singapore is today one of the most densely populated countries in the world, with a population density of 6,520 population per sq. kilometre. In line with population and economic growth, the volume of waste disposed has increased sixfold over the past thirty years.

With the population and industries housed within a small land area of only 700 sq. kilometre, every bit of land is a valuable resource. Singapore does not have large tracts of land for waste disposal, unlike some other countries where landfilling is still the norm today. This land constraint has been a key consideration in most of the government's policy decisions and strategies for solid waste management, and resulted in the ensuing search for "land-saving" waste disposal methods.

Singapore's climate is another key factor influencing the government's waste management strategy. Waste putrefies and decomposes rapidly under the hot and humid weather in Singapore, making it conducive to the breeding of disease-carrying vectors. Daily waste collection is, therefore, essential to the prevention of disease outbreaks and for maintaining a high standard of public health.

In the early years, the priority was to achieve a high standard of public health by collecting and disposing of the waste generated in a prompt, efficient, and reliable manner. Hence, the government wanted to build a system that integrates effectively the various waste collection and disposal functions, including scheduled refuse collection from residential estates, and transportation of collected waste to the disposal sites.

WASTE COLLECTION

Waste collection prior to the 1970s was very different from what it is today. The refuse collection system was rudimentary, involving workers shovelling refuse from open bin points along the roadside onto pushcarts. The waste on the pushcarts was then loaded onto open wagons for transportation to the dumping ground for disposal. Collection was irregular and inefficient, resulting in frequent accumulation of refuse along roads, backlanes, and other public areas.

Environmental public health standards were severely compromised by widespread littering, smell, and housefly nuisance of decomposing waste. Rodents were also commonly seen rummaging through piles of refuse. Then Prime Minister Lee Kuan Yew had to intervene personally, convening a special meeting of senior officers and supervisors of the health services in 1964. The objective was simple: He wanted the situation to improve.

The environmental health services were reorganized in 1965. In particular, the priority was to overhaul the haphazard waste collection system and put in place an efficient and robust system to ensure that waste was properly collected and disposed of in a safe and hygienic manner. In 1972, the responsibility of managing Singapore's solid waste was centralized under the Environmental Health Department of the newly formed Ministry of the Environment. Daily refuse collection services were provided by workers operating from seven District Offices under the Environmental Health Department. Collection of refuse collection fees through the consolidated utility bill was also introduced to make the payment of the fees more convenient.

As Singapore underwent rapid industrialization, rural areas were cleared to make way for more intensive land uses. High-rise residential apartments were built to house rural dwellers who were affected by the resettlement programme. Ensuring that waste could be collected from each apartment efficiently was a consideration in the design of the flats. Hence, each residential unit in the new high-rise apartments was provided with a refuse throw-point in the kitchen that was connected to a common vertical refuse chute. Refuse from high-rise apartment blocks could then be simply collected daily from the refuse chamber at the bottom of each chute. This also made the job less labour intensive compared with door-to-door collection of refuse. To further improve the efficiency of the waste collection services, new public high-rise apartment blocks built after the late 1980s were installed with a centralized refuse chute system in which the refuse throw-point is located in the common area on each floor and a mechanized screw conveyor is located at the bottom of the chute. This modification has resulted in greater efficiency as waste collectors only need to collect from one chute per block instead of the multiple chutes (typically five to seven) previously. There was some resistance from the residents at first as they no longer had the convenience of refuse disposal in their homes, but many residents quickly warmed to the proposal as there were no longer pest and smell problems associated with refuse throw-points in their homes. This system is well accepted today, and the centralized refuse chute is now used for all new public apartment blocks.

For the trade, industrial, and commercial sectors, legislation was enacted to ensure that every development incorporates a refuse collection system. This is done at the building plans stage to ensure that a robust system for waste collection is implemented for all premises. Licensing of general waste collectors that service the trade, industrial, and commercial sectors was also introduced in

1989 to require the use of proper vehicles and equipment for collecting and transporting waste from the collection points to the disposal facility. This further enhances the reliability and quality of the refuse collection service.

Corporatization and Privatization

By the 1990s, the waste collection system for households had been transformed into a well-established system that was reliable and efficient, with waste collection services still provided by the government. During this period, there was a concerted effort across all sectors to privatize public services that the private sector could adequately provide. The aim was to introduce greater market discipline into these services and further improve their efficiency.

However, the Environment Ministry had to ensure that policy objectives and service levels to the public were not compromised before embarking on the privatization of household waste collection services, particularly when private companies could charge higher refuse collection fees.

To address these concerns, a two-step approach was adopted for the transition from public to private provision of the waste collection service. The refuse collection arm of the Ministry was first corporatized and the newly created entity was given a three-year moratorium to be the sole provider of waste collection services for all households in Singapore. During this period, the Ministry closely monitored the situation. Satisfied that there was no deterioration in service quality and no undue increase in service fees, the Ministry decided to proceed with the next phase where the monopoly status given to the corporatized entity was terminated to allow the entry of more market players.

In 1999, Singapore was divided into nine sectors, each with about 100,000 households and trade premises. The rights to collect domestic and trade waste from each sector were competitively tendered for by pre-qualified waste collection companies. There were no restrictions placed on whether the companies were local or foreign, but to be pre-qualified, the companies had to demonstrate considerable experience, expertise, and financial capabilities in the waste collection business. The successful tenderers were appointed by NEA as the public waste collectors (PWCs) for the respective sectors.

Through regulatory and licensing conditions as well as a transparent fee structure, the privatization of Singapore's domestic waste collection has resulted in considerable efficiency improvements in this sector. As a result, the majority of consumers enjoyed a lower refuse collection fee after privatization. In the second round of tender for waste collection licences in 2004 to 2006, the average refuse collection fee fell by approximately 30 per cent for residential flats and 15 per cent for landed premises, resulting in lower refuse collection fees for residents. Despite the lower fees, the service quality of refuse collection services was well maintained as shown by customer satisfaction surveys conducted by the Ministry.

A way forward is the Pneumatic Refuse Conveyance System, where refuse is collected in a clean, hygienic, and efficient way. The system conveys refuse by air suction from individual buildings through a network of pipes to a central location for collection. Many countries have found this system advantageous to improving the quality of living as there would no longer be any open handling of refuse. Many individual private residential developments in Singapore have adopted this system, and NEA is exploring opportunities to implement this system on a wider scale in Singapore.

WASTE DISPOSAL

Back in the 1970s, refuse was disposed of at landfills in swampy areas in Kolam Ayer, Koh Sek Lim Road, and Lorong 3, Geylang. Later on, more landfill sites were opened in Lorong Halus, Choa

Chu Kang, and Lim Chu Kang. However, the government soon realized that an alternative to landfilling was needed to conserve the fast-diminishing landfills.

Development of Modern Incineration Plants

This need for an alternative disposal method led to a thorough evaluation of various methods of refuse disposal, such as high-density compaction, composting, and incineration. A fact-finding study team, led by the Permanent Secretary of the Ministry, visited Japan in 1973 to learn from the Japanese experience of operating compaction and incineration facilities.

Following the study, options such as composting, baling, and incineration were considered in greater detail. Due to the lack of land on mainland Singapore for waste disposal, it was crucial that the selected waste disposal solution achieved maximum volume reduction of the waste in order to reduce landfill needs. Baling involves the compaction of refuse before landfilling but it was not suitable for Singapore as it can only reduce waste volumes by about 40 to 50 per cent. Composting involves the decomposition of organic waste producing compost. However, the domestic demand for compost was small given the lack of an agricultural sector in Singapore. Furthermore, the volume reduction from composting was not substantial.

As for incineration, there were three main types of technology available — mass burn, pyrolysis, and fluidized bed. Many modern incineration plants around the world were based on the mass burn technology. Pyrolysis and fluidized bed incineration required pre-treatment of refuse prior to incineration as these types of plants could only accept waste that was largely homogeneous. Hence, the study team ascertained that pyrolysis and fluidized bed incineration technologies were less suitable for Singapore as its municipal waste was mainly mixed. In addition, pyrolysis and fluidized bed incineration were not technologically proven for municipal waste beyond demonstration plants during the 1970s. The alternative left for consideration was mass burn incineration technology.

At that time, modern refuse incineration plants based on mass burn technology had been built and put into operation in Japan and European countries such as Denmark and Germany. Properly designed and operated, such incineration plants did not cause any nuisance to their surroundings, and refuse was reduced to about 10 per cent of its original volume. The volume reduction was most advantageous in a land-scarce country like Singapore. With suitable smoke and dust abatement devices such as electrostatic precipitators, there was also no smoke pollution. Moreover, the heat liberated from the combustion of refuse could be used to generate electricity that can be used internally, with the excess sold to the electricity grid. Ferrous metals in the ash could also be extracted for sale as scrap iron. At the same time, these modern incinerators were clean and highly automated. Thus, refuse incineration using the mass burn technology was assessed to be the most cost effective method for Singapore.

The decision was taken in 1973 to build Singapore's first modern incineration plant at a cost of S$94 million for the first three incinerator-boiler units. A fourth unit was added in 1982 at a cost of about S$36 million, a hefty infrastructure investment by the government at the time. To assist in the financing of the project, the government took a US$25 million loan from the World Bank. It was the first incineration project in the world to have obtained the support of the World Bank. However, the government recognized that waste disposal through incineration was not the perfect solution since incineration ash would still need to be disposed of. Therefore, in recent years, it has been actively promoting waste minimization and recycling (these efforts are elaborated on later in this chapter).

While the incineration technology of mass burning was an established method in many developed countries, the decision to adopt incineration in Singapore was one taken with a fair amount of calculated risks. This was because waste generated in Singapore was much wetter than that in the European countries, mainly due to food waste, and thus might not be suited for incineration. Consultants from Germany were, therefore, engaged to design an incineration plant that could operate effectively under a wider range of operating conditions.

Having a high-quality infrastructure without a team of skilled operators and experienced managers would be futile. To build up the necessary "software" to run the plant, training of staff began as early as three years prior to the completion of the plant. The first batch of fresh graduate engineers and technicians were recruited and trained at the local Pasir Panjang power station to familiarize them with the operations of steam and power generation, which was considered fairly similar to waste incineration operations. In addition, engineers were sent to Germany for hands-on training at a modern incineration plant. On their return to Singapore, these engineers in turn shared their knowledge and experience with their colleagues. The engineers and staff concerned were enthusiastic in sharing and learning about the new incineration technology in offices amidst the noisy construction activities at the Ulu Pandan site.

The preparations went beyond classroom training and hands-on practical training. When the installation and subsequent commissioning work commenced, staff were deployed to work closely with the contractors. This gave them the opportunity to learn first-hand the construction of the different equipment and the series of tests and calibrations required to ensure a safe and proper working environment. This team who had been so actively involved in the plant construction went on to become the Ulu Pandan Incineration Plant's (UPIP) pioneer batch of operation and maintenance personnel in 1978. By 1979, the plant was fully operational.

The first incineration plant was well received by waste collectors, and there were often long queues outside the plant. For the same waste disposal fee, waste collectors preferred going to the UPIP as it was connected via a network of well-paved roads, compared with the uneven terrain at the dumping grounds. This reduced the damage to and downtime for the waste collection vehicles. Refuse disposal could also be carried out under all weather conditions in the sheltered refuse reception hall at the plant.

The UPIP proved that incineration was, indeed, a viable solution for Singapore's solid waste management problem. Soon afterwards, planning for a second incineration plant at Tuas began and the Tuas Incineration Plant came into operation in 1986. The Kim Chuan Refuse Transfer Station (KCTS) in eastern Singapore was also constructed as the majority of Singapore's population resided in the east. Refuse would be collected and dumped at the transfer station, compacted, and loaded onto large container trailers before being sent to the incineration plants located in the west. This concept led to cost savings in manpower, fuel, and vehicle requirements, while also reducing traffic congestion as each trailer can take the load of three to five refuse collection vehicles.

With the development of additional infrastructure such as vehicular expressways, the third incineration plant in northern Singapore (Senoko Incineration Plant in 1992), as well as the use of larger capacity refuse trucks incorporating built-in compaction mechanisms, waste collectors eventually found it more cost effective to transport their waste directly to the incineration plants, rather than paying for the additional haulage services at KCTS. The KCTS was, therefore, decommissioned in 2001 after operating for more than fifteen years.

Environment officers worked with technical consultants from the very start to specify the operating parameters and performance standards of each new incineration plant. The close working relationship allowed the staff to appreciate the technical considerations and intricacies behind the plant designs better. Coupled with the experiences gained from operating existing plants, the staff could suggest and make improvements to each successive plant.

For instance, because of its design, the UPIP had to be shut down entirely once in two years for maintenance work to keep the plant in good working condition. During these times, incineration capacity was drastically reduced and waste had to be diverted to the landfill. To avoid this situation, the newer plants at Senoko and Tuas South were designed to operate all year round through a modular design.

Other technical and design improvements to the plants include increasing the storage capacity of the refuse bunkers from two to four days to allow time for moisture in the waste to be drained off, thereby achieving better combustion. The increase in bunker size also helps to cater for seasonal fluctuation in refuse loads such as during Chinese New Year when waste volumes can be 30 to 35 per cent higher than on a typical day. This also provides a buffer in case of equipment shutdown (e.g., refuse cranes), so that the plants can continue receiving refuse and not turn away refuse trucks.

With increasing affluence, the characteristics of waste in Singapore have also changed over the years. The increased usage of plastic products has bumped up the heat values of the refuse. To prevent high temperature corrosion of the incineration and boiler equipment, improvements were made to line the furnace walls with refractory tiles and inconel overlay (high temperature corrosion resistant nickel-based alloy layer) on furnace ceiling boiler tubes.

Electricity generation was also enhanced with the installation of condensing turbines that offer higher efficiency than back-pressure turbines. At the Tuas South Incineration Plant, 600kWh of electricity can be generated for each tonne of waste burnt, compared with Ulu Pandan's generation rate of 180kWh per tonne of waste, representing a threefold improvement in electricity generation capacity. Today, the four incineration plants supply between 2 to 3 per cent of the island's electricity needs. Automation and the introduction of digital control systems also played a key role in keeping the manpower requirements for each plant at approximately 140 staff despite the fact that Tuas South's capacity is more than two times that of Ulu Pandan.

Besides the lack of landfill space, the scarcity of water resources is another constraint that Singapore has to grapple with constantly. Therefore, water conservation features were incorporated in the two newest incineration plants for the quenching of hot ashes, area washing, and fire fighting. The newer incineration plants were also built with large underground reservoirs to collect and store rainwater for service use. Through these initiatives, the plants were able to reduce the consumption of town water, which can then be channelled for other uses.

In the late 1980s, there was a growing concern about the danger of dioxins, which were found to be carcinogenic. In many countries, citizens have protested against the construction of incineration plants, citing dioxin emissions from the plants as an environmental and health concern. Nevertheless, these opposing voices may also have been a manifestation of the "not-in-my-backyard" syndrome, in which people see the benefits of and the need for modern facilities such as incineration plants, yet do not like them sited near their homes.

Dioxins can cause cancer through the food chain. The probability of getting cancer is higher for people who consume foods that have been contaminated with dioxins. As Singapore is not an agricultural country, the risk of food contamination by dioxins was assessed to be low. Nonetheless, a series of measures was put in place over the years for the incineration plants to mitigate the potential public health impact of their dioxin emissions.

Incineration plants built after the UPIP were judiciously sited in industrial areas on the fringes of the island. Air monitoring systems were also put in place to monitor the emissions from the incineration plants. Stringent regulatory controls were imposed by the government on the disposal of polyvinyl chloride (PVC) at the incineration plants as dioxins are produced when material containing PVC is burnt. Technological solutions were also implemented to remove dioxins from flue gas. Catalytic baghouse filters and catalytic reactors were installed.

Stringent standards for dioxins were introduced in the Environmental Pollution Control (Air Impurities) Regulation in 2001 to ensure that the incineration plants comply with permissible dioxin levels.

Another common concern from incineration plants is mercury emissions. Mercury is mainly found in electronic wastes, especially batteries. In order for batteries to be safely disposed of at the incineration plants without polluting the environment, import controls have been set to ensure that the mercury content of batteries imported is limited to 0.025 per cent by weight for alkaline batteries, and 0.001 per cent by weight for mercury oxide and zinc-carbon batteries. Thus, over the years, the Ministry has established a robust regulatory and air monitoring system (described in Chapter 2) to mitigate possible health concerns arising from waste incineration.

The fourth plant, Tuas South Incineration Plant (TSIP), was conceptualized in the early 1990s to ensure that there was sufficient incineration capacity for all incinerable waste. During the planning phase, the Ministry explored the feasibility of locating the new plant in underground rock caverns in an attempt to free up land space further for other uses. The feasibility study ascertained that the cost of such a proposal would be prohibitive, both in terms of engineering and construction costs, as well as the insurance cost for staff safety and equipment. The net amount of land space saved from having the plant below ground was also questionable, given that there would still be a need for numerous large above-ground structures for vehicular access, chimneys, ventilation, and emergency evacuation routes. Therefore, the idea for an underground incineration plant was rejected. When TSIP was completed in 2000, it was one of the largest incineration plants in the world, capable of incinerating 3,000 tonnes of refuse each day.

With sufficient incineration capacity in place, it became a regulatory requirement in Singapore for waste collectors to dispose of all incinerable waste at the incineration plants. Only non-incinerable waste and the ash generated from the incineration process (incineration bottom ash) can be disposed of at Singapore's only landfill at Semakau. While it is the responsibility of waste collectors to separate waste into incinerable and non-incinerable waste, a pricing mechanism was also put in place to deter the mixing of incinerable waste and non-incinerable waste. The disposal fee at the incineration plants for incinerable waste and the disposal fee at the Tuas Marine Transfer Station for non-incinerable waste are set at parity. The rationale is that if the incineration plant disposal fee for incinerable waste is priced lower than the disposal fee for non-incinerable waste at Tuas Marine Transfer Station, waste collectors may want to save on the disposal fee by mixing some non-incinerable waste with the incinerable waste that is sent to the incineration plant. As the incineration plants are not designed to receive non-incinerable waste, proliferation of such acts could severely damage plant equipment.

Private-Public-Partnership Approach for Waste Disposal Services

Solid waste disposal facilities had traditionally been developed, owned, and operated by the government. Given the capital-intensive nature of constructing and operating an incineration plant as well as the need to ensure reliable incineration services, the government had hitherto borne all the financing, design, and operational risks.

However, following the successful privatization of refuse collection services in 1999, the government decided to also look into liberalizing the incineration plant industry. The objectives were to increase efficiency in the sector further by injecting competition, and to develop the environmental engineering industry by transferring expertise residing with the government to the private sector. The plan was to liberalize the sector in phases, starting with the development of a fifth IP by the private sector on the design, build, own, and operate (DBOO) model.

In 2001, an open tender was called for the development of the fifth incineration plant with the potential developer having to undertake the financial, design, and demand risk. The tender was not well received by the market with only one non-compliant bid submitted. On studying the tender results, it was ascertained that the primary reason for the poor response was that potential bidders felt they were unable to bear the demand risk associated with uncertain waste growth and a non-guaranteed waste stream, in tandem with the high capital outlay associated with incineration plants.

Subsequently, a more in-depth study of the industry structure was commissioned, taking into consideration lessons from the failed tender. A decision was taken to adopt a DBOO scheme with a full take-or-pay approach. Under this structure, NEA, as the market-maker, would enter into take-or-pay agreements with the private operator to buy 100 per cent of the incineration capacity at a price determined through the DBOO tender. The government now bears the demand risk by giving the DBOO operator full capacity payment, regardless of the actual utilization rate of the incineration plant. This addressed the concerns of the market and allowed private sector participants to bid more competitively. The government's interest in the provision of incineration services is safeguarded through an Incineration Services Agreement, which clearly states the commercial terms and conditions governing the services to the government.

The tender for the fifth IP was called again and attracted good response from the market, with Keppel Seghers Engineering Pte Ltd being awarded the tender in November 2005. The plant is currently being constructed and scheduled to be ready for commercial operation in mid-2009 to replace the UPIP, which will then be decommissioned after more than thirty years of operation.

Just as Singapore had studied the best practices and technologies available in more developed countries when the waste management system was in its infancy, many countries have now started to look at the integrated waste management system in Singapore today. These countries are keen to adapt the Singapore system to cope with their rising waste volumes. In 1994 and 1998, experienced technical staff from Singapore's incineration plants were seconded to Taiwan to provide technical advice for the construction, commissioning, and initial operation of several of their incineration plants. Two batches of Taiwanese operators, from engineering staff to technicians, were also trained in Singapore on the operation and maintenance of incineration plants.

In 2005, Qatar invited international companies from Japan, Greece, Spain, Malaysia, and Singapore to tender for the right to provide an integrated waste management system ranging from collection to disposal. Qatar, like Singapore, is a small country with increasing waste growth due to the rising affluence of the population. The Singapore concept of integrated waste management was well received by the Qatari government. A Singapore company, Keppel Seghers, was awarded a S$1.7 billion contract in 2005 to implement the Domestic Solid Waste Management System in Qatar. Currently, NEA is training the Keppel Seghers operators in batches for the operation of the fifth IP in Singapore and some will be sent to operate the incineration plant in Qatar.

Semakau Landfill

The strategy of volume reduction by incineration helped to extend the life span of dumping grounds. However, with the rapid growth of waste, the Lim Chu Kang Dumping Ground became depleted by 1992 and it was projected that the Lorong Halus Dumping Ground would also be exhausted by 2000. The initial plan was to convert neighbouring Punggol into the next landfill to serve Singapore for the next generation. However, the government subsequently decided to earmark Punggol as a new housing estate instead, given the increasing housing demand.

An alternative site had to be sourced for the new landfill. After taking into consideration the competing needs for land space on the mainland and the experiences of other countries with similar land scarcity problems, the idea of an offshore landfill — similar to land reclamation which Singapore had much success and experience in — was conceived.

Feasibility studies were initiated in the early 1990s to ascertain the possibility of developing an offshore waste disposal site off Pulau Semakau, an island 8 kilometres off the coast of mainland Singapore. The study encompassed technical feasibility and design, operational planning, and cost estimation. Consultants were also invited to study the potential impact of the development on the surrounding environment. The study concluded that with the incorporation of pollution control measures in the design and construction stages, an offshore landfill would have minimal impact on the surrounding marine ecosystem.

A study trip to the world's largest landfill, Fresh Kills Landfill, in New York City was conducted to study how offshore landfills were operated. Waste was transferred from New York City to the landfill via barges. The barges used were often not covered and the smell and environmental nuisance were significant. However, in some parts of the United States, waste was loaded onto containers and then transported in barges. This would be cleaner and more hygienic as the waste is not exposed to the elements during transportation. However, establishing container operations at Semakau Landfill would require massive facilities such as container handling yards and cranes, and a logistic chain that would comprise about 400 people for the landfill operations. Thus, due to massive cost and manpower requirements for the container system, it was decided that the waste should be transported directly on barges instead. However, the barges had specially designed covers not only to minimize smell and bird nuisance, but also to prevent the penetration of rain water during transportation.

Approval was granted in 1994 to construct the offshore Semakau Landfill as well as the Tuas Marine Transfer Station on mainland Singapore from which the waste would be barged to Semakau. In addition, a fleet of sea transport and landfill equipment was also purchased. The total cost of constructing and equipping Semakau landfill was S$610 million. Semakau Landfill is the world's first man-made offshore landfill created entirely out of sea space. It was created by enclosing the 350 hectares of sea space between Pulau

Sakeng and Pulau Semakau with a 7-kilometre perimeter bund. The construction was an extraordinary engineering feat given the challenges of constructing a landfill in deep sea — at the deepest point, the landfill is more than 20 metres deep. To overcome the challenges, engineers had to devise engineering solutions that were creative and yet prudent, so as to ensure minimal impact of the landfill construction on the surrounding marine ecosystem. Silt screens were installed to prevent the migration of silt from the construction areas. Constructing Semakau Landfill was a massive exercise in terms of labour and materials. At the peak of the construction, there were more than a thousand workers on the island. A total of 20 million cubic metres of sand, 2.5 million cubic metres of rock, and 2 million square metres of geofabric and membrane were used in the construction of the perimeter bund.

During the construction, some parts of the mangrove swamp on Pulau Semakau had to be removed. As a commitment to nature conservation and environmental protection, two plots of mangroves with a total of 400,000 saplings and covering an area of 13.6 hectares were later planted to replace those removed during the construction. In addition to conserving the biodiversity of the area, the replanted mangrove plots also serve as biological indicators of any leakage of waste. The mangroves are thriving today — a living testament to the safety and ecological soundness of the landfill.

The project was completed successfully and on schedule, and on 1 April 1999, one day after Lorong Halus Dumping Ground was closed, Semakau Landfill was opened for waste disposal.

Great care is taken during the landfill operations to ensure that the landfill is clean, free of smell, and the surrounding water not polluted. The marine ecosystem on and around Semakau Landfill is thus well preserved and protected. It is home to rich marine life such as barracuda, trevally, sea bass, and milk fish. It also has fifty-five species of birds such as the endangered great-billed heron, the Pacific reef egret, and the Malaysian plover. Its mangrove mudflats are rich with seagrass, giant sea anemones, and sea urchins.

Contrary to popular belief that landfill sites are often dirty and smelly, Semakau Landfill is an idyllic and scenic attraction. It is now used to educate the public, especially the youth, on the need to manage Singapore's waste in a sustainable manner. Since 2005, Semakau Landfill has also been opened to members of interest groups such as the Raffles Museum of Biodiversity Research, Nature Society (Singapore), Sport Fishing Association (Singapore) and Astronomy Society of Singapore, for recreational activities. To enhance the sustainability of Semakau Landfill further, a renewable green energy system comprising a wind turbine and solar panels has been installed and successfully commissioned in 2006.

RECYCLING

Ensuring that waste is collected and disposed of in the most efficient and cost-effective manner possible is not enough. The government believes that priority must also be accorded to reduce, reuse, and recycle waste, as this will allay the need to build new waste management infrastructure indefinitely, which is not only costly, but also takes up precious land. Hence, the solid waste management system encompasses two additional initiatives, namely, waste recycling and waste minimization.

The manufacture of products and packaging consumes resources. Throwing these products and packaging away after a single use constitutes a waste of resources since much of the materials that go into their production can be reused, or can be processed for other uses. Developed countries, such as the European Union countries and Japan, have emphasized the need for recycling as it not only helps to conserve limited resources, but also reduces stress on the waste management system. Similarly, in Singapore, the segregation and recycling of recyclable materials help to reduce the dependence on incineration plants and landfill for the disposal of waste.

About half the waste disposed of in Singapore comes from the industrial and commercial sectors. The government has, therefore, put in place a framework to encourage recycling among industries. First, waste disposal is not subsidized in Singapore, and industries are required to pay for disposing waste that they produce. Through market forces, industries would be incentivized to recycle if the cost of recycling is lower than that of waste disposal. Already results for the recycling of construction and demolition waste, as well as used slag, are visible, with recycling rates for both waste streams hitting more than 90 per cent as there is a viable market for the recycled products.

The next step is to target households. Informal channels such as the "rag and bone" man have for a long time been providing door-to-door collection of recyclables such as newspapers, clothes, and old electronic products. However, these services were provided in a *laissez-faire* and often ad hoc manner and thus do not provide a sustained level of service expected by residents.

Singapore's overall recycling rate had been stagnant at 40 per cent for many years and the Environment Ministry realized that more had to be done to get Singaporeans to recycle. In 2001, the National Recycling Programme (NRP) was launched to provide a convenient means for residents living in public and private landed housing estates to recycle. Under the programme, recycling bags or bins are distributed to each household for residents to store their recyclables. These recyclables are then collected by the appointed recycling companies fortnightly from residents' doorsteps. Even though the door-to-door collection of recyclables is a much more labour-intensive programme than the provision of centralized recycling bins, it makes recycling convenient for residents. Residents have responded positively to these recycling programmes. Survey results show that many households have indicated that they are actively participating in the NRP.

To put in place the programme, public waste collectors were required under their licensing conditions to provide door-to-door recycling collection services. The waste collectors also benefit from the recycling programme. If more households recycle, less waste is collected by the waste companies for disposal, and this lowers their operational costs. In addition, the recyclables collected have value and are a source of additional revenue. The government's policy of bundling waste collection and waste recycling thus resulted in the public waste collectors promoting recycling as well since they saw this resulting in a win-win outcome.

The participation rate by households in NRP was 15 per cent at the start in 2001 and has since increased to 63 per cent in 2007. To further enhance accessibility of recycling facilities for households, centralized recycling bins have been deployed in HDB estates so that the majority of residents can find a recycling bin not more than 150 metres from their apartment blocks. NEA has seen the total recyclables collected from households double since the introduction of the centralized recycling bins. Public recycling bins have also been deployed at public places with high human traffic such as outside some mass rapid transit stations, food centres, bus interchanges, the airport, and shopping malls.

While efforts were made to provide Singaporeans with convenient access to recycling facilities, the government realized that this was not sufficient to raise the recycling rate. Public education was equally, if not more, important, and the first target group was the young. In September 2002, the Recycling Corner Programme for schools was launched with the aim of educating and inculcating good 3R (Reduce, Reuse, and Recycle) habits in students. Recycling bins for paper, drink cans, and plastic bottles are placed at Recycling Corners located within school premises. To instil a sense of ownership of the recycling programme in the students, some are identified and trained to be Environment Champions in their schools. These Champions are responsible for conducting talks on the environment and assist in organizing environmental activities. By the end of 2007, 90 per cent of schools had joined the Recycling Corner Programme, while another 5 per cent had their own recycling programmes.

Sustaining the recycling industry is the next important step. Many of the companies in the waste management and recycling industry in Singapore are small and fledgling. However, with targeted aid to help them grow and upgrade their professionalism, many of these companies would have the potential to become regional players. For this reason, the government facilitated the formation of the Waste Management and Recycling Association of Singapore (WMRAS) for the industry. WMRAS has been active in building capability, sharing of best practices among the industry, and establishing networks among local companies as well as with overseas associations such as the International Solid Waste Association.

To promote the adoption of innovative environmental technologies, NEA has set up a S$20 million "Innovation for Environmental Sustainability" (IES) Fund. The IES Fund provides financial grants to assist Singapore-based companies to defray part of the cost of test bedding innovative environmental technologies, such as recycling technologies that can contribute to environmental sustainability. Waste recycling projects supported by the IES Fund include the production of precast drainage channels from recycled aggregate. Market acceptance of the recycled products is crucial so the IES Fund also provides industries with financial incentives to improve the quality of recycled products.

An example is the recycling of raw materials such as horticultural and wood waste into wooden pallets used for the storage and transportation of goods. The wooden pallets made from recycled raw materials are able to handle loads comparable to those handled by pallets made from virgin materials and thus have been widely used by the industry. Another project involved the recycling of incineration bottom ash into road base for a stretch of road in the Jurong Industrial Estate. The road has been in use since May 2002 and found to be safe and without any impact on the surrounding environment. Despite the technology breakthrough in recycling the incineration bottom ash into useful materials, the cost of recycling the ash is still high compared with landfilling the ash. NEA is constantly monitoring various technologies that would help bring down this cost so that recycling of the ash can be implemented on a large scale in Singapore.

Recently, some Singapore companies have deployed new waste recycling technologies, which will not only add to the vibrancy of the recycling industry in Singapore, but will also contribute to increasing the recycling rate. A plant capable of handling 300 tonnes per day of food waste has been set up to recycle food waste into compost and biogas. The biogas can be burnt to generate electricity. Another plant has also been set up to further recover recyclables such as plastics and ferrous metals from municipal waste.

All these strategies have helped improve the recycling rate from 40 per cent in 2000, to 54 per cent in 2007. Table 4.1 shows the breakdown of the recycling rate according to various waste streams in 2007. The aim is to achieve a target of 60 per cent recycling rate by 2012.

WASTE MINIMIZATION

Incineration and recycling have helped prolong the lifespan of the landfill. However, many countries such as those in the European Union and Japan have developed a waste hierarchy where the reduction of waste at source is the top priority. Thus, it is important to move upstream to target waste generation at source and close the waste loop.

The key enabler to push for waste minimization is the concept of product stewardship. This means that all the various stakeholders along the supply chain such as manufacturers, distributors, retailers, consumers, waste collectors, and recycling companies should be responsible for the afterlife management of the products and their packaging. Waste minimization can be promoted through either mandatory or voluntary means. In the European Union, industries are required to recover packaging waste under the extended

TABLE 4.1

2007 Recycling Rates (by waste streams)

Waste Stream	Waste Generated (ton)	Waste Recycled (ton)	Waste Recycling Rate in 2007 (%)
Construction & Demolition	778,300	759,300	98
Ferrous Metal	736,500	668,000	91
Food	558,900	51,200	9
Glass	65,300	5,800	9
Horticultural Waste	224,600	91,100	41
Non-ferrous Metal	92,300	75,600	82
Paper/Cardboard	1,202,900	619,000	51
Plastics	659,800	75,000	11
Scrap Tyres	25,500	22,000	86
Sludge (from industries)	124,600	0	0
Textile	110,100	6,000	5
Used Slag	527,200	520,000	99
Wood/Timber	246,200	127,800	52
Others	248,600	14,000	6
Total	5,600,800	3,034,800	54

Source: NEA.

producer responsibility scheme, where producers set up take-back systems to collect waste associated with their products at the end of the product lifecycle. In New Zealand, a voluntary approach has been adopted to encourage industries to reduce and recycle their packaging waste.

Plastic bags have become the latest environmental problem in recent years as they are non-biodegradable and remain in landfills for thousands of years. Many countries have introduced legislation to either charge for plastic bags or ban certain types of plastic bags. Ireland, where plastic bags are charged for, has succeeded in reducing the amount of plastic bags used by up to 90 per cent. Other countries such as Bangladesh and China have banned certain types of plastic bags that can only be used once. In Singapore, the problem is a different one. Since all incinerable waste is burnt, plastic bags are incinerated and thus do not cause a problem to the landfill. Many residents also reuse their plastic bags to bag their refuse — this is a practice to be encouraged as it contributes to a higher standard of public health. Nevertheless, to deter the excessive wastage of plastic bags, NEA embarked on an educational campaign to educate the public about not wasting plastic bags and only taking plastic bags that they need. The Singapore Environment Council partnered major retailers and supermarkets in 2007 to launch the "Bring Your Own Bag" Campaign to raise awareness of not wasting plastic bags and to encourage shoppers to bring their own bags when doing their shopping.

As much as one-third of household waste in Singapore is packaging waste, of which a major part comes from the food and beverage sector. After studying the various options, NEA, together with the industry players, set up a voluntary programme to reduce packaging waste in Singapore. The voluntary approach was adopted as it gives industry more flexibility and allows market efficiencies to find their equilibrium, although the results would likely take a longer time to be realized, compared with simply putting in place waste minimization legislation. After a year of negotiation, NEA signed the first Singapore Packaging Agreement with major players in the food and beverage industry in 2007. This is still relatively new for Singapore, but already some companies such as Nestle, Boncafe, and Chinatown Food Corporation have reviewed the design of their packaging and started to reduce the amount of packaging used. For example, Nestle has reduced the thickness of its Milo tins from 0.25 mm to 0.22 mm, saving about 9.5 tonnes of materials annually. Boncafe has also reduced the thickness of its coffee powder packaging from 140 microns to 120 microns, which will result in a reduction of 1.5 tonnes of packaging material each year. In the long run, NEA hopes that this Packaging Agreement will serve as a platform for industry to share their best practices in reducing packaging and thus reducing the amount of waste generated.

CONTROL OF HAZARDOUS SUBSTANCES AND TOXIC INDUSTRIAL WASTE

Chemicals are essential in modern living. Chemicals are used to make plastic and resins which form the basic materials in many household products, ranging from personal computers and hi-fi sets to furniture and utensils. However, chemicals not managed properly would not only pose potential hazards to the environment, but would also affect the general population. The by-products of hazardous substances form toxic industrial waste, which if improperly disposed of, would also be potentially detrimental to human health and the environment. In Singapore, both hazardous substances and toxic industrial waste are regulated and controlled strictly with the aim of avoiding their spillage, leakage, or improper disposal.

In managing hazardous substances and toxic industrial waste,[1] the Ministry adopts a four-pronged approach: Planning and Development Control, Licensing Control, Enforcement, and Education and Partnership.

Planning and Development Control

The government adopts a "cradle-to-grave" approach in the management of hazardous substances and toxic industrial waste. Only companies that can demonstrate their ability to manage, store, and handle hazardous substances safely as well as dispose of their waste effectively are allowed to be set up in Singapore. The deliberate policy of locating such industries away from residential areas and water catchments is also crucial to minimizing potential public exposure and protecting Singapore's precious water resources.

In 1994, the Ministry implemented a scheme that requires industrial projects involving large volumes of hazardous substances to submit Quantitative Risk Assessment (QRA) study reports. This report would help to identify and quantify hazards and risks due to possible accident scenarios that would lead to fire, explosion, or accidental toxic release. Taking into account the scenarios, these projects are required to incorporate measures in the design and operation of their plants to keep the risks to as low a level as practical.

Licensing Control

The hazardous chemicals controlled by the Ministry are those that pose a mass-disaster potential, are highly toxic and pollutive, generate wastes which cannot be safely and adequately disposed of, and have long-term environmental impacts. Licensing controls began in 1985 with just thirty-two industrial chemicals regulated under the Poisons Act. These provisions have since been subsumed under the Environmental Protection and Management Act (EPMA) and there are now more than 530 industrial chemicals under control.

Licensing controls implemented under the EPMA prevent unauthorized persons from handling such substances and ensure proper safeguards are taken at all times in the handling of the substances to prevent accidental releases, and mitigate adverse effects if they occur. Licences are only issued to persons who have undergone a training course conducted by the Singapore Environment Institute (SEI), and passed the prescribed examination.

As hazardous substances pose huge risks during the transportation process, measures have been put in place to ensure the safe transportation of such substances. Firstly, the containers and tankers used for bulk chemical transportation must be designed, manufactured, and tested in accordance with internationally-accepted standards. To minimize the risks posed during their transportation only certain approved routes and timings are allowed for transportation of hazardous substances. Transportation routes are designed such that they avoid water catchments areas, densely populated areas, and road tunnels.

Enforcement

Planning and development control and licensing control alone are not enough to ensure that Singapore is safe from the hazards and risks associated with hazardous substances. A rigorous enforcement programme is devised to ensure that industries comply with the requirements stipulated by the regulatory controls.

In 1991, the Ministry put in place a Safety Audit Scheme requiring companies with large inventories of hazardous substances to identify and rectify systematically (once every two years) weaknesses in their management systems and practices of handling hazardous chemicals.

Education and Partnership

Education and partnership is an important component in Singapore's four-pronged strategy for managing hazardous substances. In this respect, the Ministry worked with the Ministry of Manpower to design a four-day "Management of Hazardous Substances" course to train industries on the legislation and tools for the management of hazardous substances in Singapore and the workplace.

The Ministry also works in partnership with the Singapore Chemical Industry Council (SCIC) to promote co-regulation and self-regulation within the chemical industry. Together with SCIC, NEA conducts workshops, seminars, training courses, and community outreach programmes to raise awareness on chemical safety.

Biohazardous Waste

Concerned that the improper management and disposal of biohazardous waste could give rise to the spread of diseases, the inter-Ministry Joint Coordinating Committee on Epidemic Diseases[2] set up an ad hoc Committee in 1987 to formulate guidelines for the management, handling, and disposal of biohazardous waste. The objective of the guidelines was to protect the health and safety of health care workers, waste disposal workers, and the general public. The guidelines, which were based on WHO standards as well as practices adopted by developed countries such as the United Kingdom, the United States, and Australia advocate the "cradle-to-grave" approach via requirements for the safe and sound management of biohazardous waste from the point of generation in hospital and other medical facilities to the point of disposal.

Hospitals are required to segregate biohazardous waste from normal waste streams through a colour-coded system of waste labelling which ensures that proper precautions are observed when handling the different types of biohazardous waste. Currently, biohazardous waste is controlled under the Environmental Public Health (Toxic Industrial Waste) Regulations. This waste must be properly segregated and contained in special biohazardous waste bins for disposal by licensed biohazardous waste collectors for incineration at dedicated medical waste incinerators.

With a comprehensive and robust system for the disposal of biohazardous waste put in place over the past decade, Singapore was able to react swiftly when Severe Acute Respiratory Syndrome (SARS) broke out in Asia in 2003. Proper segregation and disposal of waste, together with other measures and the cooperation of all Singaporeans, helped contain the spread of SARS in Singapore.

The "cradle-to-grave" approach ensures accountability in the management of hazardous substances, toxic industrial waste and biohazardous waste, and has served Singapore well in safeguarding its environment and public health from adverse impacts arising from improper management of such substances and waste.

CONCLUSION

Today, Singaporeans enjoy a clean and healthy living environment, made possible, in no small way, by an effective solid waste management system that has undergone constant improvements over the past few decades. Singapore's current waste management system is depicted in Figure 4.1. (Map 2 shows the locations of the incineration plants and Semakau landfill.)

FIGURE 4.1

Waste Management System in Singapore (2007)

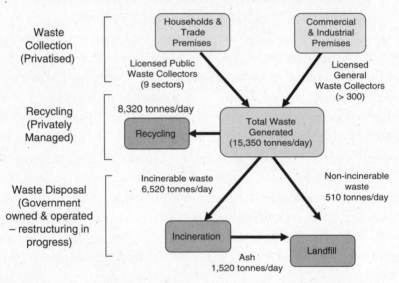

Source: NEA.

Singapore's leaders had the vision of a clean and green city with a high standard of environmental public health. To achieve this vision, the execution of new policies and initiatives was key. For instance, the entire waste collection system was overhauled to provide for daily collection of waste for disposal. Environmental infrastructure ranging from basic refuse chutes in apartments to mechanized collection vehicles to capital intensive incineration plants and landfill were introduced. However, investments in environmental infrastructure only account for half the success story. The other half lies with the people — from the group of dedicated and well-trained staff responsible for the day-to-day operations of the waste disposal facilities, to those who constantly review the system and policies to see how they can be improved upon.

The government has also learnt that allowing private sector participation in the waste collection and disposal sector does not necessarily lead to a reduction in service quality. However, the risks involved, such as operational risk and demand risk, have to be apportioned between the government and the private sector to ensure that these risks are borne by the best party, and that service fees charged are fair and competitive.

Going forward, the government will continue to invest in new infrastructure for waste disposal and will bring in the best available technologies for Singapore's needs, with the objective of moving Singapore towards zero waste. Technologies such as pyrolysis, gasification, and plasma arc are being looked at as the next generation of waste disposal solutions since the end products of these processes are inert and can be reused immediately (e.g. as construction aggregates). However, as these waste disposal technologies are in the infant stages of development and have yet to become cost effective, they have not been implemented on a large scale for treatment of municipal waste. NEA will continue to monitor such new technologies for implementation in Singapore.

Singapore has done well in recycling certain waste streams such as construction and demolition waste, and copper slag (as shown in Table 4.1) as there is a ready market for such recycled materials. However, there are also some waste streams such as plastics and food where recycling rates are still low. In Japan, food waste recycling is mandatory for businesses that generate more than 100 tonnes of food waste annually. Singapore is currently studying various options to promote the recycling of food waste.

In the future, waste minimization should be the main strategy to curb waste growth. Having started a Packaging Agreement for the food and beverage industry, NEA hopes to extend the agreement to other industries such as the electronics sector. These efforts will move Singapore closer to the vision of having a sustainable waste management system.

Map 1. Locations of air quality monitoring stations in Singapore. The 15th station is a mobile station with no fixed location.

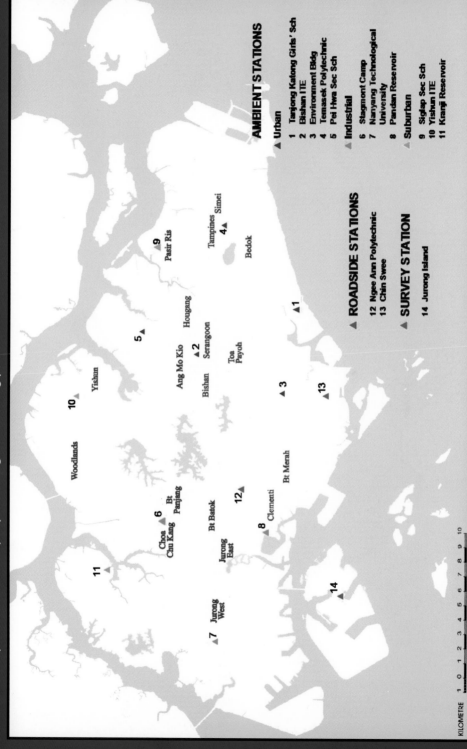

AMBIENT STATIONS

▲ **Urban**
1 Tanjong Katong Girls' Sch
2 Bishan ITE
3 Environment Bldg
4 Temasek Polytechnic
5 Pei Hwa Sec Sch

▲ **Industrial**
6 Stagmont Camp
7 Nanyang Technological University
8 Pandan Reservoir

▲ **Suburban**
9 Siglap Sec Sch
10 Yishun ITE
11 Kranji Reservoir

▲ **ROADSIDE STATIONS**
12 Ngee Ann Polytechnic
13 Chin Swee

▲ **SURVEY STATION**
14 Jurong Island

KILOMETRE 1 0 1 2 3 4 5 6 7 8 9 10

Source: NEA.

Map 2. Locations of incineration plants and Semakau Landfill.

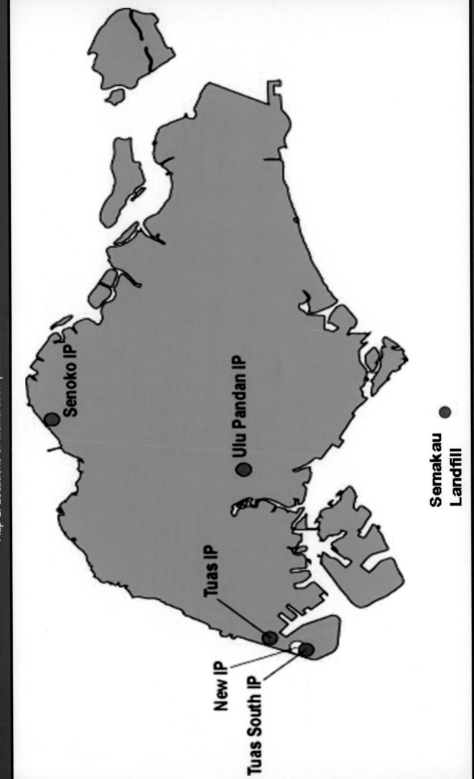

Source: NEA.

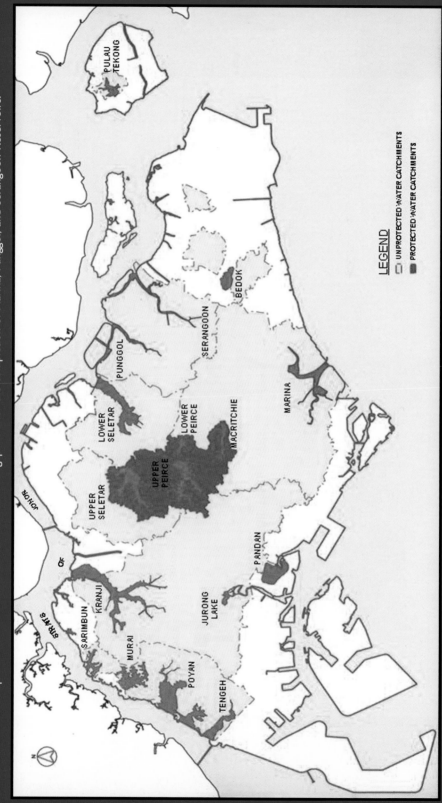

Map 3. Reservoirs and water catchments in Singapore after the completion of Marina, Punggol, and Serangoon Reservoirs.

LEGEND
☐ UNPROTECTED WATER CATCHMENTS
■ PROTECTED WATER CATCHMENTS

Source: PUB.

Map 4. Map of Singapore showing the Deep Tunnel Sewerage System and Water Reclamation Plants.

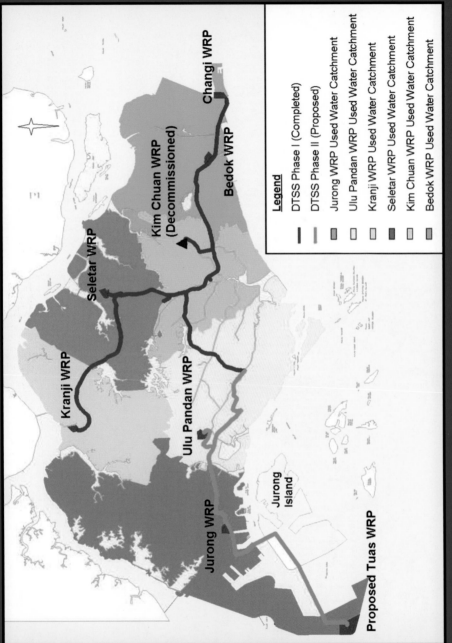

Changi WRP

Kim Chuan WRP (Decommissioned)

Bedok WRP

Seletar WRP

Kranji WRP

Ulu Pandan WRP

Jurong WRP

Jurong Island

Proposed Tuas WRP

<u>Legend</u>

DTSS Phase I (Completed)

DTSS Phase II (Proposed)

Jurong WRP Used Water Catchment

Ulu Pandan WRP Used Water Catchment

Kranji WRP Used Water Catchment

Seletar WRP Used Water Catchment

Kim Chuan WRP Used Water Catchment

Bedok WRP Used Water Catchment

Source: PUB.

Map 5. Blue Map of Singapore showing the network of reservoirs and waterways.

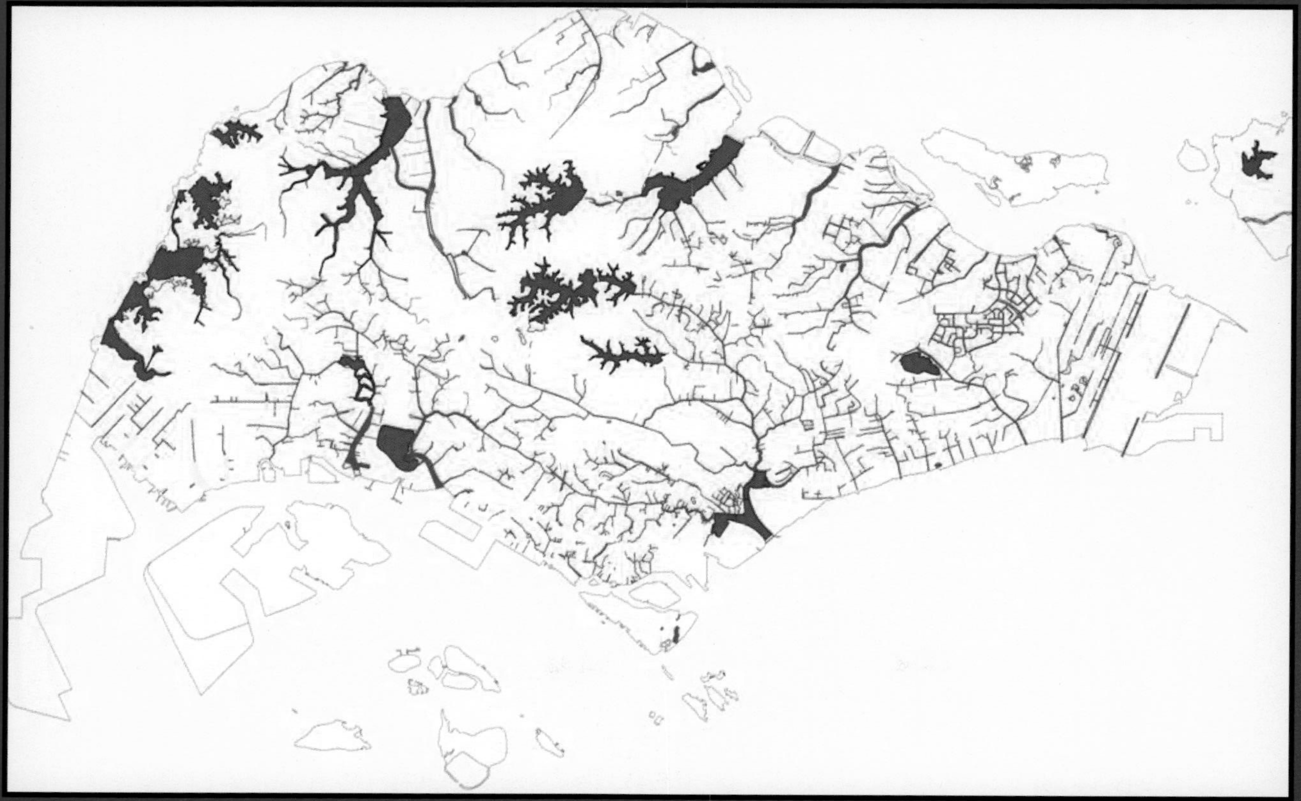

Source: PUB.

Map 6. Singapore's green cover grew from 35.7 to 46.5 per cent between 1986 and 2007.

1986

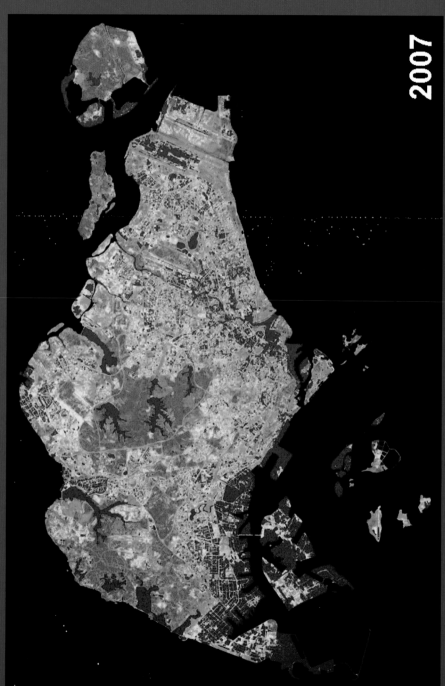

2007

PART III

CLOSING THE WATER LOOP

5

ENSURING WATER SUSTAINABILITY
The Supply Side

The smooth progress of NEWater, the construction of our first desalination plant at Tuas and the enlargement of our local catchments through projects such as the Marina Barrage have certainly strengthened our water supply for the long term.

However, this does not mean that our water challenge is now over and that we can relax and become complacent. On the contrary, it is important that we press on with our efforts in making sure that every drop, every dollar and every idea will always count. This is the best and only way forward for us to ensure that Singapore will stay on the right side of the global water divide, today, tomorrow and well into the future.

Minister Lim Swee Say, Minister for the Environment,
at the official opening of Seletar NEWater Plant on
18 June 2004

Singapore suffered one of its worst droughts in 1963, when water stocks dropped to dangerously low levels. Water rationing was introduced in April 1963 and was only lifted ten months later in

February 1964, with the return of heavy rainfall. What started off as zone rationing for six hours a day, four times a week, was soon extended to islandwide rationing for twelve hours a day, three times a week. It was a painful episode. Singaporeans had to be conscious of when the rationing periods were, and wake up early or stay up late to store the water they needed. Otherwise, they would have to collect their water from public stand pipes during rationing hours. The usual routines were disrupted and the cost of food went up.

During this period, with the dissolution of the City Council, the Public Utilities Board (PUB) was established in May 1963 as a statutory board to coordinate the supply of water, electricity, and piped gas. With regard to water, PUB was charged with improving and expanding the available water assets to keep pace with population expansion and industrial development. To the fledgling PUB, the drought of 1963 left deep and indelible impressions among its officers which remain to this day. So far, through its efforts in building up supply and managing demand, there have not been any further water rationing episodes in Singapore (except for mock exercises), even during the dry spells in 1971, 1990, and more recently, in 1997 due to El Nino.

STATE OF WATER IN SINGAPORE

At first glance, it may seem surprising that Singapore would have an issue with water. Lying on the equatorial belt, it receives its fair share of rain, with some 2,400 mm falling each year (well above the global average of 1,050 mm). Unfortunately, Singapore is a small island with only 700 sq. kilometre of land. Its growing population and economy exert pressure on land use, so that water catchments have to compete for land with activities such as housing, commerce, industry, transport, recreation, and schools. It is this lack of land, and thus, limited catchment size to collect and store rainwater, as well as high evaporative losses, that result in Singapore being classified by the United Nations as a water scarce country.[1] Together with the lack of natural aquifers or groundwater, these factors have led to Singapore being ranked 170th among a list of 190 countries in terms of fresh water availability.[2] Nevertheless, over the years this disadvantage has been turned into a source of motivation, which has inspired not only a "can do" but a "must do" mentality in Singapore's continual quest for innovative water solutions to ensure its sustainability as a nation.

DEVELOPMENT OF CONVENTIONAL WATER RESOURCES

Early History[3]

The earliest sources of water on the island were inland streams and wells. These were small sources, sufficient for the few inhabitants on the island. After its founding in 1819, as Singapore grew as a port city, a small reservoir was constructed at Fort Canning in 1822 to supply water to ships which called at the port.[4] By 1850, the island's population had grown to more than 50,000 without provisions made to supply these residents with water. Planning for Singapore's water supply became an issue. It was only in 1857 that philanthropist Tan Kim Seng made a donation of S$13,000 for the building of Singapore's first waterworks and piped water supply. This provided the impetus for the construction of an impounding reservoir in Thomson Road in 1868. It was expanded in 1891 and named MacRitchie Reservoir in 1922, after Municipal Engineer James MacRitchie who oversaw the expansion.

As colonial Singapore's population grew, steps were taken to enlarge and improve the water supply. In 1910 the Singapore Municipality built the Kallang River Reservoir, which was later renamed Peirce reservoir in 1922, after Municipal Engineer Robert Peirce who was in charge of its construction. Seletar Reservoir, the third impounding reservoir, was named after a Malay word that refers to coastal dwellers called Orang Seletar, and was built within the central catchment in 1920 and later expanded in 1940.

These were, in a nutshell, the main water sources in Singapore at the time of PUB's formation in 1963. Singapore also imports water from Johor through two agreements (concluded in 1961 and 1962) for the supply of water for fifty years and ninety-nine years respectively (this is described later in this chapter). As a young PUB went about building the infrastructure to supply water from Johor under the two water agreements, it recognized the need to build up local water sources and storage capacity in Singapore also.

Protected Catchments

The first three reservoirs — MacRitchie, Peirce, and Seletar — are located in what are called protected catchments, within the central nature reserve. These catchments are protected in the sense that they are left in their natural states as far as possible and development is not allowed. This preserves the sensitive ecological balance in these areas, and minimizes the risk of an accident that could pollute the pristine waters. Consequently, raw water from protected catchments is generally of a higher quality than that from non-protected catchments, and hence supplying water from these areas is the preferred strategy.

To effect this, PUB embarked on a project to expand the catchment of Seletar Reservoir. This was done through a system of stream intakes and ponds to abstract raw water from the seven adjacent streams, which is then pumped into Seletar Reservoir. At the same time, the storage capacity of Seletar Reservoir was enlarged through the construction of a larger dam, and Woodleigh Waterworks was expanded to increase its treatment capacity to produce drinking water. The project, which was completed in 1969, was also noteworthy in that it was one of only two PUB projects, the other being sewerage infrastructure (see Chapter 7), that was developed through a World Bank loan. The loan instilled in PUB the organizational and financial discipline to achieve high standards of investment and operational performance, including full accounting and recovery of costs for its water products.

At Peirce Reservoir, a higher dam was constructed upstream of the existing one, and the Upper Peirce Reservoir scheme was completed in 1975 to increase storage capacity. Even today, Seletar Reservoir (renamed Upper Seletar Reservoir in 1992) and Upper Peirce Reservoir are still the largest reservoirs in Singapore.

Although protected catchments provided an excellent source of high-quality raw water, it was not possible to expand them indefinitely. In the 1970s and 1980s, the rapid growth of industries and residential estates placed increasing pressure on the scarce land in Singapore. This compelled PUB to look into new and innovative ways to develop more water sources.

In 1971, a Water Planning Unit was set up under the Prime Minister's Office to study the scope and feasibility of new conventional sources such as unprotected catchments, and unconventional sources, such as water reuse and desalination. This was a significant move, signalling the importance that the political leadership accorded the issue. The outcome of the study was the first Water Master Plan in 1972. The Water Master Plan outlined plans for the local water resources in Singapore, including water from local catchments, recycled water, and desalinated water, to ensure a diversified and adequate supply of water to meet future projected demand. It would serve as the blueprint to guide the long-term development of water resources in Singapore.

Unprotected Catchments

The need to balance competing land needs led to the creation of unprotected catchments, where, unlike protected catchments, development was allowed. However, such development was limited to residential estates and industries with clean and light uses, for example, those that did not involve the heavy use of chemicals. In addition to land-use planning, stringent pollution control was also required, as Singapore's first Prime Minister Lee Kuan Yew summed up in his memoirs, *From Third World to First, The Singapore Story: 1965–2000):*[5]

> One compelling reason to have a clean Singapore is our need to collect as much as possible of our rainfall of 95 inches a year. I put Lee Ek Tieng, a civil engineer, then the head of the Anti-Pollution Unit, in charge of a plan to dam up all our streams and rivers (Estuarine Reservoirs Scheme). The plan took about 10 years to implement. He had to ensure that all sewage, sullage and other soiled water from homes and factories emptied into the sewers. Only clean rainwater runoff from the roofs, gardens and open spaces was allowed into the open drains that flowed into dammed-up rivers.

Estuarine Reservoirs

The unprotected water catchments began with the river estuaries in northern and western Singapore. However, the estuaries led to the sea and were often subject to salinity and tidal influence. Hence, the idea was to create large bodies of freshwater to store and regulate the supply, by damming up the estuaries and flushing out the salty water over time.

A number of new reservoirs were formed in this way. In 1975, Kranji Reservoir was created through the damming of the Kranji River, while Pandan Reservoir was created from a tidal swamp to store water abstracted from Pandan River. Under the Western Catchments scheme, dykes or dams were built across the mouths of four rivers — Murai, Poyan, Sarimbun, and Tengeh — to convert them into reservoirs by 1981. To treat the water from the Kranji, Pandan, and Western Catchments, a waterworks was built at Choa Chu Kang in 1976.

A number of settlements and farms (in particular, pig farms) were located in the Kranji catchment in the earlier days, resulting in the discharge of untreated human and animal wastes into the watercourses. These were tackled with the relocation of the farms, extension of the sanitation system, and introduction of anti-pollution legislation. Nevertheless, the raw water from these catchments would still be of lower quality than that in the protected catchments, and higher in organic matter. Traditionally, chlorine is used for disinfection. However, to deal with the lower raw water quality, a more powerful disinfectant, ozone, was used to supplement the conventional water treatment at the Choa Chu Kang waterworks. To achieve a consistently high quality of treated water, the treatment process was further enhanced recently to include membrane filtration to replace the conventional sand filters.

Urbanized Catchments

Developing water resources, however, did not stop there. With demand growing, there was a need to capture every economically viable drop of water. This would not be limited to forested catchments and dammed-up rivers. In land-scarce Singapore, PUB had to find ways to marry the multiple uses of land for housing, transport, commerce, or industry. Bolder and more innovative methods were needed to tap water that flowed through urbanized areas — and this gave rise to the creation of urbanized water catchments.

Even today, urbanized catchments are not the norm. In many other countries, water is still collected in undeveloped areas and transported hundreds of kilometres to supply urban centres. Back in the 1980s, the idea of tapping water from urbanized catchments was deemed risky and unconventional since the water run-off from urbanized areas would tend to be polluted and of low quality. There were many potential sources of pollution — rainwater could flow onto various surfaces, picking up contaminants on its way; household waste, industrial discharge, sewage from leaking sewers, and litter could find their way into the drains that were connected to the reservoirs. In all, a heady cocktail of challenges!

Nevertheless, there were not many viable alternatives then. Desalination techniques were energy-intensive and significantly more costly. Water reuse was still in its infancy, the only available technology being unreliable and expensive. Short of any reliable and proven technology, there would also be a psychological barrier in getting the public to accept recycled water. In comparison, embarking on urbanized catchments first, while monitoring developments in water reuse and desalination technologies, was more feasible.

Sungei Seletar-Bedok Water Scheme

The Sungei Seletar-Bedok water scheme was developed in 1986. Sungei Seletar was dammed to form Lower Seletar Reservoir (the original Seletar Reservoir was renamed Upper Seletar Reservoir). The raw water would be conveyed through pipelines to fill Bedok Reservoir, which was constructed out of a sand quarry. Bedok Reservoir would also be filled with water collected in storm water abstraction ponds constructed in the highly urbanized New Towns of Bedok and Tampines, including Yan Kit. The storm water collection system in such urbanized catchments was specially designed to allow the more polluted dry weather flow and the "first flush" of wet weather flow to bypass the collection facility, while the cleaner part of the storm water was diverted into a holding pond and pumped to the reservoir.

At its time, the technical complexity of the storm water collection system was a feat in itself. However, what was more noteworthy was the integrated planning by various government agencies for such an extensive system, which had to be carried out on various fronts — this was long before "inter-agency coordination" became the buzzword.

The most important task was to tackle pollution at source. In this instance, the different characteristics of the catchments at Sungei

Seletar and Bedok required different approaches. In the Sungei Seletar area, existing developments included fish ponds, farms, residential premises, and some small industries. In fact, some of these farms had earlier been relocated here when Kranji Reservoir was developed in the 1970s.[6] Pig farming was phased out in 1984 with the help of the Primary Production Department (now Agrifood and Veterinary Authority), and other forms of farming were relocated.[7] In fact, close to a fifth of the budget for the Sungei Seletar-Bedok water scheme went to resettlement costs for farmers.

In Ang Mo Kio, which was also within the Sungei Seletar catchment, less than 2 per cent of latrines were connected to the public sewerage system. Used water was mostly sent to the localized sewage treatment plants, where it was treated and discharged into drains and canals. The Sewerage Department under the Ministry of the Environment was charged with the extension of the sewage network to ensure that all used water was collected and centrally treated.

On the other hand, the Bedok catchment was largely a green field site where it would be easier to stipulate development and land-use guidelines from the outset. Here, the Urban Redevelopment Authority (URA) played a key role in planning the land use, keeping pollutive developments away from the water sources from as early as ten to fifteen years prior to the construction of the reservoir scheme. Farming activities were not allowed, and the area was largely earmarked for residential development and light industries. The need for an extensive sewerage network for Bedok New Town was also incorporated at the planning stage, involving multiple agencies such as the URA and the Housing and Development Board (HDB). The various measures would be important for safeguarding the water quality of urban run-off. Similar to Choa Chu Kang waterworks, ozonation was employed at the Bedok Water Treatment Plant. The reservoir itself was formerly a sand quarry that HDB had used for its development programme. To allow for the timely conversion of the quarry into a reservoir, HDB excavated the sand that it required for its future projects and created a stockpile at Tampines. This was another example of how integrated planning could bring about seamless coordination, even for development works that cut across various agencies.

Since its commissioning in 1986, the Sungei Seletar-Bedok water scheme has proven itself capable of delivering water of a comparable quality to that obtained from the protected central catchment. The scheme illustrates how good quality water from urban catchments can be possible through a combination of factors — understanding the nature of the catchments, implementing bold policies to remove existing sources of pollution, upfront and long-term planning to minimize future sources of pollution, proactive enforcement, harnessing technology, and perhaps most important of all, a strong determination to succeed and integrate planning amongst different government agencies to make things happen.

Conjunctive Use of Land

The construction of storm water collection ponds to collect storm run-off from the catchments continues to be a key component of the water supply system today. However, these require large tracts of land amidst competing demands on scarce land. In some cases where the land was developed later on, innovative approaches were found. For example, four of the storm water collection ponds for the Upper Seletar Reservoir scheme were rebuilt: one was located under the viaduct of the Seletar/Bukit Timah Expressway and had a huge storage capacity of 18 million gallons (equivalent to more than twenty-five Olympic-sized swimming pools); two others were constructed beneath school fields; the fourth was built as part of a community pond.

Reservoir Integration

The story so far on how Singapore has developed its catchments and reservoirs may give the impression that the size of catchments and reservoirs is all that matters. To some extent, this is true, but it is not the full picture.

Water catchments and reservoirs come in various sizes. Some reservoirs, for example, Kranji, have smaller storage capacities relative to the size of their catchments. When a lot of run-off flows into these reservoirs, they fill up quickly and the water spills over, resulting in wastage. On the other hand, some reservoirs, such as Upper Seletar, have larger storage capacities relative to the size of their catchments.

It is not always possible to expand the reservoir or the catchment to improve the effective yield of each reservoir. However, the overall water supply can be increased by transferring water from one reservoir to another, without the need to expand the catchments or reservoirs. This was achieved through the Reservoir Integration Scheme (RIS), which commenced construction in 2004 and was completed in 2007. The scheme allows PUB to operate the reservoirs in a flexible and integrated way by interconnecting them through a system of pumps and pipelines so that excess water in one reservoir can be pumped into another for storage. This not only helps to optimize the yield of the reservoirs, it also maximizes the capture of rainwater. In fact, some of the older schemes, such as the storm water collection system in the Sungei Seletar-Bedok water scheme, were early versions of the RIS.

Marina and Punggol-Serangoon Reservoir Schemes

Marina Reservoir Scheme: Until the 1990s, half of Singapore still remained untapped as water catchment — most notable was the Marina Catchment, which covered some 10,000 hectares or about one-sixth the total land area of Singapore. Perhaps it was not surprising that this catchment had been largely untouched, since it included some of the oldest and most densely populated parts of the city.

A huge effort had been undertaken in the 1970s to clean up the Singapore River. This led to a significant improvement in the water quality, but it was still not good enough for the production of drinking water. There were still too much nutrient and bacterial loads in the water, caused by the washing of land-based pollutants into the river during heavy rain and the presence of old and leaking sewers. In fact, when plans were made in the 1990s to build a barrage across the Marina Channel, the intention was for the resulting Marina Reservoir to serve as a potential source of second grade water — water to meet non-potable uses.

The advancement in membrane technology in the late 1990s made it possible and cost effective to treat the water in Marina Reservoir to potable water standards. Once this was established, plans quickly unfolded to bring forward the construction of the barrage and the idea of a three-in-one city reservoir was conceptualized — for water supply, flood alleviation, and recreational purposes. With the switch to develop Marina Reservoir as a source of water, plans were put in place to transfer raw water from Marina Reservoir to Upper Peirce Reservoir for storage. This would in effect be another reservoir integration project to increase the yield from Marina Reservoir.

Punggol-Serangoon Reservoir Scheme: In addition to the Marina Reservoir, Singapore's sixteenth and seventeenth reservoirs are also being built — they are formed by damming the mouths of the Punggol and Serangoon Rivers in the northeastern part of Singapore. The Punggol-Serangoon Reservoir Scheme has a catchment area of some 5,500 hectares.

The Punggol and Serangoon Rivers had not been considered for potable water supply earlier due to the poor quality run-offs from their associated catchments. This arose from pollutive industries within their catchments and other potential sources of contamination such as the Lorong Halus dumping ground and Serangoon Sludge Treatment Works. In addition, treated effluent from the Kim Chuan Water Reclamation Plant was also discharged into the Serangoon River.

A number of developments helped to change this. With the completion of the Deep Tunnel Sewerage System (DTSS), the Kim

Chuan Water Reclamation Plant and Serangoon Sludge Treatment Works were decommissioned, removing two sources of pollution. Both the Punggol and Serangoon Reservoirs were dredged to remove contaminated materials such as heavy metals. A cut-off wall will also be constructed as part of the Serangoon Reservoir development to isolate the leachate from Lorong Halus dumping ground, and wetlands will be built to pretreat the leachate. With these and the availability of advanced membrane technology to treat raw water to drinking water quality, the two rivers can now be dammed up and integrated with the rest of the reservoirs to increase Singapore's total water supply. With the completion of Marina, Punggol, and Serangoon Reservoirs in 2009, Singapore's catchment area will have increased from half to about two-thirds of Singapore's land area (as shown in Map 3).

Maximizing Water Supply from Singapore's Catchments

Singapore's combined water catchment will make up two-thirds of its land area with the completion of the Marina and Punggol-Serangoon Reservoir schemes in 2009. Rainwater within these catchments will eventually flow into drains which culminate in reservoirs.

As for the remaining one-third that remains untapped, these are mainly in the industrial areas in the west and east. In time to come, when the technology and cost are right, further ideas to develop them will be explored. One example is the Variable Salinity Plant, which is discussed later in this chapter.

Overcoming the Environmental Challenges of Reservoir Creation

Damming a water body typically introduces a series of possible social and environmental problems. These could include the displacement of people living along the river banks, build-up of silt behind the dam which could lead to flooding, changes in the landscape, and impact on biodiversity. In the case of estuarine reservoirs, the desalting of the water changes the ecosystem drastically, leading to habitat loss and elimination of certain saltwater species. Hence, when building a barrage, it is important to consider not only the financial costs, but also the environmental consequences.

Great care has been taken in the planning and design of reservoir projects to ensure that they will have minimum impact on the coastal waters and the environment. At the planning stage of the Punggol-Serangoon Reservoir scheme, PUB conducted a biodiversity study, followed by an Environmental Impact Assessment (EIA) by international consultants, in order to develop suitable mitigating measures to address any impacts which may arise from the project. The Nature Society was also consulted on the scope of the EIA, and thereafter briefed on the findings of the study.

The EIA concluded that apart from small, localized, minor impacts that could be addressed by mitigating measures, the project would have a negligible effect on the water level and flow velocities in the coastal waters. Hence, the impact on navigation, sediment transport and seabed morphology, flooding, water quality, aquaculture, and fisheries in the coastal waters were assessed to be negligible. Although the overall findings of the EIA showed that impact would be minor and localized, PUB, in line with best practices, implemented a series of environmental management and monitoring measures as the works were carried out.

For example, to minimize the impact of dredging, contractors were required to minimize the dispersal of sediments in the water. They also used silt screens to contain sediments and installed online turbidity monitoring equipment, so that remedial actions could be taken immediately if the turbidity exceeded the preset criteria.

To mitigate the loss of mangrove species, the saplings and root cuttings of the mangroves were transplanted to other suitable sites, such as the Sungei Buloh wetlands and Pasir Ris Park. Studies concluded that the bird and fish species could be found in many other parts of Singapore such as the nature reserves and coastal waters. Nevertheless, floating islands would be constructed, which could serve as habitats for birds. Biodiversity surveys were also carried out on a monthly basis throughout the works to monitor the possible impact of construction works on the ecosystem.

IMPORTED WATER

Imported water has always played an important role in meeting Singapore's water needs. In 1961, an agreement was concluded with the State of Johor in Malaysia for the supply of water to Singapore from the Gunong Pulai and Pontian catchments, and Tebrau and Skudai Rivers, until 2011. The City Council (predecessor of PUB) was given the full and exclusive right and liberty to take, impound and use the water within these catchments and rivers.

A second agreement was concluded in the following year (1962) for the drawing of up to 250 million gallons of water per day from the Johor River, until 2061. Under the Water Agreements, the price of raw water was fixed at 3 sen per 1,000 gallons of water. However since 1961, Singapore has been paying for the water infrastructure, such as dams, pipelines, plants and equipment. It also pays for the operational and maintenance costs which add up to millions of dollars a year. All these payments, including costs incurred under the Linggiu Dam Agreement (which is discussed in detail below), total more than S$1 billion. In addition, Singapore supplies treated water to Johor under both agreements at a price of 50 sen per 1,000 gallons of water when it costs Singapore about RM2.40 to treat every 1,000 gallons of water.

To facilitate the abstraction of water from Johor River, an agreement with the Government of the State of Johor and PUB was signed in 1990 that allowed for the construction of the Linggiu Dam upstream of the Johor River waterworks. The idea was to collect the run-off from that part of the Johor River catchment in a large body of water, which could be used to regulate the flow in the Johor

River. By collecting and storing storm water from this part of the catchment, this reservoir also helps alleviate flooding during heavy rain in the downstream reaches of the Johor River.

At the time, the Linggiu Dam was the largest dam project undertaken by PUB for water supply, and it took three years to construct. The land within which the Linggiu Dam, reservoir and catchment area is located has also been designated a protected place by the Malaysian Government to safeguard water quality. PUB also made Malaysia a one-time upfront payment of some RM320 million in compensation for the permanent loss of use of the land, the loss of revenue from logging and also for the lease of land. In addition, an environment impact assessment was also conducted to ensure that impacts to the environment were minimized.

Water from local catchments together with water imported from both these agreements are adequate for Singapore's needs. But it has, nevertheless, decided to supplement them with NEWater and desalinated water. In this way, by 2011, when the 1961 Water Agreement expires, Singapore will not need to renew it. By 2061 when the 1962 Agreement expires, Singapore can be self-sufficient in water if there is no new water agreement with Malaysia.

BEYOND CONVENTIONAL SOURCES

Singapore's First Foray into Water Recyling: Industrial Water

Industrial water was first introduced in 1966 with the construction of Jurong Industrial Water Works (JIWW) by the Economic Development Board (EDB) as a cheap source of low-quality water for industries. The objective was to help conserve potable water by reclaiming the final effluent from Ulu Pandan Water Reclamation Plant (UPWRP).[8] The industrial water thus produced served as an alternative source of water for the industries in Jurong/Tuas Industrial Estate, Tuas View, and Jurong Island.

The then Ministry of the Environment (ENV) took over JIWW in 1971. To replace potable water that was being channelled for non-potable use, HDB and ENV embarked on a pilot scheme to supply industrial water for toilet flushing. In 1973, industrial water was supplied to 600 units of flats in the Taman Jurong housing estate. This was extended to over 6,000 residential flats by 1989, including flats in Pandan Garden and Teban Garden. Unfortunately, the lower water quality resulted in high maintenance and replacement costs which made the scheme not viable, leading to the discontinuation of the scheme in 1990.

Nevertheless, industrial water demand from industries continued to grow. At its peak, JIWW was supplying more than sixty customers who used it mainly for washing and cooling purposes. However, with the introduction of NEWater to the Jurong/Tuas Industrial Estate in 2007, most of the industrial water users switched from industrial water to NEWater. The high quality of NEWater, with its wide acceptance for non-potable use, heralded a new era in Singapore's water supply story, particularly in terms of the approach toward meeting non-potable water demand.

Water Reclamation: The Thirty-year Wait

Most Singaporeans will remember the "birth" of NEWater in 2002, in particular, the toasting with NEWater at the National Day Parade that year. It was a rapturous moment of great pride, for it symbolized Singapore's founding of a sustainable solution to its long-term water needs and its coming of age as a country capable of delivering breakthroughs in water technology.

However, NEWater, or reclaimed water, was not conceived overnight. Since the 1970s, then ENV and PUB were well aware that used water could be reclaimed and purified to high-quality water of drinking standards which would potentially increase the yield of the water supply system and ease demand for more land as water catchments.

In 1974, the first water reclamation plant, a joint ENV-PUB pilot project, was built at JIWW to test various water treatment technologies including reverse osmosis (RO). The pilot study confirmed that high-quality drinking water could be produced from treating used water. However, technologies such as RO membranes were then in the early stages of development, and expensive. There were also doubts on the reliability of the technologies. The plant was, therefore, decommissioned, although PUB continued to keep abreast of technological developments in this field.

Another opportunity resurfaced in the late 1990s when pilot tests and research studies done overseas, as well as technical publications, confirmed that the development of membrane technologies had become more reliable and cost efficient to operate and maintain. In 1998, then Chairman (PUB) Lee Ek Tieng and then Permanent Secretary (ENV) Tan Gee Paw felt that the time was ripe to revisit the project. Two young engineers, one from PUB and the other from ENV, were sent on a study trip to the United States. The findings from the trip showed that water recycling was viable, and a study team was formed. This led to the construction of a dual-membrane demonstration plant of 2.2 million gallons per day at Bedok in May 2000. The modern-day journey of NEWater thus began.

History of Water Reclamation and Reuse

Reclamation of used water as a source of water supply is not unique to Singapore and has, in fact, been going on in several parts of the United States for more than twenty years. At Water Factory 21, Orange County Water District in Southern California, high-quality water reclaimed from treated used water has been used to recharge groundwater since 1976.[9] Similarly, in North Virginia, the Upper Occoquan Sewage Authority has since 1978 been putting high-quality reclaimed water into the Occoquan Reservoir which serves as a source of water for more than a million people living in the vicinity of Washington, D.C.[10]

In large countries, many cities are currently also using water from rivers that contain effluent discharged from upstream sewage treatment plants. In England, large towns such as Oxford, Reading, Swindon, and Bracknell upstream of London, discharge their treated sewage into the Thames River that supplies downstream London with water. This is also done in the United States where the Mississippi River serves as both the destination of sewage treatment plant effluent and a source of potable water.

Two Years of Study

When used water reclamation and reuse was considered in the 1970s, questions were raised pertaining to not just the reliability and costs of the technology, but also public health risks, safety assurances, and other technical issues. Used water contains microbial pathogens that pose a major concern for human health. Major groups of pathogens include bacteria (e.g., *Escherichia coli, Salmonella spp*), viruses (e.g., *Enterovirus, Rotavirus, Hepatitis A*), protozoa (e.g., *Giardia lamblia, Cryptosporidium parvum*), and helminths (e.g., tapeworm). Furthermore, although most used water is from household sources (more than 90 per cent), there were concerns about the presence of trace organics such as pharmaceuticals and hormones, and toxic wastes such as cyanide in recycled used water. Unless a comprehensive set of risk management practices was in place to ensure a "fail-safe" system, recycling of used water was unlikely to materialize in Singapore.

In view of the concerns, a comprehensive two-year study was conducted by PUB/ENV from 2000 to 2002 when the demonstration plant was built. An independent expert panel was convened to advise PUB and ENV on the study. Among other areas, the expert panel was tasked to review the sampling and analysis of NEWater, conduct toxicological and carcinogenic risk assessment and other relevant health studies, as well as evaluate the findings of the PUB/ENV study in order to make recommendations on the suitability of NEWater as a source of raw water for potable use. The expert panel comprised local and foreign experts across multiple disciplines, including engineering, water chemistry, toxicology, epidemiology, and microbiology.

The expert panel ensured that the latest methodologies, analytical tools, and international best practices were adopted to investigate the robustness of membrane technology to produce NEWater of drinking water standards consistently. Following more than 20,000 tests carried out on some 190 water quality parameters, the extensive results showed NEWater quality to be well within the USEPA and WHO drinking water standards. The expert panel also reviewed studies on the toxicity and estrogenic[11] effects of NEWater as carried out on mice and fish, which showed that short- and long-term exposure or consumption of NEWater concentrated at 500 times did not produce any tissue abnormalities or health effects in mice, nor was there evidence of carcinogenic or estrogenic effects on fish.

Having evaluated the data and study reports, the expert panel concluded that NEWater was safe for potable use. The expert panel also concluded that Singapore should consider the use of NEWater for indirect potable use (IPU) as it was a safe supplement to the existing water supply. Three reasons were offered for IPU: first, blending with reservoir water would provide trace minerals which had been removed in the treatment process; second, reservoir storage would provide additional safety beyond the advanced technologies used to produce safe and high quality NEWater; and last but not least, gain public acceptance.

How NEWater is Produced

The production of NEWater involves the systematic reduction of risk to human health posed by water-borne contaminants through a series of robust, multiple safety barriers to chemical contaminants and microbial pathogens. This is known as the "multiple barrier" process. Adopting this principle, the multiple barrier processes in NEWater production include the following steps:

(i) Used water is first treated through conventional treatment processes to meet globally recognized standards suitable for discharge into rivers.

(ii) The first stage of NEWater treatment involves micro-filtration (MF) or ultra-filtration (UF). This involves the use of membrane filters to remove suspended solids, colloidal particles, disease-causing bacteria, some viruses, and protozoan cysts. Only dissolved salts and organic molecules go through to the next stage. The second phase is reverse osmosis (RO), where a membrane with even smaller pores is used to filter out or remove dissolved salts (including inorganic ions) and organics to produce ultra-clean water.

(iii) To provide a safety back-up to the RO stage, a third stage is used where high-intensity ultraviolet (UV) disinfection is carried out to ensure that any residual micro-organisms are inactivated. Some alkaline chemicals are then added to restore the pH balance to stabilize NEWater before it is piped for use.

In spite of the proven technology, there has been no complacency. PUB continues to adopt a vigilant monitoring and surveillance programme to ensure a high level of safety and reliability in the production process. The NEWater quality is continuously monitored through a comprehensive water sampling and monitoring programme. The parameters monitored include physical characteristics, organic and inorganic contaminants, radiological and microbiological quality, as well as emerging contaminants. The original list of some 150 water quality parameters has been enlarged to 290 parameters, far exceeding the 140 parameters listed in the WHO and USEPA drinking water standards.

The water quality test results, plant operation and competency of NEWater plant operators are audited every quarter by an Internal Audit Panel (IAP) and biannually by an External Audit Panel (EAP)[12] comprising local and foreign experts.

Tests conducted by the National University of Singapore (NUS) and supervised by a panel of local and international experts have established that NEWater is of a higher purity than PUB water. NEWater is clearer and more sparkling than water from river or reservoir sources, which have more colour as they contain more minerals and organic substances. Organic substances in NEWater are also extremely low, at the parts per billion level. Because of this, industry users find NEWater more attractive. For example, wafer fabrication plants have switched from PUB water to NEWater and reported savings in their operation because of the higher purity of NEWater.

Uses for NEWater

NEWater is supplied for both direct non-potable use (DNU) and indirect potable use (IPU). It is able to serve as an effective substitute for PUB tap water for use in manufacturing processes that require ultra-clean water such as wafer fabrication in the semiconductor industry as well as air-con cooling of commercial buildings. This frees up a large amount of PUB water for potable purposes.

NEWater is well within WHO and USEPA Drinking Water Standards and is safe for human consumption. However, it is not piped for potable use. NEWater has only been bottled for public sampling, albeit reaching 10 million bottles currently (in 2008). Nevertheless, the direct supply of reclaimed water for potable use is not adopted worldwide except in Windhoek, Namibia. In Singapore, NEWater is incorporated into the drinking water system via IPU, which involves the injection of NEWater into reservoirs for mixing with reservoir water, and thereafter the mixed water is treated through the conventional water treatment process. In effect, this adds another barrier process and provides an important and psychological assurance that NEWater for IPU is safe for drinking. This "naturalization" process also reintroduces natural minerals into the NEWater through the reservoirs. Convinced that NEWater IPU was safe, the government announced in September 2002 that it had accepted the recommendations by Expert Panels to introduce NEWater for IPU.

From an initial volume of 1 million gallons per day in 2003, the target is to steadily increase NEWater IPU to 10 million gallons per day by 2011. In so doing, PUB has effectively closed the water loop through recycling of used water to produce NEWater. This is strategically significant, as NEWater IPU can be ramped up in times of need to boost water supply. NEWater is also independent of fluctuations in rainfall, hence it can enhance Singapore's resilience against prolonged periods of low rainfall or drought.

The Multiplier Effect of Water Recycling

Apart from freeing up large amounts of potable water for other purposes, NEWater has a role in "multiplying" the water supply achieved through recycling. What this means is that if 50 per cent of water is recycled, the water supply could theoretically be doubled. From recycling 1 drop of water, 0.5 drops of water can be obtained. This 0.5 drops can in turn be recycled to get 0.25 drops, and then 0.125 drops, and so on. Theoretically, recycling 1 drop of water results in another drop of water ($0.5 + 0.25 + 0.125 + \ldots = 1$) produced. This is a multiplier of two. At a higher recycling rate, a higher multiplier effect, mathematically equal to $1/(1-R)$ where R is the recycling rate, can be achieved.

This means that instead of building new capacity of 100 million gallons per day (mgd) through catchment expansion, which is difficult in land-scarce Singapore, or desalination, which is costly, only half the required new capacity (50 mgd in this case) needs to be built and the rest made up through the multiplier effect of recycling.

Spreading the Message to the Public — It is Safe!

While all steps were taken to ensure the quality and viability of NEWater, there was also a need to convince the public that NEWater was safe for consumption. As PUB and the then ENV delved into the public communications aspect of NEWater, it noted that in other parts of the world, public acceptance of reclaimed water had been mixed at best. A number of cities had failed to introduce reclaimed water, not for lack of funding or water purity, but because of the public's negative perception towards the idea of turning "used water" into potable use.

Having come so far, the Singapore Government wanted to avoid a situation where NEWater would be rejected by the public. Singaporeans had to be convinced that NEWater was safe to use, with no negative long-term health implications. If they could not be convinced, the price to pay would be costly, given that Singapore's demand for water would continue to rise and land needed for water catchment areas was already severely limited.

In May 2002, PUB prepared a Public Communications Plan for NEWater to engender public acceptance, which sought to convey the following messages:

> Water reclamation was not new and had been practised in other countries, for example the United States, for more than two decades without any significant health concerns in the long run. On the whole, NEWater was a safe and valuable source to supplement the potable water supply.
>
> NEWater was "WHO+" and "PUB+", meaning its quality was comparable to, or even exceeded, international drinking water standards, and it was even purer than PUB water. The public had to be assured that NEWater was safe and consistently of the best quality, even though it would not be used directly as potable water. Mixing it with raw water in the reservoir prior to further treating the water into drinking water was akin to supplying water the traditional way and hence would not change the social habits that Singaporeans were used to.

NEWater was a cost competitive source of water supply compared to desalinated water and probably other conventional sources of water supply in the future, as its cost of production was expected to come down with further advances in membrane technology.

In putting out the public communications messages, it was felt that the focus should not be purely on the technical considerations. While international experts had a vital role to play in terms of providing an independent and objective assessment on the technical issues, local experts and officials would be better placed to understand and address the sentiments and sensitivities of the local community on the issue. For example, a series of briefings were planned and "tested" on the Members of Parliament (MPs). Their reactions and feedback, both as non-technical persons and political leaders, were used to fine-tune the presentations before they were put to the media and general public.

As the media would play a key role in conveying the details and objectives of NEWater to the public, it was important that they had an accurate picture and appreciation of the issues related to reuse. An open and transparent approach was taken to provide the media with information. In May 2002, a study trip was organized for journalists to visit areas in the United States where reclaimed water had been tried and tested, so the media could see first-hand their experience in harnessing and reclaiming water for potable and other uses. Thereafter, in July 2002, the findings and independent evaluation of the expert panel were released to the media. To help journalists grasp the details, a press conference was held where local and foreign experts fielded questions from them on NEWater. Visits to the NEWater demonstration plant at Bedok allowed the media to see for themselves what went on at the plant.

Telling the facts about reclaimed water and increasing understanding about the water cycle became an exercise of national proportions. Ministers and civil servants went public with the findings of the expert panel on NEWater. Exhibitions, briefings, advertisements, posters, and brochures were used to get the message across that NEWater was not only safe to drink, but also a sustainable source of water supply. MPs and grassroots leaders, having been convinced themselves, helped to spread the messages further to the community.

In a greater attempt to reach out to the community, NEWater was bottled to allow the general public to sample the taste of NEWater. Then Prime Minister Goh Chok Tong gave his personal endorsement after drinking a bottle of NEWater following a tennis game, a footage that reflected the strong support for NEWater at the highest levels. It was aired on national television on 6 August 2002, and would set the stage for the "mass toast" event at the National Day Parade three days later, where 60,000 people celebrated Singapore's national birthday with NEWater.

A survey carried out pointed towards an overwhelming public acceptance of NEWater, with 82 per cent of respondents indicating they were prepared to drink it directly and an additional 16 per cent prepared to drink it indirectly, after mixing with reservoir water. It was a resounding show of support from all Singaporeans,[13] and with it, the country could take a quantum leap in its quest towards achieving water sustainability.

The public education campaign continued in schools, community centres, and workplaces. Education leaflets and posters were distributed to explain what NEWater was. In February 2003, the Bedok NEWater Visitor Centre was launched as a primary avenue for public education on NEWater. At the centre, visitors learned about water technology and experiences of water reuse around the world, and viewed the operation of the various technologies in the production of NEWater. It helped to bridge the gap between scientific understanding and public perception.

Convincing the Wafer Fabrication Industry

Convincing the wafer fabrication industry (or wafer fabs) to convert from potable water to NEWater was no easy task, given the sensitivity of the wafer fabrication process. These plants are typically fitted with a pretreatment facility that treats incoming (potable) water to ultra pure water (UPW), which is required for the wafer fabrication process. Even with pretreatment facilities and technical reports on the quality of NEWater, wafer fabs were reluctant to switch from potable water to NEWater. The reason was simple — there was no wafer fabrication facility in the world that used recycled water. Theoretically, the higher grade NEWater would be more suitable than potable water since wafer fabs would have to spend less money and chemicals treating it to UPW standards. Other practical considerations such as the reliability and security of NEWater also played a major role in the customer's decision to use NEWater.

In order to increase wafer fabs' confidence level, a pilot plant that could simulate "real" conditions at the wafer fabs was built. Since different wafer fabs produced UPW using different process configurations, PUB proceeded to build a "plug and play" pilot plant that would simulate different configurations of the UPW system. This was built following close consultations with the wafer fabs.

PUB engaged the services of the Centre for Advanced Water Treatment (CAWT) to conduct pilot studies and analyse the UPW quality. The pilot plant was installed at Bedok NEWater Demonstration Plant and was designed to study three different configurations. The plant was run over twelve months, from 2001 to 2002, during which the UPW produced from this plant was tested for its quality, to the satisfaction of wafer fabs. Following additional tests conducted for another six months, the wafer fabs were fully convinced of the reliability and security of NEWater. In fact, by using NEWater instead of potable water, the wafer fabs achieved 20 per cent savings[14] in their chemical cost for UPW production. Today, some 14 mgd of NEWater is supplied to eleven wafer fabs in Singapore.

Rolling it out — NEWater Clusters

As of March 2008, NEWater has been supplied to more than 290 customers, including wafer fabrication plants, petrochemical complexes and refineries, power stations, electronics companies, and commercial premises. These companies use NEWater for their wafer fabrication processes, process cooling, air-con cooling, boilers, and general washing purposes. Collectively, this accounts for some 40.5 mgd of NEWater demand.

To meet the demand, NEWater factories were constructed next to the existing water reclamation plants, which provide the treated effluent feedstock for the production of NEWater. The first NEWater factories were built at the Bedok and Kranji Water Reclamation Plants. They were completed in January 2003 and supplied wafer fabrication plants in Woodlands, Tampines, and Pasir Ris, and other industries. A third NEWater factory at the Seletar Water Reclamation Plant was commissioned in January 2004, supplying NEWater to industries in Ang Mo Kio.

A significant milestone in the history of NEWater was the facilitation of private sector participation in NEWater supply, through the adoption of a Public-Private Partnership (PPP) approach for subsequent NEWater plants. What this means is that the private sector would design, build, own, and operate (DBOO) the NEWater plant, producing and supplying NEWater to PUB based on a tendered price. This would allow PUB to focus on acquiring the private sector's services at the stipulated level of quality and at the most cost-effective price. Such an approach would encourage greater innovation to enhance production and operational efficiency, and in the longer term, help to develop the water industry into a more vibrant, innovative, and export-oriented sector. A tender was successfully awarded in December 2004, and in March 2007, the first NEWater factory to be built under the DBOO model was commissioned by Prime Minister Lee Hsien Loong. The factory, adjacent to Ulu Pandan water reclamation plant, was built by Keppel Seghers to supply PUB with 32 mgd of NEWater for a period of twenty years.

To meet the growing demand for NEWater, PUB in 2008, brought forward the construction of a 50 mgd NEWater factory at Changi

Water Reclamation Plant, through a twenty-five-year DBOO contract with Sembcorp Utilities. At the same time, plans are underway to build pipelines across the island so that NEWater from the Changi plant (also the largest plant) can supplement and back up the supply from the other plants. This will enhance the robustness and reliability of NEWater supply.

With these developments, Singapore would have sufficient NEWater capacity to meet 30 per cent of its water demand by 2011. This would be achieved within a relatively short span of ten years from the inception of NEWater in 2002 — no mean feat and a clear signal that NEWater is here to stay.

As NEWater production has been expanding rapidly, economies of scale, productivity gains, as well as more effective membrane technologies have brought down the cost of NEWater. With lower costs of production, PUB could pass the savings on to customers, which resulted in NEWater prices being reduced from an initial price of S$1.30 per cubic metre in 2003 to S$1.15 per cubic metre in January 2005. This was further lowered to S$1.00 per cubic metre in April 2007, with further efficiency gains and lower costs of production from the Ulu Pandan NEWater plant. This would in turn provide more incentive for non-domestic consumers to make the switch from PUB water to NEWater.

Singapore's NEWater Journey

The successful development of NEWater would not have been possible without the strong support from both the government and the public. In many ways, the NEWater journey is an important milestone in the management of water supply in Singapore and the communication of public policy. NEWater has also allowed the water loop to be closed — treated used water which would have been discharged into the sea is now further treated to produce NEWater. It was with this in mind that PUB was transferred from the Ministry of Trade and Industry to the Ministry of the

Environment in 2001 and the used water and drainage functions of the Ministry of the Environment were taken over by a reconstituted PUB. In so doing, Singapore was able to leverage the synergies of having a single agency to manage its water resources effectively across the entire spectrum of the water loop in an integrated and sustainable manner.

Apart from placing Singapore on the path towards water sustainability, NEWater (or water reclamation in general) is poised to be a strategic concept and viable solution to many of the water challenges in the region and beyond. As summed up by Professor Saifuddin Soz, India's Minister for Water Resources: "NEWater is beautiful as it is in itself a great hope not only for Singaporeans but for the world at large."[15] Singapore can share its knowledge and experiences with its partners from around the world, and has already begun to do so.

With the development of NEWater, PUB has closed the water loop by recycling used water for consumption purposes. The closure of the water loop has also enabled PUB to manage all aspects of the water cycle in an integrated manner — from the collection of rainwater to the supply of water, the collection and treatment of used water, water recycling and the desalination of seawater, which will be described in the next section (see Figure 5.1).

Seawater Desalting

Ultimately the world would need to turn to the seas and oceans for water solutions. Globally, freshwater constitutes only some 3 per cent of all water resources, much of which, even with global warming, is locked up in glaciers and ice caps. The rest — more than 90 per cent of our water resources — make up the oceans and seas. Singapore has over 190 kilometres of coastline — almost five times the width of the island. The island is surrounded by salt water — the South China Sea to the east, the Straits of Johor to the north, and the Singapore Straits to the south. With limited land to

FIGURE 5.1
The Concept of a Closed Water Loop

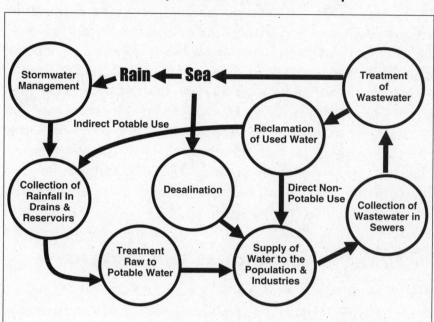

Source: PUB.

develop catchments and the sea at its doorstep, it is inevitable that Singapore would harness some of it for its water supply.

How can this resource be tapped? As early as the first Water Master Plan in 1972, desalination was already considered. The technology then consisted mainly of multi-stage flash distillation, which involves evaporation of seawater and condensation of freshwater on a surface, leaving the salts behind. Quality-wise, this technology was effective, producing clean and safe drinking water, but at a huge cost. The process was highly energy-intensive. Thus, it was favoured among oil-rich countries in the Middle East. Membrane technology was also in use in the 1970s, but like the water reclamation trial, membranes were often unreliable. Thus, producing desalinated water at that time was not viable.

In the 1990s, advancements in membrane technology significantly improved the effectiveness and reliability of membranes. With more widespread use of membranes, the cost also came down. In 2001, PUB held a pre-qualification exercise to select private suppliers to tender for the DBOO of a 30 mgd desalination facility in Tuas. Eleven suppliers were shortlisted, out of which four submitted tenders in 2002. Eventually, SingSpring Pte Ltd, a wholly owned subsidiary of Hyflux, a home-grown company, was awarded the contract. The SingSpring desalination plant, using reverse osmosis membranes, was successfully commissioned in September 2005.

THE FOUR NATIONAL TAPS STRATEGY

The successful development of NEWater (in 2002) and desalinated water (in 2005), together with local catchment sources and imported water, form what is now known as Singapore's "Four National Taps" strategy. It was a concept that was introduced in 2002 by then Minister for the Environment Lim Swee Say to explain to the public the different ways in which Singapore's long-term water needs would be met.

It is instructive to note that of the four taps, three (local catchments, imported water, and desalinated water) are primary sources, which are, in effect, the "first drops" derived from the water catchments or the sea. On the other hand, NEWater is a secondary source that is created from the recycling of used water from primary sources. Therefore, both desalinated water and NEWater have an important role to play in meeting long-term demand — one as a primary source of water, and the other by providing a multiplier effect through recycling. Both also have the advantage of being independent of fluctuations in rainfall, which will increase Singapore's resilience against the vagaries of the weather. This is particularly reassuring in the face of uncertainties that climate change would bring.

LEVERAGING FURTHER TECHNOLOGICAL INNOVATIONS

The Challenges of Desalination — Energy Consumption and Brine Discharge

Despite the "limitless" potential and promise of desalination, it currently still has some shortcomings. Firstly, desalination is energy-intensive, as high pressure is required to drive water molecules through membranes. Due to the high salinity of seawater, desalination is more energy intensive, and hence more costly than NEWater or conventional water treatment. With rising oil prices, this will be further accentuated.

Therefore, future development in desalination technology lies in reducing the energy consumption. One way to do this is through membrane distillation. This involves the use of a special membrane (called a hydrophobic membrane) to bring the water vapour from heated seawater, and condense it on a cool surface as freshwater. The advantage of membrane distillation is that it can occur at lower temperatures (50°C to 60°C) than boiling point (100°C). Hence, previously untapped energies, for example, waste heat from industrial processes can be used, as well as natural energies such as solar energy. PUB is exploring the feasibility of test bedding this technology on a larger scale. If successful, it will help to reduce the energy consumption and hence the cost of desalination.

The second issue with desalination is that extracting freshwater from seawater leaves behind brine or concentrated saltwater that will negatively affect the marine ecosystem when improperly dumped back into the sea. Currently, most brine is discharged back into the sea. Often, scientific models are used to determine how far offshore the brine must be discharged so that tidal dispersion dilutes the brine and minimizes its impact on the marine ecosystem. Although this method is widely used and is effective, an alternative method might be to close the brine loop in the same way the water loop was closed with NEWater.

In Singapore, used water is treated to international discharge standards, after which, much of the secondary treated used water is used for the production of NEWater. However, treated used water that is not required to produce NEWater to meet demand is discharged into the sea. The "base" of the treated used water is, of course, freshwater. If the brine loop could be closed by combining treated used water and brine, it could be possible to "create" or "reconstitute" seawater that could be returned back to sea.

This idea is currently being explored by the Marin and Santa Cruz counties in California, and if successfully developed, will indeed reduce the environmental impact of desalination dramatically. It will also be particularly relevant in Singapore, given its long-term plans to centralize the used water collection and treatment system into two main water reclamation plants east and west of Singapore, where adjoining land sites have been safeguarded for the future development of desalination plants.

Variable Salinity Plant

With the completion of the Marina and Punggol-Serangoon reservoir schemes in 2009, two-thirds of Singapore's land area will become major water catchments feeding the seventeen reservoirs. The remaining land comprises small catchments around the fringes of the island which experience bouts of heavy rain, but dry up when rainfall is low. Rain in these fringe catchments is currently not collected and flows into the sea, as it is not economically viable to construct large dams there to support large water treatment plants.

In 2003, a team of PUB engineers was formed to develop a water treatment process using advanced membrane technology to harness water in the fringe catchments, rather than let it go to waste. As the small rivers in the fringe catchments have daily incursions of seawater, such a water treatment plant would need to be able to treat water of variable salinity.

The project team developed a small pilot plant, called a variable salinity plant, which is basically a two-in-one plant that can treat either freshwater or seawater to produce drinking water. Such a treatment concept would be the first of its kind, as current water treatment processes are only able to treat brackish water or seawater, but not both. The success of the pilot plant has prompted the construction of a larger municipal-sized (1 mgd) demonstration plant at Sungei Tampines, which was completed in 2007. The demonstration plant has since produced high-grade water suitable for drinking, and initial results have been promising, achieving a production cost that is cheaper than desalination. The success of the plant will enable the extraction of surface run-offs at fringe catchments around the island. This could further increase water catchments, from two-thirds to as much as 90 per cent of Singapore's land area.

CONCLUSION

Professor Asit K. Biswas, winner of the Stockholm Water Prize in 2006, observed that "If the world faces a crisis it will not be due to physical scarcities of water, but... it will be due to sheer mismanagement of water."[16] In the case of Singapore, its vulnerability in not being blessed with abundant water sources fuelled a national hunger and desire to overcome it. Instead of being constrained by the country's natural disadvantages, the government believed that solutions were possible with the right commitment, an open mind towards innovation, and investing in research and development. In the relatively short span of forty to fifty years since the water rationing in 1963, the Singapore water story has progressed by leaps and bounds. From being a water-scarce country that was ranked 170th among a list of 190 countries,

Singapore has developed the Four National Taps strategy and ensured a sustainable water supply to meet the long-term needs of Singapore.

As water was not readily available, the need to increase and diversify water resources was supported at the highest political levels, with the formation of the Water Planning Unit and development of the Water Master Plan in the 1970s. This translated into integrated planning across various government agencies such as URA and HDB, as exemplified in the Lower Seletar-Bedok reservoir scheme. Given the sheer extensiveness of the scheme (stretching from Ang Mo Kio to Bedok), it would never have been possible to set aside land for the catchments, the stormwater collection ponds system and the reservoir itself if not for long-term planning and proper land zoning.

Preventing pollution to the catchments was also critical. Some countries have no lack of water resources, but the amount available for drinking is low due to pollution. In Singapore, this was tackled through upfront measures such as proper land use planning, separation of the drainage and sewerage systems, and a robust anti-pollution legislative framework and enforcement regime. With these, Singapore was able to tap urbanized catchments such as Bedok and Marina, uncommon even in developed countries.

Innovation and the use of technologies also play a key role in the sustainability of the water supply system. The successful development of NEWater would effectively double water sources through recycling, an important multiplier in water scarce Singapore, while efforts in piloting desalination would ensure that a sustainable primary source of water was always available. Together, they will put Singapore in a strong position to meet its long-term water needs.

In going forward, it is important to be on the lookout for new innovations and continue to push the boundaries. As more and more countries in the world grapple with water shortages, it is the hope that any solutions found for Singapore would also bring benefits to others beyond its shores.

6

ENSURING WATER SUSTAINABILITY
Water Demand Management

Proper water management is ever more crucial in those places where little water is available. Moreover, with freshwater resources strongly affected by, and vulnerable to, climate change, finding solutions to these challenges becomes all the more pressing... Singapore is an exemplary model of integrated water management and WHO hopes to work closely with Singapore to share such expertise in water management with its Member States.

Mrs Susanne Weber-Mosdorf, the World Health Organization's (WHO) Assistant Director General for Sustainable Development and Healthy Environments, at a signing ceremony where the Government of Singapore and WHO signed a new partnership agreement[1] to promote jointly the safe management of drinking water globally, August 2007

Developing new water sources through the Four National Taps constitutes half the strategy to ensure a sustainable water supply in Singapore. The other half is managing water demand and encouraging water conservation. Arguably, this can even be regarded as the more important half, given the physical and cost limitations of building new water sources indefinitely.

A single user increasing his water consumption may have little impact on the country's water resources, but if the entire population behaves likewise, this will not be sustainable. Furthermore, the prudent use of water involves important social habits and behaviours that take time to be inculcated, and hence any desired behavioural outcomes cannot simply be achieved overnight. Therefore, the thrust of any effective water demand management strategy must be to reach out to each and every user, be it an individual or organization, and ensure that such efforts are sustained over time.

SINGAPORE'S WATER DEMAND

Water consumption for the domestic sector in the last few decades has increased as a result of rapid industrial, economic, and social developments in Singapore. Up until 1995, the growth in domestic water consumption outpaced population growth. In 1965 when the population was at 1.9 million, domestic demand for potable water was 142,000 cubic metres per day (75 litres per capita per day). By 1994, the population had gone up by about two times, but domestic water demand had increased by more than four times (175 litres per capita per day). Such high demand growth puts a huge strain on Singapore's limited water resources and is not sustainable. Fortunately, more recent initiatives have helped to lower the growth in demand. In 2007, the population was 4.6 million and domestic water demand was 724,000 cubic metres per day (157 litres per capita per day).

LOW RAINFALL AND WATER SHORTAGES

Perhaps the value of water is most keenly felt during dry spells. Between 1963 and 1964, Singapore imposed water rationing for a ten-month period due to a severe and prolonged drought. While low rainfall was the key trigger, the problem would not have been as severe if not for the high consumption of water in the 1960s due to population growth, industrialization, housing development, and the rising standards of living.

Singapore was divided into several zones, and people in each zone could not receive water during predetermined time slots of the day. These time slots were later extended, as repeated calls for the reduction of water usage yielded little result and water levels in the reservoirs continued to dip further. By the time the rationing ended in 1964, water consumption had dropped by 13.4 per cent — perhaps an indication of the level of "non-essential" demand. Nevertheless, when heavy rains returned in 1964, consumption shot back up. Singaporeans, it appears, have short memories.

When Singapore once again experienced a long spell of dry weather in 1970, history would have repeated itself if not for PUB having quickly developed more water sources — Seletar Reservoir had been completed in 1969 and infrastructure to bring in more water from Johor was in place. Nevertheless, Singaporeans still came very close to another water rationing exercise but were saved when the heavy rains returned.

SAVE WATER CAMPAIGNS IN THE 1970s

The huge inconveniences and difficulties arising from water rationing, as well as the potential public health ramifications, spurred PUB to look into more permanent solutions to conserve water resources. Nationwide campaigns were launched in the 1970s aimed at reducing water consumption by raising public awareness of the need to save water.

In 1971, the first "Water is Precious" campaign was launched. With rationing looming in the background, the campaign had an immediate impact. It succeeded in bringing down water consumption by 4.9 per cent and helped to tide the country through the drought without the need for water rationing. Over the next few years, campaigns continued to encourage people to adopt water saving habits through small but practical ways, at the same time driving home the message "To save water only when there is a drought is not good enough for us in Singapore. Saving water must become a daily habit for us."

WATER CONSERVATION PLAN

In the 1980s, however, water demand continued to outpace population growth. It was clear that campaigns alone were not enough. The first Water Conservation Plan was drawn up in 1981, setting out Singapore's water conservation strategy along three key approaches: pricing, mandatory requirements, and public education. The plan called for water conservation measures that included the use of water saving devices, checks on wasteful use of water, reduction of excessive pressures, and recycling of water used in processes.

The same year, a Water Conservation Unit was formed within PUB, tasked with managing water demand and promoting water conservation to the public. The unit introduced various initiatives, such as talks to schools, visits to waterworks, and water conservation messages in the school syllabus. The Save Water campaigns in the 1970s continued into the 1980s with the "Let's Not Waste Precious Water" and the "Let's Save Precious Water" campaigns. Flow restrictors were installed at the meter positions of high-rise residential buildings and were successful in reducing water consumption in those premises by about 4 per cent.

As they accounted for about 40 per cent of total water consumption, the commercial and industrial sectors were another key target group. Mandatory requirements such as approvals for water consumption above 500 cubic metres per month for industries were institutionalized together with JTC and EDB. Low-value industries that were huge water guzzlers, such as pulp mills, were phased out. The Water Conservation Unit also reached out to the non-domestic sector by conducting water audits for large users, in order to advise them on measures to reduce their water consumption.

PRICING — WATER TARIFF AND WATER CONSERVATION TAX

Singapore practises a policy of metering and charging for water sold to all customers. A water tariff is levied on the volume of water metered at the customers' premises. As water was deemed to be a social good and had to be made available to all for public health reasons, potable water was sold at a much lower rate to domestic than non-domestic customers. The low price of water amidst rising affluence among the population resulted in rapid growth in demand in the 1980s and early 1990s.

In 1991, the government introduced a Water Conservation Tax (WCT) as a pricing tool to discourage excessive consumption of water. A 5 per cent tax was levied on water used in residential premises in excess of 20 cubic metres per month, while a higher 10 per cent tax was levied for all water used in the non-domestic and shipping sectors. Despite the introduction of the WCT and its subsequent increases in 1992 and 1995, domestic water consumption continued to grow, even on a per capita basis.

The 1997 Pricing Review

A fundamental pricing review was conducted in 1997, following which water was priced not only to recover the full cost of production and supply, through the water tariff, but also to reflect the higher cost of alternative water supply sources, through the WCT. This introduced an important concept to consumers of water, that is, when demand goes up and existing sources of supply run out, the next drop of water, or the marginal source, will come at a higher cost.

With the price set, the question was then how to structure it. One way would be to let both the water tariff and the WCT go to

PUB, but this would result in PUB collecting revenue in excess of what it needs for production and supply of water. Hence, the decision was for WCT to be channelled into the government consolidated fund managed by the Ministry of Finance, which can then be used to fund national projects that would benefit everyone.

At the same time, to equalize potable water tariffs for domestic and non-domestic customers, the potable water tariff was doubled to bring the domestic water tariff on par with the non-domestic water tariff, eliminating any cross-subsidy between them. The government also adopted a new philosophy which regarded even the first drop of water as precious. The WCT would, therefore, apply to the first drop and was pegged to the difference between the water tariff and the cost of the marginal source (which was desalinated water). To further disincentivize higher consumption by households, a second tier water tariff and WCT would apply on household consumption exceeding 40 cubic metres per month. The changes were gradually phased in over four years from 1997 to 2000.

With the water tariffs reflecting the true cost of water production, supply and treatment, revenue could be ploughed back into R&D to identify novel and more efficient ways of treating and distributing water, and to construct new water supply sources to meet future demand.

Helping the Low Income on Water Bills

The experiences of other countries have shown that subsidizing water leads to over-consumption. More water sources will have to be developed to meet the higher demand, and more subsidies have to be given. This is not sustainable with regard to water resources and the ever increasing subsidies will have to be funded through other forms of taxes or revenues.

In Singapore, there have also been calls for the WCT to be waived on an initial block of consumption, on the grounds that a minimum level of consumption is required for basic needs. This is an attractive but naïve argument. First, defining the "minimum" level of consumption can be subjective. Unless it is set very high, which defeats the purpose of the WCT, it is unlikely to satisfy most people. Second, this also breeds an entitlement mindset that within this block, conservation is not necessary. However, water conservation ought to start from the very first drop since every drop of water is precious. Most fundamentally, when demand increases and more costly water sources are necessary, the first drop will also be more expensive.

For the low-income groups, targeted help is provided to those who have difficulty paying their water bills. Such assistance is given in the form of Utilities Save (U-Save) rebates. U-Save rebates are structured so that they are quasi-cash, that is, the amount is placed in the qualifying household's utilities account, which can be drawn upon at any time to pay its utilities bills, including water. If the rebates are not used completely in the first month, they remain in the account and can be used in subsequent months. Rather than grant low-income households a direct waiver on their water bills, the government chose to adopt this method of decoupling its assistance from consumption, so that it will not lead to over-consumption of water.

COMMUNITY-LED INITIATIVES FOR THE DOMESTIC SECTOR

The Save Water campaigns in the 1970s and 1980s continued into the 1990s. Campaigns in 1995, 1996, and 1997 reminded Singaporeans that water is scarce and encouraged the public to "Use Water Wisely". In 1998, the "Turn It Off. Don't Use Water Like There's No Tomorrow" campaign was launched to effect the behavioural change in the way water was being used, so that people would on their own accord make saving water a way of life.

While the various Save Water campaigns helped in managing water demand, they were not sustainable on their own. Often, the conservation messages would wear off and be forgotten soon after the campaign ended. PUB realized that what was needed were continual initiatives and efforts at the community level, rather than annual month-long campaigns at the national level.

In 2002, a master plan for water demand management in the domestic sector was drawn up, with emphasis on the adoption of community-led initiatives. The first of such initiatives was the Water Efficient Homes (WEH) programme, launched in 2003. The WEH programme was run by grassroots organizations and their advisers, who would encourage residents in their constituencies to install water-saving devices and adopt good water-saving habits. Residents were taught how flow restrictors could be installed at taps and shower hoses to reduce excessive flow rates, while those with the old 9-litre flushing cisterns were taught how to install water-saving bags to reduce the amount of water stored in the cistern for flushing.

As part of the programme, do-it-yourself (DIY) water saving kits consisting of flow restrictors, cistern water-saving bags, and leaflets on water conservation tips were supplied to grassroots organizations for distribution to residents free-of-charge. Mobile exhibitions were also set up to brief residents on installation procedures and demonstrate the effectiveness of water-saving devices. The WEH programme reached out to about 370,000 households in all eighty-four constituencies.

The cascading of outreach efforts from a national level to the community level greatly improved the sustainability of water conservation efforts. Riding on the success of the WEH programme, a "10-Litre Challenge" was introduced in 2006, to encourage every individual to reduce his or her daily water consumption by 10 litres. Various new initiatives were also launched the same year to support the "10-Litre Challenge".

To extend the WEH programme, PUB, together with the People's Association and the Community Development Councils, worked closely with grassroots organizations to form Water Volunteer Groups (WVG). These WVGs conduct visits to households to educate them on water conservation practices and help them with the installation of water-saving devices. The WVGs also visit lower-income and needy families to help them save on their water bills. This proved to be effective, as the education and persuasion were done by volunteers and members of the community themselves. It also allowed PUB to harness the growing support for its programmes, empower groups to take meaningful actions, and, through their efforts, help the community to internalize the values and good habits.

Studies have shown that people believe in doing good, and they want to do so. However, they may not be sufficiently informed to take the correct actions. In today's knowledge-based society, making information available is one way in which the conservation message can be spread. In reaching out to the individual, a web portal was set up to educate the public on simple means to save 10 litres of water a day. The website allowed the user to gain insights into his water usage behaviour and understand the efficacy of water conservation devices.

Another initiative to close the information gap was the Water Efficiency Labelling Scheme. The scheme sought to provide consumers with information on the water consumption and efficiency of water products, which they could factor into their purchasing decisions and make better informed choices. The scheme was launched in 2006 on a voluntary basis. However, it enjoyed only limited success since most suppliers and manufacturers registered only the more water-efficient models, constituting only 16 per cent of the market. To further elevate consumer awareness about water efficient models, the scheme will be made mandatory in 2009.

WATER CONSERVATION INITIATIVES FOR THE NON-DOMESTIC SECTOR

With a good programme in place for the domestic sector, the attention turned towards the non-domestic sector, especially since they constitute close to half of the water usage in Singapore. Unlike in the domestic sector, the nature of operations and businesses result in different usage patterns across the non-domestic sector. For example, water-intensive manufacturing industries will have a usage pattern that is different from that of a commercial office building. Hence, various initiatives were introduced targeting specific groups of users in this sector.

The introduction of NEWater as Singapore's third National Tap in 2003 opened up opportunities to reduce potable water demand from the non-domestic sector. Since then, many industrial and commercial premises have substituted potable water with NEWater for their processes, in cooling towers, and general washing, thus reducing national demand for potable water. To encourage manufacturing industries to recycle their process water or improve on their existing recycling rate, the Water Efficiency Fund was launched in 2007 to provide financial incentives for companies to look into efficient ways to manage their water demand through recycling, and assist them in defraying a portion of the initial capital outlay, as well as overcome the difficulty in obtaining commercial funding.

Attention was also placed on "domestic" usage in non-domestic premises, such as toilet flushing and wash basin use. The approach was similar to the domestic sector, where control of flow rate was the key in managing water consumption, coupled with good management and maintenance practices. This was the basis for the Water Efficient Buildings programme that was launched in 2004. By the end of 2007, more than 1,000 buildings had reduced their water consumption by lowering the flow rates at the taps and the flush volume at the urinals in their staff and public toilets.

To further enhance the Water Efficient Buildings programme and encourage the non-domestic sector to play a bigger role in reducing water consumption, the "10% Challenge" was launched in 2008 to motivate the non-domestic sector to work towards saving

10 per cent of their monthly water consumption. Under the scheme, there are targets for non-domestic users to lower their water consumption through benchmarking across the industry and sharing of best practices. These will be complemented by capacity-building initiatives, such as guides for the design of water-efficient building systems, and courses for facilities and operations managers to equip them with the knowledge to undertake water conservation measures in their premises.

PUB's water conservation initiatives also inspired the private sector to play a more active role in managing water demand. In the non-domestic sector, water supply applications with anticipated potable water requirements exceeding 500 m^3/month are submitted to PUB for approval. As part of the approval process, PUB encourages the industries to recycle their process water and substitute potable water with non-potable water such as industrial water, high-grade industrial water, seawater, or more recently NEWater. Industries can also receive financial support through the Water Efficiency Fund to look into efficient ways of managing their water demand. As a result of PUB's efforts, wafer fabrications plants, which are large water users, have contributed significantly towards the conservation effort. Their recycling rate of 50 to 60 per cent helps to cut their water demand by more than half. The use of NEWater has also created a win-win situation for them: the industry values NEWater for its ultra pure quality which is required in their processes, and in doing so, frees up large quantities of potable water for potable use.

Many industries such as refineries, petrochemical complexes, and power stations also use seawater for cooling purposes. On Jurong Island, SembCorp Utilities (SUT) produces high-grade industrial water (HGIW) from recycled effluent to meet the demand of users. Some power stations have even installed desalination plants, tapping synergies in their operations, such as by utilizing waste heat from their generation process.

MANDATORY REQUIREMENTS

So far, under the pricing and community-led approaches, individuals and businesses are encouraged to lower their water consumption through economic incentives or persuasion. Nevertheless, effecting behavioural change has its limits. For example, a person does not reduce the number of times he or she visits the toilet just to save water.

Hence, there is also a need for structural or technical changes to save water, independent of the actions of each person. Where PUB has assessed that cost-effective technical or technology solutions are available, it has imposed some mandatory requirements on the adoption of these solutions.

Since 1983, the installation of water-saving devices such as constant flow regulators and self-closing delayed action taps has been made mandatory in all non-domestic premises and common amenities areas of all private high-rise residential apartments and condominiums; bathtubs and jacuzzis larger than 250 litres in volume also require a water recirculation system. Low-capacity flushing cisterns (LCFCs) that use not more than 4.5 litres of water per flush have been installed in all new public housing units since 1992. This was later made mandatory for all new and ongoing building projects, including all residential premises, hotels, commercial buildings and industrial establishments in 1997. In future, dual-flush LCFCs which offer the option of a half flush (not more than 3 litres of water) when the full flush (not more than 4.5 litres of water) is not necessary, will be made mandatory for all new developments and premises undergoing renovation from 2009.

To prevent excessive flow rates, PUB limits the maximum allowable flow rates at water fittings. A review was conducted in 2003 and the maximum allowable flow rates were reduced by between 25 to 33 per cent to prevent water wastage. The requirement on limiting the maximum allowable flow rates at water fittings was also extended to all domestic premises.

MANAGING LEAKS IN THE
WATER DISTRIBUTION SYSTEM

In a water supply system, the key infrastructure that operators are most concerned with usually relates to the supply sources, such as reservoirs, waterworks, and treatment plants. However, as experience has shown, the "less visible" components such as the supply networks are equally, if not more important, in determining the success of the supply system. Networks that are not well maintained will result in frequent supply disruptions or high system losses. This leads to inefficiency, under-recovery of charges, and unprofitable operations. This drop in revenue in turn leads to further cutbacks in provision and maintenance, and a vicious cycle begins. Ultimately, customers are left unhappy as they are faced with interruptions in their water supply and poor customer service.

One critical measure of network maintenance is the management of leaks in the water distribution network. Singapore has one of the lowest number of leaks, at fewer than seven leaks per 100 kilometres per year. Singapore's low leak rate was not accomplished overnight. In the early 1980s, there were more than 100 leaks per 100 kilometres per year. Efforts were made to improve the situation through using good pipe materials, systematically replacing old unlined cast iron mains and unlined galvanized iron connections, as well as the active detection of underground leaks.

Minimizing Unaccounted-for-Water

In Singapore, pipe leaks are mainly caused by earth movement rather than direct material failure such as corrosion. Soil subsidence accounts for 60 per cent of leaks, mainly from brittle asbestos cement pipes. The asbestos cement pipes also created water quality problems when conveying piping water that contained high chloride levels, which was the case for treated water supplied from the Kranji and Pandan Reservoirs. To improve the reliability of supply and water quality, more durable and corrosion-resistant piping materials were used, such as copper, stainless steel, and steel/ductile iron pipes that were internally lined with cement mortar. The use of such materials helped prevent leaks in the water distribution network. Besides offering durability and corrosion-resistant characteristics, metallic pipes also helped in acoustic leak detection/tracing due to the better sound and electrical conductivity of metallic materials compared with plastic materials. Asbestos cement pipes now form less than 1 per cent of the over 5,000 kilometres of water network.

The pressure in the network is also being optimized to increase the durability and lifespan of the pipes, as well as minimize leakages from non-identified underground leaks. Detailed studies are conducted to identify the demand of each supply zone before the pressure is reduced using pressure-reducing valves.

PUB's various initiatives to reduce pipe leaks in the water network are primarily motivated by its efforts to provide high levels of service to customers through the reliable supply of good quality water. This has resulted in Singapore having one of the lowest unaccounted-for-water (UFW) rates in the world. At 5 per cent, this is half the level of many developed cities and way below the average of 30 to 60 per cent in most Asian cities. Low UFW rates are also achieved in Singapore through the use of accurate meters in premises (this minimizes the discrepancies between measurements taken at the upstream bulk meters and the aggregation of downstream meter readings from individual premises, which contribute to UFW), and an active leak detection programme to detect and fix leaks early.

A low UFW rate means that more of the water produced actually reaches the customer and less is lost along the way. As an example, at a UFW of 50 per cent, twice the amount of water resources will be needed to meet the same demand. Hence, an effective network and leak management system will not only reduce wastage, but also operating costs as well. This in turn defers the need for investment in new capacity. In the long run, this is a more sustainable and cost-effective system.

Besides using better quality pipes and fittings for new networks, PUB also looks into new technologies to improve its current way of laying watermains. One such initiative is participating in the Common Service Tunnel (CST) project to house the water services for the New Downtown in Marina South. Together with electricity services, telecommunications services, district cooling pipes, and pneumatic refuse conveyance systems, some 5 kilometres of potable watermains and NEWater mains were also laid within the CST. Besides the prevention of accidental damage to the water pipes, there is easier accessibility to the water pipes for maintenance, which can be done without causing traffic disruption.

CONCLUSION

Long-term sustainability in water cannot be achieved by boosting water supply alone. Critical and complementary to this is the management of water demand, which has been a key thrust of Singapore's water management policy from the outset.

The government realized that encouraging the public to conserve water *per se* would not be enough, and that a holistic approach that tapped various levers would improve the chances of success. In 1997, water was priced not only to recover the full cost of production and supply but also to reflect the higher cost of alternative water supply sources. This sent a strong signal to Singaporeans on the need to conserve water. Apart from pricing and voluntary efforts, mandatory requirements and technical solutions were also explored and imposed, covering maximum flow rates for fittings, as well as labelling schemes to inform and educate consumers.

Water conservation efforts evolved in tandem with growing public awareness and active citizenry, moving towards more community-based initiatives such as the Water Efficient Homes/

Water Efficient Buildings and 10-Litre Challenge/10% Challenge in the 2000s. With a slew of initiatives for the domestic and non-domestic sectors, Singapore's average annual water demand growth rate since 1995 has been kept low at about 1.1 per cent despite a GDP growth of 5.1 per cent per annum and population growth of 2.2 per cent per annum. This helped to reduce domestic per capita water consumption, from a peak of 176 litres per person per day in 1994, to 157 litres per person per day in 2007. In future, more bottom-up approaches will be needed, where Singaporeans not only learn to embrace environmentally conscious lifestyles, but also actively champion them.

PUB will also do its part to improve water supply quality and reliability, through the holistic management of the water supply network. This reduces wastage and defers the need for investment in new capacity.

In a land- and resource-scarce country such as Singapore, it is the efficient use of scarce resources that will ensure that growth in the population and economy can be accommodated in a sustainable manner — through a holistic approach to managing resources from both a supply and demand perspective, creative and innovative ideas, as well as garnering the support and participation from the public, private, and people sectors.

7

MANAGING USED WATER

Access to sanitation is deeply connected to virtually all the Millennium Development Goals, in particular those involving the environment, education, gender equality and the reduction of child mortality and poverty.

United Nations Secretary General Ban Ki-Moon at the launch of the International Year of Sanitation, November 2007[1]

Singapore's journey in used water management started during the early twentieth century when the country was faced with the urgent need to tackle its hygiene and sanitation problems — issues brought about by rapid population growth in its tropical environment and concerns over public health.

After independence in 1965, the government realized that the development of a world-class used water management system was crucial not only in improving the quality of life for its people but also in sustaining the economic growth of the country. A comprehensive Sewerage Master Plan was thus developed and the necessary investments made to extend the used water infrastructure so that 100 per cent of the population would have access to modern sanitation.

Increasing water demand has also necessitated reclaiming water from used water to augment water supply. Singapore's fully sewered system offered the opportunity for large-scale used water recycling and water reclamation to be carried out. Recent breakthroughs allowed for the development of more advanced water reclamation facilities, namely, the NEWater factories, which are located adjacent to the Water Reclamation Plants (WRPs). These were formerly known as Sewage Treatment Works but they were renamed WRPs in 2001 to reinforce the idea that used water is a resource to be reclaimed. The NEWater factories receive the treated used water effluent and treat (reclaim) it further using advanced membrane technology. The resulting product is high-grade water known as NEWater, which is channelled for both direct non-potable and indirect potable uses. Chapter 5 elaborates on NEWater.

This chapter provides insights into how the management of used water in Singapore evolved over the years and the key considerations behind the government's decisions in adopting various solutions as the country progressed from a simple fishing village to one which was rapidly industrializing, and eventually to the modern, cosmopolitan city of today.

KEY DESIGN FEATURES OF SINGAPORE'S USED WATER MANAGEMENT SYSTEM

There are several key features in the design of Singapore's used water management system, namely: (1) clear separation of storm water and used water streams and systems, (2) leveraging technological developments, and (3) strict regulation through legislation. The effective implementation of these key features has served Singapore well through the years and instilled the discipline that shaped its approach to the management of this municipal service. These are elaborated on in the sections below.

Separation of Storm Water and Used Water Streams and Systems

First, ensuring that used water goes into a central used water system and is kept separate from storm water has been critical in keeping the waters in and around Singapore clean. This system, inherited from the colonial days, is a more effective and economical approach in the long run as it ensures that the inland waterways, reservoirs, and the sea surrounding Singapore are not polluted through the indiscriminate discharge of untreated or semi-treated used water and trade effluent; and can be collected to produce potable water. The separation of the systems also prevents storm water from entering the used water systems and causing overflows, as may happen in the case of combined storm sewers.

Over the years, sewerage engineers continued to improve the sanitary system to enhance its efficiency and functions. These include having distinct and separate piping systems, provision of water seals in bathrooms and kitchen sinks, and proper certification for all water-service professionals. This proved to be a wise and life-saving move as seen from Singapore's experience during the Severe Acute Respiratory Syndrome (SARS) outbreak in 2003 (see details later in this chapter).

Leveraging Technological Developments

Second, greater value was derived from used water systems and their environmental impact minimized by leveraging technological developments. These are put into the planning and design of used water facilities to optimize land use, minimize the level of nuisance to the public, and reduce negative impact on the environment. Examples include: (1) effective treatment of used water to recognized international standards prior to its discharge into the sea, (2) adoption of advanced sludge treatment technology to recover energy and minimize waste generated, (3) use of compact-and-covered designs for the WRPs and equipping them with odour treatment facilities so as to reduce the footprint and buffer zones, and (4) employment of "trenchless" technologies for the laying of sewers and the renewal of old pipes under the sewer rehabilitation programme to save costs and minimize disruption to users. As described later in this chapter, these efforts were inter-related and introduced in a coordinated fashion.

Strict Regulation through Legislation

Third, in addition to putting in place good infrastructure, legislation was also enacted to ensure that the infrastructure is properly used. For instance, all premises are required to connect to public sewers where these are available. Developers of housing and industrial estates have to incorporate a central used water facility to collect and convey used water effectively into the public used water system. Proposals for development are scrutinized to ensure that they do not encroach on the public used water system (i.e., sewers, pumping, mains, etc.). This helps to avert any potential damage to the public used water system and, in turn, prevents pollution resulting from overflow or leakage of used water. In addition, stringent pipe laying and sanitary work requirements are also imposed through legislation enacted by the PUB.

SINGAPORE'S USED WATER SYSTEMS THROUGH THE YEARS

Used water management systems in Singapore have progressed from relying on the primitive night soil buckets of the early 1900s, to the shallow sewers cum pumping network of the pre-independence years, and finally to the modern deep tunnel sewerage system of today. Despite these changes over the years, the underlying motivation for these systems has remained the same, that is, to find practical and sustainable solutions for Singapore.

In the early years, sanitation and used water management systems focused mainly on tackling pollution to watercourses, to prevent the spread of water-borne diseases and maintain a high standard of public hygiene. The early solution to the sanitation problem was through the night soil (that is, human waste) collection service where night soil would be collected by bucket for disposal, sometimes indiscriminately. It was not until the 1910s that the first water-borne sanitation system was constructed to handle, treat and properly dispose the waste. Consisting of sewers in a small section of the city, this system conveyed used water to a central Sewage Disposal Works at Alexandra via three pumping stations at Park Road, Albert Street, and River Valley. At the Alexandra Sewage Disposal Works, the used water was treated through trickling filters and humus tanks before being discharged into the Singapore River.

Although various extensions and improvements were made to the Alexandra Sewage Disposal Works, it was often overloaded as the flow increased, resulting in odour which proved offensive to other developments in the vicinity. It was then decided that a used water system and disposal works be established for the eastern sector of Singapore, away from the congested city vicinity. As a result, the Rangoon Road and Paya Lebar Pumping Stations, the Kim Chuan Sewage Treatment Works, and the Serangoon Sludge Treatment Works were designed and constructed towards the end of the 1930s. These facilities served the growing population well until the early 1960s, when further construction works were required to expand and enhance the used water system.

Effective treatment of used water at the treatment works was necessary to minimize pollution, not only to the waterways but ultimately the coastal waters. With this in mind, proper treatment of used water by the activated sludge method had been introduced to improve the quality of the treated effluent. Rapid population growth and development plans for the island in the 1950–60s called for new satellite towns to be built in the then rural areas and new sewage treatment works in the western part of Singapore. The used water system was fast becoming overloaded. Thus, in 1955, the City Council commissioned the development of a new sewage treatment works, that is, Ulu Pandan Sewage Treatment Works, which was constructed on a completely new site well away from the city centre. At this new facility, used water was treated fully before being discharged into the Jurong River.

After Singapore achieved independence in 1965, rapid industrialization, the sprouting up of new housing estates, and intense urban redevelopment propelled the further development of its used water infrastructure. With the City Council (of pre-independence days) dissolved, the fledgling government undertook major investments in used water infrastructure development as it realized that this was necessary to improve the quality of life for Singaporeans and to facilitate further housing and industrial development.

DEVELOPING A BLUEPRINT — THE USED WATER MASTERPLAN

The Sewerage Master Plan (later renamed the Used Water Master Plan) was therefore conceived in the late 1960s, and tied to Singapore's overall land-use Concept Plan, which was developed using a multi-agency approach involving urban planners and housing and economic agencies, amongst others. Drawing from the apportionment of proposed land uses under the Concept Plan, the Used Water Master Plan served as a detailed guide for the development of used water facilities, specifying corresponding projected used water flows based on pre-determined zoning, and even micro-level design considerations of sewers and the layout of the used water facilities. It formed the foundation for planning the management of used water in Singapore.

Under the Master Plan, Singapore was divided into six used water catchment zones, based on the contours of the island. Each zone was served by a centralized water reclamation plant where the used water was treated to international standards before the treated effluent was disposed to the sea. Within the used water catchments, pumping stations were installed to transfer used water flows to the plants.

These plans were implemented through the 1968–73 and 1973–78 investment programmes, with assistance from the World Bank. As a condition for the loans, the World Bank required that the Government of Singapore adopt a proper charging mechanism that would sufficiently recover costs from consumers so as to ensure sustainability. In doing so, financial discipline was instilled from the outset, thus facilitating the smooth implementation of the used water plans.

These significant investments led to the provision of a comprehensive used water network and treatment services to about 98 per cent of premises by 1991. By 1997, 100 per cent of Singapore was served by a modern sanitation system. In comparison, just thirty-two years earlier in 1965, proper sanitation was available to only about 45 per cent of the population.

MANAGING AN EXPANDING AND AGEING INFRASTRUCTURE

With the Used Water Master Plan, Singapore had put in place a comprehensive used water network. Over the years, many of the older sewers have degraded through wear and tear, due to a variety of causes such as ageing, ground movements, or tree-root intrusions. In addition to the risk of structural failure, the infiltration of ground water into the sewer pipe would add to the volume of used water carried. This additional volume increases the risk of overflows in the network system. Renewal is, therefore, needed to restore the structural integrity of the sewer pipes and mains, as well as to prevent infiltration so as to preserve the capacity of the sewers, pumping stations, and treatment facilities. As part of the effort to ensure a sustainable sanitation system, Singapore has, since the 1980s, been renewing its ageing used water infrastructure.

The Sewer Rehabilitation Programme

Sewer rehabilitation in the early days involved large amounts of excavation work. Back then, sewers were rectified mainly by the open trench method which involved excavating the affected site and creating an open trench so as to access the segment of sewers that required rehabilitation. The operation, while necessary, was time-consuming and often caused inconvenience to the public. To minimize the inconveniences, PUB has, since the early 1980s, been exploring the use of "trenchless" technologies. These technologies can be grouped into two main types. First, pipe laying technologies such as pipe-jacking, where new pipes are installed with minimal excavation under the new sewer schemes. Second, *in situ* renewal processes are used where existing pipes are restored. Some of these methods include Cured-In-Place Pipe lining (CIPP), pipe bursting, and spiral wound lining methods.

The more common method of CIPP cleverly uses a process involving inserting a flexible resin-impregnated felt liner via a manhole into the existing host-pipe under water pressure. Once in place, the soft material forms a lining against the original pipe. The lining is then cured using hot water. Once cured, the liner forms "a pipe-within a pipe", functioning like a new pipe. CIPP requires no excavation, resulting in minimal site disturbance and no adverse environmental impact. "Trenchless" technologies such as these have greatly saved time and costs, resulting in cost reductions of as much as 40 per cent. Employing these methods has also lessened the inconvenience to the public as most of the work happens underground, with less disruption to traffic flow and no significant interruption to used water services for the residents living in the vicinity.

The development of new reservoirs in highly urbanized areas such as the Marina Reservoir brought new challenges for sewer maintenance. Diffused leaks, especially from shallower sewers, had to be minimized to reduce the adverse impact on the aesthetic and recreational quality of the water bodies after the regular seawater flushing is removed with the completion of the Marina Barrage. To meet these challenges, a new phase of the sewer rehabilitation programme was launched in 2006, to focus on rehabilitating the shallower public sewers that were found to be leaking.

Whilst it is the government's responsibility to maintain public sewers, a significant portion of the ageing sewers are under private ownership, channelling used water from individual premises to the public sewers. To assist private owners in ensuring that their sewers are functioning properly, PUB also embarked on a Private Sewer Rehabilitation Programme as part of the overall sewer rehabilitation programme to conduct free checks on the condition of private sewers and advise owners on any rectification work required. As a start, these efforts focus on developments that are more than ten years old and located within the highly urbanized water catchment of the Marina Reservoir. Should repairs be needed, the government helps to defray part of the costs, and the services of PUB's contractors are also made available to the owners of private sewers so as to ensure that cost is kept to the lowest through aggregation. Other forms of financial assistance rendered include allowing owners to pay through monthly instalments if they engage PUB for the rectification works.

Since the implementation of the private sewer rehabilitation programme, leaks were found in the private sewers of many older buildings. These were subsequently rehabilitated, and the leaks fixed. This reduces the pollution load in the Marina catchment, and helps to improve water quality in the Marina Reservoir. PUB will continue with the programme to maintain the operational reliability of the sewerage network and improve water quality.

IMPROVING THE DESIGN OF WRPs

A concerted effort has been made in the planning and design of used water facilities to maximize land use and minimize the level of negative impact to the public.

Reducing the Buffer Zones

The WRPs are located in areas that were once rural. Conventional design meant that open tanks were used, and given the tropical climate, odour nuisance was inevitable. Hence, these WRPs had a 1-kilometre buffer zone within which only limited development was allowed. As the urban area expanded, demand for more land led to a need to reduce the large buffer zones and the footprint of treatment plants. Thus, four of the six WRPs were progressively covered up in the 1990s and the foul air extracted for treatment in specially developed odour control facilities. As a result, the buffer zone for WRPs was reduced from 1 kilometre to 500 metres from the fence line of the WRP.

Compact Covered Plants

The designs of WRPs were further optimized in the late 1990s when three WRPs needed to be expanded to meet the increased used water treatment needs. The extensions for the Kranji, Ulu Pandan, and Seletar WRPs were completed in 1999, 2000, and 2001 respectively, based on the compact-and-covered design concept. This concept allows the rectangular treatment units to be stacked on each other, making the final structure compact. Deep reactor tanks were also used to further reduce the footprint. In addition, these compact units are also enclosed and the odorous air extracted and treated to render it odourless before being discharged into the atmosphere.

Odour Control Facilities

The treatment of foul odour from the WRPs has been extensively carried out to mitigate smell nuisance affecting developments near the plants. At the WRPs, comprehensive odour control facilities comprising odour containment covers over the treatment units, extensive odorous air extraction systems, and odour treatment plants, are introduced to contain and treat the foul air from covered treatment units prior to its discharge. The end result is an improved ambience within the plant and minimized odour nuisance to the surrounding areas. With the odour control systems in place, the odour buffer zone around the WRP is reduced and more land can be released for higher value developments.

In recent years, there has been increasing interest in the use of biomass to treat odour. Replacing the chemical scrubbers with bioscrubbers for odour treatment in the WRPs eliminates the use of hazardous chemicals and reduces the operating cost of odour treatment. In Singapore, bioscrubbers have been installed in the Ulu Pandan, Bedok, and Kranji WRPs. Recently, locally developed biocarbon technology (which combines the odour treatment functions of the bioscrubbers and activated carbon) is being tried out with the installation of three biocarbon scrubbers at the Kranji WRP. It is the first of its kind in the world and further eliminates the need to replenish activated carbon. If successful, it promises to reduce further the capital and operating costs for odour treatment.

THE DEEP TUNNEL SEWERAGE SYSTEM

Despite having achieved 100 per cent access to modern sanitation facilities for its entire population, Singapore is constantly challenged by the demands of its ever increasing population and growing economy. The existing conventional used water infrastructure and systems were reaching their maximum capacities and economic lives. To ensure the long-term sustainability of the systems, one option was to continue expanding and upgrading these conventional water reclamation plants. The second option was to embark on a totally novel approach that would employ new technologies that were both cost effective and able to meet the more stringent environmental requirements. After much deliberation, the government decided in

1995 to opt for the second approach and took the bold step of transforming its used water system by putting in place the Deep Tunnel Sewerage System (DTSS).

To be implemented in two phases, this long-term project consists of two large, deep tunnels criss-crossing the island, two large centralized water reclamation plants located at the eastern and western ends of the island, deep sea outfalls, and a link-sewer network. The two deep tunnels are designed with diameters of up to six metres, making them as big as a typical Mass Rapid Transit (MRT) tunnel! Also, these tunnels are built at depths ranging from 20 to 50 metres below ground, which are deeper than a fifteen-storey building, and are connected to the existing used water reticulation system through a network of smaller link sewers.

Given the scale of the DTSS, it is constructed and implemented in phases. Construction of Phase I, commenced in 1999 and completed in 2008, involved the construction of the North and Spur Tunnels, Changi Water Reclamation Plant, and the Changi Outfall, as well as link sewers diverting the flows to the main tunnel sewers. Phase II, which will be implemented over the next ten to twenty years, will involve the construction of the South Tunnel, a link sewer network, another large water reclamation plant, and an outfall, located at the southwestern part of Singapore. The total cost of Phase I is about S$3.65 billion. The DTSS is considered a great engineering feat, having been awarded the Institution of Engineers Singapore (IES) Prestigious Engineering Achievement Award, as well as the ASEAN Outstanding Engineering Achievement Award in 2005 and the International Water Association's Project Innovation Award in 2008.

Cost-effectiveness, Land-use, and Environmental Considerations

The large and deep sewers of the DTSS allow large volumes of used water from the growing domestic and industrial sectors to be conveyed to large centralized water reclamation plants for treatment.

Population and economic growth were taken into consideration in the sizing of the large tunnels and the design of the water reclamation plants. This also eliminates the need for continual upgrading and expansion of the existing intermediate used water pumping stations, and the six aged water reclamation plants (along with their attendant outfall discharges) to cater to increasing demands while meeting more stringent environmental requirements.

With the completion of the DTSS, used water flows from the sewerage system to the centralized water reclamation plant will be achieved through gravity flow. This will result in the phasing out of 134 sewage pumping installations and smaller water reclamation plants scattered over the island, freeing up some 880 hectares of land, including buffer zones around the facilities, for residential and other high value developments. This is about 1.5 times the size of Choa Chu Kang New Town, located in the northwestern part of Singapore. In fact, the new Changi Water Reclamation Plant takes up only one-third of the land area of the existing plants. Further land savings can be achieved, as the roof of the Changi Water Reclamation Plant is used to house a NEWater plant.

Furthermore, the risk of used water overflows arising from failures in the intermediate pumping system will be eradicated. The phasing out of the pumping stations and mains will greatly enhance the operational reliability of the used water system, and, in turn, protect water quality, especially in water catchments that will cover two-thirds of Singapore by 2009. Project Director of the DTSS, Chiang Kok Meng, commented:

> Some might also recall that in 1987 both sewage pumping mains from one of our sewage pump stations had ruptured and seriously polluted the Kallang River. Our existing sewerage system is a combination of gravity and pumping mains, and half of these are located in water catchments! Can you imagine the consequences of any breakage?[2]

The treatment processes installed in the Changi Water Reclamation Plant are also able to treat used water to effluent standards that are better than the existing plants so that treated used water effluent discharged through the Changi Outfall will not have any adverse impact on the water quality or ecology in the surrounding waters. With the gradual phasing out of existing WRPs and their discharges of treated effluent, the water quality of the seas surrounding Singapore will be further enhanced for recreational activities.

Opportunities to Develop Singapore's Water Industry

The construction of the DTSS involves excavating and constructing some 48 kilometres of concrete tunnels, of diameters between 3.3 metres to 6 metres and at depths between 20 to 50 metres below ground level. Further work includes lining the tunnel walls with corrosion-resistant membranes, constructing link sewer systems, as well as building a large (800,000 cubic metres a day capacity) centralized water reclamation plant with a 5-kilometre-long deep sea outfall. This mammoth challenge required the dedicated work of 49 main contractors and consultants, more than 300 subcontractors and suppliers, and 4,000 workers, featuring contractors, design consultants, and project supervisory teams from many countries including Singapore, Austria, China, Japan, Korea, Germany, India, the United Kingdom, and the United States.

Rather than packaging the DTSS project into one or two large contracts, PUB decided to carve the project into a number of smaller contracts. This gave more contractors, both local and international, the opportunity to participate, and also built up PUB's close partnership with the local private sector. Under Phase I of the DTSS project, PUB awarded fifteen link sewer contracts, with local contractors participating in twelve of them.

At the DTSS Pumping Station completion ceremony at Changi Water Reclamation Plant on 28 August 2006, Dr Yaacob Ibrahim, Minister for the Environment and Water Resources, said:

With the completion of this DTSS pumping station, it is yet another step forward in our journey to ensure the long term sustainability of our water resources... It will act like a superhighway, efficiently linking the many intricate but extensive tributaries of public and private sewers in homes and buildings to the water reclamation plant... The impending completion of the whole DTSS (Phase I) is indeed the apex in our ongoing efforts to ensure that Singapore continues to have a first class used water network.[3]

With the completion of Phase I of the DTSS, used water flows in the eastern part of Singapore will be diverted into the DTSS in phases. In tandem, the existing WRPs and pumping stations in this sector will also be phased out (refer to Map 4).

THE SARS OUTBREAK OF 2003 — AVERTING A CRISIS

When Singapore was afflicted with the Severe Acute Respiratory Syndrome (SARS) in 2003, the spread of the virus was mainly thought to be via airborne transmission. However the spread of the virus within large residential tower blocks at Amoy Gardens in Hong Kong led authorities to suspect that the sanitary system could be the culprit allowing "faecal droplets" containing the virus to enter bathrooms and apartments.

It was reported that the water seals for floor traps[4] had dried up, allowing passage of foul air into the apartment from the vertical sanitary pipe (called the stack) that links all apartments in the block. In such situations, exhaust fans could even accelerate the extraction of the foul air and circulate it into the living unit.

In a press release titled "Inadequate Plumbing Systems likely Contributed to SARS Transmission" issued by the World Health Organization (WHO) (Press Release WHO/70, 26 September 2003),[5] the Technical Consultation concluded that "inadequate plumbing was likely to have been a contributor to the spread of SARS in residential buildings in Hong Kong". It added that "in the absence of proper maintenance and without consistent monitoring, reviewing, enforcing and updating of building standards and practices, inadequate plumbing and sewage systems could continue to enhance the potential of SARS and some other diseases to spread".

The Singapore Ministry of National Development (MND) and the Environment Ministry took swift action to reassure the Singapore public and issued a joint statement (in April 2003) to explain the intricate differences between the sanitary systems in Singapore and Hong Kong (as shown in Figure 7.1). Although both Hong Kong's and Singapore's sanitary systems had the same roots in the original British design, these systems have developed

FIGURE 7.1

Sanitary Systems of Buildings in Hong Kong and Singapore

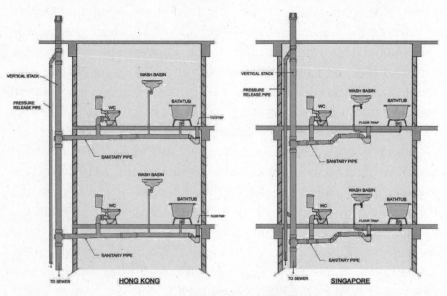

Source: PUB.

differently. In Singapore, as the concern was with the possible loss of water in the seal, floor traps were configured to be constantly replenished by discharge from the wash basin and bathroom shower. This ensures that the water seal in the floor trap is maintained and prevents foul air in the sanitary pipes from entering the premises. The sanitary system in buildings in Singapore, therefore, did not pose a SARS risk.

Whilst the Housing and Development Board and Town Councils under MND have standard operating procedures to tackle and address sewage leaks swiftly and appropriately, PUB and the Environment Ministry had adequate measures specified in the Code of Practices on the Sanitary Drainage and Plumbing Systems for the exclusion of foul air from the sanitary drainage system. These include stipulating that water seals of sufficient depths be provided at appropriate sanitary appliances discharge points and floor traps. The design of sanitary drainage and plumbing systems must also avoid the loss of water seals in these traps due to pressure fluctuations. This could be done by providing ventilating pipes/ stacks or adequate sizing of discharge stacks so that the water seals would always be kept in place. This example shows how the two ministries worked together to ensure that public housing sanitation systems are well designed.

EFFECTIVE USE OF LEGISLATION

While the government provides the essential infrastructure required to manage used water, industries and private owners also have to do their part in controlling water pollution and managing their used water. In order to ensure that the various industrial activities do not have an adverse impact on water quality or the management of used water, a number of acts and regulations were enacted, with strict penalties to control pollution of watercourses. These acts and regulations are further elaborated below.

Sewerage and Drainage Act and Its Subsidiary Legislations

The control of trade effluent discharge into sewers and watercourses was first legislated under the Local Government (Disposal of Trade Effluents) Regulations, passed in 1970, and the Environmental Public Health (Prohibition on Discharge of Trade Effluents into Water Courses) Regulations, passed in 1971. These were subsequently consolidated under the Water Pollution Control and Drainage Act (WPCDA), 1975, to improve the effectiveness of overall water pollution control. Later in 1999, the WPCDA was disaggregated into the Sewerage and Drainage Act (SDA) and the Environmental Pollution Control Act (EPCA), administered by the then Environment Ministry, with stipulations on the control of discharge into public sewers and watercourses respectively. The SDA was subsequently transferred to the PUB upon its reconstitution as the national water agency in 2001, while the EPCA (renamed the Environmental Protection and Management Act in January 2008) went under the purview of the National Environment Agency (NEA) in 2002.

The SDA empowers PUB to control the discharge of used water from domestic, industrial, agricultural, and other premises. Under the Act, the government may require all used water generated to be discharged into public sewers if they are available. The Act also provides for penalties for offences that have resulted in serious water pollution. Regulations made under the Act guide the provision of sanitary works in all premises, provision of small sewage treatment plants (STPs), control of trade effluent discharged into the sewerage system, and collection of fees to maintain the public sewerage system. Some of the regulations that are part of the SDA are described below.

Trade Effluent Regulations (TER)

Trade effluent is defined as "any liquid, including particles of matter and other substances in suspension in the liquid, which is the outflow from any trade, business or manufacture or of any works of engineering or building construction". The Trade Effluent Regulations, 1977, was enacted to allow certain industries which produced biodegradable waste water to discharge their effluent into the public sewer, as long as they were in accordance with specified water quality limits. The Trade Effluent Tariff Scheme allows applicants to discharge biodegradable used water with higher concentration into the public sewer, subject to a fee. Furthermore, industries could also dispose their organic sludge at designated water reclamation plants for a fee. This provision offers a choice to industries that produce biodegradable wastes of higher concentration, but find it undesirable or impossible to install, operate, and maintain a trade effluent treatment plant on its premises.

Sanitary Works Regulations

The Sanitary Works Regulations explicitly stipulate the separation of rainwater from used water, and the diversion of rain water into a surface storm water drain and away from any opening connected to a used water system. Furthermore, all sullage water from premises such as motor workshops, eating establishments, car washing bays in petrol stations, refuse chutes and bin centres, and backwash water from swimming pool filters are to be discharged directly to the used water system, via a grease trap where necessary. Sullage water should be kept out of the rain water collection system as they contain pollutants such as detergents, organic material (food waste, oil, and grease) and other harmful substances such as heavy metals from scrap metal yards, which will contaminate watercourses and catchments.

Surface Water Drainage Regulations

The Surface Water Drainage Regulations govern discharges into the storm water drainage system. These regulations, first enacted in 1999, prohibit the discharge of silt or suspended solids into open drains in concentrations greater than 50 milligrams per litre. The regulations require that every person carrying out earthworks or construction works should provide and maintain effective earth control measures and take adequate measures to prevent "any earth, top soil, cement, concrete, debris, or any other material to fall or be washed into the storm water drainage system". This is particularly challenging with all the development works that are taking place around the island. Nevertheless, effort has to be made to protect the storm water drainage system from silt and debris, which not only cause siltation and impede the effectiveness of the drainage systems, but also contribute to the unsightly brown water in waterways and reservoirs.

CONTROL OF USED WATER QUALITY AT SOURCE

Used water is no longer a waste product that is treated before release to safeguard the environment. It is now a national resource for the production of NEWater. Used water, particularly trade effluent that does not comply with the legislation, if discharged into sewers can have an adverse impact on the used water reclamation process. Such trade effluent may be potentially toxic to the biological process in the WRPs, or may disrupt the NEWater production process. To ensure robustness and reliability in the production of NEWater, it is critical to have effective source control measures to manage the trade effluent discharged from industries into the sewers.

Discharge of trade effluent into sewers is regulated by legislation and PUB's prior approval is also required. Despite the legislation in place, there is a need to ensure that trade effluent discharged into sewers complies with the requirements. PUB carries out surveillance and enforcement activities to meet this need. However, it is difficult to detect violations as such surveillance is not continuous. One approach to enhance the surveillance of trade effluent discharged into sewers is to leverage technology.

Organic solvents are one of the main groups of substances of concern. There are no direct instruments to detect these solvents. But as these solvents are volatile, they can be detected indirectly by volatile organic compounds (VOC) meters. VOC meters are the best available detection technology for solvents now. PUB has installed VOC meters at strategic locations in the used water network. Such locations include pumping stations that serve significant industrial clusters, and at the WRP inlets. The meters are configured as online VOC monitoring units that measure the VOC level at regular intervals. They will also set off alarms at certain preset levels. The readings are sent to a central monitoring system for data logging. Together, this constitutes a remote VOC monitoring and warning system. PUB also has a few mobile VOC monitoring units that can be set up at different locations, including factory clusters and factories. These movable units also have a sampling pump system to collect a sample in the event of high VOC, and will send alerts to the central monitoring station. The samples can also be analysed for other substances of concern besides VOCs, and will facilitate taking enforcement action where appropriate.

Use of technology and legislative enforcement aside, PUB also conducts dialogue sessions with factories to share with them good practices pertaining to trade effluent discharge.

The evolution of Singapore's environmental legislation reflects efforts to address the changing needs of used water management — from the early days of providing basic sanitation, to controlling used water discharged and maintaining effluent quality for water reclamation.

HARNESSING NEW TECHNOLOGIES

PUB is constantly on the lookout for new and emerging technologies that would enhance its existing used water management processes. The DTSS alone has provided immense opportunities for PUB to partner industry players in R&D work, as well as employ new groundbreaking technologies, processes, and equipment. In addition, PUB's keen and forward-looking attitude towards test bedding and pilot testing new technologies in its existing WRP facilities enhances its efforts to be at the forefront of used water management and operations. In addition to the technological innovations that have been described earlier in this chapter, the following sections highlight more of such initiatives.

Sludge Management

The solid by-product of used water treatment, or sludge, has to be properly treated and disposed of so it does not cause contamination to the environment. Since the commissioning of the Kim Chuan WRP in 1948, the raw sludge collected from the primary sedimentation tanks and excess activated sludge from the secondary treatment process were treated using anaerobic sludge digesters to break down the organic matter in the sludge to render them inoffensive for disposal. This produces biogas that enables electricity to be generated in the plant and thus reduces electricity required from the grid. In fact, the biogas produced at the WRPs is presently able to generate, through PUB's dual-fuel generators, up to 25 per cent of their plants' electricity needs.

Prior to 1980, treated sludge was dried under the sun at the sludge drying beds. This was possible then as the only two sites at Ulu Pandan and Serangoon were located in remote rural areas. By the end of the 1970s, as the volume of sludge had significantly increased and more developments encroached towards the facilities, the drying beds were phased out with the installation of mechanical sludge dewatering facilities.

Up to the 1980s, the treated sludge could be disposed of via its use as a soil conditioner for reclaimed land, landscaping, and tree planting. However, towards the 1990s, this sludge disposal process was re-evaluated in view of the need to protect surface water quality within the expanding water catchment areas, and to minimize odour nuisance. Also, land application at reclaimed sites outside the water catchments is not sustainable as these sites are fast running out.

This prompted PUB to search for alternative sludge disposal methods to reduce the overall sludge volume. Incineration of sludge is also adopted to reduce further the sludge to ash for disposal at the Semakau Landfill.

Membrane Bioreactor

The development of membrane bioreactor (MBR) technology bridges conventional used water treatment and the water reclamation process. The membrane barrier in the MBR process retains most of the micro-organisms and solids, resulting in effluent of excellent quality without the need for additional filters. In addition, the effluent produced is clean enough to be fed directly into the reverse osmosis system for the production of high grade industrial water, or even for NEWater production. This would eliminate the need for the micro-filtration or ultra-filtration step, further compacting the NEWater treatment process and reducing the amount of valuable land needed.

The existing process of aeration, final sedimentation, and microfiltration pretreatment can be effectively replaced by a single-stage MBR. This results in a significant reduction in total retention time, improved effluent quality, and cost savings. The MBR technology also supports much higher biomass for more effective aerobic biological treatment and reduced aeration-basin volume, thus reducing the surface area required at a WRP. In fact, with promising results from the demonstration MBR plant at Ulu Pandan WRP, there are plans to introduce the MBR process to other WRPs. Similarly, pilot testing for other treatment methods are also carried out to search for better and more efficient ways to treat and manage used water.

CONCLUSION

Singapore has come a long way in its bid to provide effective modern sanitation and used water management systems for its population. From the early days of open dumping into waterways to the night soil collection system, disposal works and sewage treatment works, the country has progressed to the present-day water reclamation plants and the integration of used water management under the DTSS.

Long-term planning led to the development of a comprehensive Used Water Masterplan. Equally important was the discipline to adhere to the key features in designing used water management systems, which allowed Singapore to achieve 100 per cent access to modern sanitation within a short span of time. In addition, the search for longer term, sustainable solutions led to the bold and innovative approach of managing used water through the DTSS. Singapore's fully sewered system also made possible large-scale used water recycling, with recent breakthroughs in technologies allowing for reclaimed water, in the form of NEWater, to be channelled to augment water supply.

The journey in managing used water may be arduous and never-ending, but it is definitely eventful. Going forward, Singapore will face new challenges that will require further improvements and innovative solutions. It will have to review the sustainability of its used water systems constantly, in tandem with economic development, and consider the best means of collecting every drop of used water for recycling, as this would contribute towards its water self-sufficiency over the long term.

Singapore hopes to share its experience in used water management with other nations as they embark on their used water management development plans. At the same time, this may also facilitate and trigger further sharing of knowledge and expertise among nations in the common pursuit of more sustainable and environmentally friendly ways to manage used water.

8

FROM FLOOD PREVENTION AND FLOOD MANAGEMENT TO ABC WATERS

Today this (drainage and reservoir) system helps us collect water, store water, and control floods. So we have taken care of the basics well. But moving on, there is further potential — if we think creatively and work together. With some planning and enhancement, the water bodies and waterways can be changed into vibrant areas for everyone in the community to enjoy. There can be more lifestyle activities and people will have more recreational choices. This in essence is the spirit of the ABC Waters Programme.

Minister for the Environment and Water Resources,
Dr Yaacob Ibrahim, at the Kallang River Fiesta "Fun & Joy"
cum Launch of PUB's ABC Waters Programme demonstration
project at Kallang River/Kolam Ayer,
16 April 2006

In the 1960s and 1970s, floods were common and widespread in Singapore, especially in the city centre, which was built on relatively low-lying land. As the ground levels of developments in these areas were usually barely above high tide level, they would flood almost every time heavy rain coincided with high tide. Floods like these not only caused great inconvenience and disruption to people's lives but also damage to property.

SEVERE FLOODS IN SINGAPORE

Flood of 1969

In December 1969, Singapore experienced 467 millimetres of rain within a 17-hour period, the second highest rainfall ever recorded in Singapore in a single day. The heavy rain, coupled with a high tide of 3.1 metres, resulted in extensive floods across the island. The most severely affected areas were Bukit Timah Valley and Potong Pasir, where several stretches of road were submerged under 2 metres of flood waters. The floods claimed the lives of five people, and more than 3,000 people were evacuated. The city transport system was paralyzed, and all roads and rail links between Singapore and West Malaysia were severed. Total damages were estimated at S$4.3 million (based on 1969 prices).

Flood of 1978

In December 1978,[1] Singapore experienced its most severe flood ever. A total of 512.4 millimetres of rain was recorded over a 24-hour period — the highest in a single day and almost a quarter of Singapore's average annual rainfall. To compound matters, the rain coincided with a very high tide of 3.2 metres (the average high tide level is about 2.8 metres). Roads were submerged under more than a metre of water, resulting in massive traffic jams as hundreds of vehicles were abandoned. The worst hit areas were the farm belts of Woodlands, Braddell Road, Potong Pasir, and Changi, where more than 2,000 pigs and poultry perished in the swollen waters. In some areas, the flood levels reached the roofs of squatter huts.

Seven people died in the 1978 flood. Altogether, more than 1,000 people were evacuated from their homes by army and police boats, with the more serious casualties transported via helicopters. Total damages were estimated at S$5.75 million (based on 1978 prices).

Causes of Floods

Many believe that flooding depends on the volume of rainfall and the size of canals and drains, that is, the capacity to convey storm waters away quickly. To some extent, this is true, but there are other factors as well.

One such factor is the intensity of rainfall, which is the volume of rainfall within a period of time, usually expressed in millimetres of rainfall per hour. Due to Singapore's location in the equatorial belt, it receives about 2,400 millimetres of rainfall each year on average, which is characteristic of a tropical rainforest climate. The rainfall occurs throughout the year, but with higher rainfall in the northeast monsoon season from December to early March, when there are frequent afternoon showers, and intense spells of widespread moderate to heavy rain, lasting from one to three days. In some cases, a huge volume of rain can fall within a relatively short period of time, such as during the flood of 1978, in which almost a quarter of Singapore's average annual rainfall fell within a single day.

With such abundant rainfall, it is not surprising for floods to occur if the storm water drainage infrastructure is inadequate. Fortunately for Singapore, careful planning and judicious implementation of an efficient drainage network has helped spare the island from major floods for more than two decades. Nevertheless, floods could still occur in Singapore during an intense storm, such as that occasionally experienced during the northeast monsoon season, when heavy or localized rains coincide with a very high tide, causing flash floods.

Besides hydrological factors, the relief and contour of the land may also increase the risk of flooding. Although Singapore is relatively flat, there are land undulations, with the lowest-lying lands located along the southern and eastern coastal fronts. These areas, which include Singapore's Central Business District, are subject to a higher risk of flooding. Some pockets of low-lying land can also be found further inland.

Furthermore, floods are not always caused by geographical elements. Blocked drains, for example, can reduce the conveying capacity of drains, compromising their conveyance function. At times, some developers may also overlook the fact that their new concrete-based structures reduce the amount of rain that can infiltrate into the ground, resulting in increased surface run-off. This is typical of areas that undergo urbanization or land development, where drains ought to be enlarged in tandem to cater to the excess surface flow. To ensure there are no chokepoints, the drains downstream will also need to have the capacity to handle the excess flow.

FLOOD MANAGEMENT STRATEGY

From close to 7,000 hectares of flood-prone areas in the 1960s, there were only about 130 hectares at the end of 2007. Furthermore, unlike the extensive floods in the past, today's floods are localized flash floods, that is, floods that occur in a small locality, which often subside quickly, within thirty minutes to an hour. How were such improvements achieved?

Because of the potential damage floods could cause, Singapore's leaders had recognized from early on that if not tackled, floods could disrupt lives and become a major impediment to economic growth. Thus, various measures were taken to tackle the flood problem along two key thrusts:

a. Flood alleviation projects were implemented to tackle and reduce the size of flood-prone areas, by improving the drainage in these areas.

b. Flood prevention measures were put in place in low-lying areas, even those that had escaped serious flooding previously. Flood prevention was also important in areas undergoing major development, as increased urbanization would reduce natural infiltration into the ground, thereby leading to increased surface run-off and a higher risk of flooding during storms.

Flood Alleviation

The earliest drainage network in Singapore began as a public health measure. In the early 1900s, malaria was very rampant as the malaria vector — the *Anopheles* mosquito — thrived in warm weather and bred easily in pools of stagnant water. To combat this, an anti-malarial drainage system was introduced in 1914 to convey seepage water and prevent formation of stagnant pools. The network comprised naturally formed earth streams, subsoil pipes, and concrete drains. With the growth and urbanization of Singapore, the anti-malarial drains also served the purpose of flood alleviation. However, as seen by the extent and severity of the floods experienced, the drainage system was inadequate to meet the needs of a rapidly growing Singapore. The immediate task then was to reduce the size of the flood-prone areas.

Early Flood Alleviation Schemes

In 1951, a Joint Committee on Flood Alleviation was formed under the Public Works Department (PWD), which was charged with improving the drainage system. As a single department was responsible for flood alleviation, from drawing up plans to carrying them out, coordination and implementation were easier and faster. A number of flood alleviation projects were carried out in the 1950s and 1960s, mainly in flood-prone areas such as Queenstown, Geylang, Bedok, Potong Pasir, Whampoa, Jurong, Tampines, and Seletar. It was important to alleviate flooding in these areas, as they were densely built up and flooding would affect a large number of residents (this was before the development of public housing estates in new towns and many Singaporeans were still living in dense squatter colonies). To improve their capacities to convey flood water to the sea, the drains serving these areas were widened, deepened, and concrete-lined.

At the same time, a tide-gate system was also designed for the Central Business District and other areas in central Singapore that were below the high tide level and faced frequent flooding during high tides. To protect these low-lying areas from tidal inundation, eighteen tide-gates were installed in the vicinity of the Singapore River, Rochor, and Katong. Nevertheless, the tide gates would have to be open when there was heavy rain, and if this coincided with high tides, the low-lying areas would still be flooded.

Bukit Timah Flood Alleviation Scheme

One of the most important and complex flood alleviation schemes was the Bukit Timah Flood Alleviation Scheme (BTFAS). The Bukit Timah Catchment had a history of flooding from as far back as the 1930s, due to the undersized Bukit Timah Canal and Rochor Canal which were the main outlets for the catchment. In particular, areas surrounding the Bukit Timah Canal experienced frequent flooding as a result of being on relatively lower ground. The problem came to a head in the 1960s when rapid development of the Bukit Timah Catchment resulted in regular overflowing of the canal.

Unfortunately, the Bukit Timah and Rochor areas had been densely built up all the way to the edge of the canals. This made it impossible to widen the canals without a highly disruptive and costly exercise to resettle and compensate those developments. To reduce flooding upstream, the PWD, therefore, decided to divert storm water by channelling it to the sea via a different route.

The BTFAS was conceived at a time when Singapore had just become independent and there were other pressing issues that had to be addressed urgently, such as education and national defence. Nevertheless, the government provided S$7 million for the scheme, but because this was insufficient to carry out the entire project, it was divided into two phases.

Phase 1 of BTFAS: Phase 1 of the scheme was implemented over six years (1966–72). Under this project, part of the storm water from 700 hectares of the Upper Bukit Timah Catchment was diverted to Sungei Ulu Pandan via a new canal. This was a huge undertaking even by today's standards, and although the budget of S$7 million was a stretch, with dim prospects of further government funding, the PWD engineers came up with innovative engineering methods to deliver the project within the approved budget.

Phase 2 of BTFAS: By the 1980s, further developments in the central part of the catchment made it necessary to implement Phase 2 of the scheme. By then, the success of Phase 1 had convinced the government of the importance of good drainage and the need for Phase 2. The speedy approval for Phase 2 was also in part due to the economic downturn in the early 1980s. The government had given the green light for many large projects in the hope that these would boost the economy and help it get back on its feet.

As the Bukit Timah Canal was flanked by major roads and services on both sides, the maximum expansion that could be achieved was limited, even for the most efficient of canal designs. Besides deepening and widening the Bukit Timah Canal, a second diversion canal (4.4-kilometre long, including 2 kilometres of tunnel) diverting water from the Bukit Timah Canal to Kallang River was constructed — from Swiss Cottage Estate to Sir Arthur's Bridge at Kallang River. A section of Kallang River was also improved to increase its drainage capacity to handle the diverted flows from Bukit Timah. Downstream of the Bukit Timah Canal, two major subsidiary drains, the Thomson Road Outlet Drain and the Pelton Canal, and several other smaller subsidiary drains, were constructed to allow for more efficient drainage of storm water.

Phase 2 of the BTFAS was hailed as ENV's largest civil engineering project then — it was a complicated affair that cut across an expressway and involved major works close to the intersection òf Singapore's two major expressways. Comprising seven separate contracts awarded to four different consultants and seven contractors, Phase 2 was rolled out in 1986 and completed in five years at a cost of S$240 million.

Given the dense build-up within the Bukit Timah Catchment, the improvements in Phase 2 would have been impossible if not for the fact that British engineers had foreseen the need for this diversion canal decades before. Although the British had not found it necessary then to implement the flood alleviation measures in the Bukit Timah Catchment, they had identified possible solutions to potential flood problems before the 1960s. In one particular report prepared by the Chief Drainage Engineer F. Pelton of the Public Works Department in the 1950s, plans for the Bukit Timah Diversion and for alterations to the Bukit Timah Canal were laid out. Having identified the solution, the British had the foresight to earmark the land for the diversion route (from Bukit Timah Canal to Kallang River) as a drainage reserve for the implementation of such a solution. If this had not been done, there would have been no cost-effective solution to the flooding problem in the Bukit Timah Catchment. It is perhaps fitting, therefore, that the Pelton Canal was named after this Chief Drainage Engineer.

The BTFAS experience offers a valuable lesson. It illustrates the importance of taking a long-term approach to planning, a key principle that continues to underpin the master planning that is done today. Anticipating challenges early provides for more options available downstream as provisions can be made upfront to cater for the solutions. This is particularly true in flood management, where drainage needs tend to grow over time with urbanization, whilst the flexibility for solutions decreases as more and more land is developed. Hence, foreseeing problems and finding ways to tackle them early is critical.

Flood Prevention

In the 1970s, as drainage infrastructure could not keep pace with new developments, flood incidents occurred across the island, even in areas that had not experienced flooding before. Rapid urbanization would lead to increased storm water flows that required corresponding expansions of the drainage system, but this was limited by the budget set aside for drainage infrastructure amidst other competing needs for government funds.

The situation would become particularly acute in the 1970s and 1980s, as it was a period of rapid expansion, spreading even to the suburban areas. New towns were being built as the Housing and Development Board (HDB) expanded its public housing programme. The Jurong Town Corporation (JTC) had also embarked on an ambitious plan to develop industries in the western part of Singapore.

Drainage Master Plan and Development Control

To cope with these challenges, the Drainage Department in ENV was designated the drainage authority responsible for spearheading and implementing drainage planning and control strategies. ENV was formed in 1972 to look into providing Singaporeans with a quality living environment and a high standard of public health. The decision was made to move the Drainage Department to ENV in recognition of the fact that besides physical infrastructure, drainage issues were linked with public health considerations (for example, stagnant water could cause water-borne diseases).

In close consultation with the Urban Redevelopment Authority (URA), HDB, JTC, and other development agencies, the Department drew up a comprehensive drainage master plan in the mid-1970s. Taking into consideration the drainage requirements based on current and projected land uses, the master plan guided the provision of drainage systems and set aside drainage reserves for future requirements. The master plan also targeted known flood-prone areas, laying out the plans to tackle them through flood alleviation projects.

In line with the administrative procedures for planning and building control, the Drainage Department would have to be consulted on drainage technical requirements at every stage of any development proposal, be it at the land reclamation phase, planning consultation, or building plan stage. With this, the Department would scrutinize all new land development proposals and impose drainage requirements[2] which were in line with the drainage master plan for effective flood control. The requirements also applied to public projects by agencies such as HDB, JTC, and the Land Transport Authority (LTA).

Road Drainage Improvement Task Force

Even today, the most commonly reported floods are those that occur on public roads, due to the extent of disruption they cause. In 1984, a Road Drainage Improvement Task Force was set up to minimize disruption to traffic during rainstorms, by alleviating ponding and localized flooding on roads. The need for integrated planning had been recognized back then, with the Task Force comprising representatives from the Drainage Department and the Environmental Health Department in ENV, and the Roads Division of the PWD.

The Task Force was structured to maximize efficiency and benefits from specialization. Different departments were made responsible for different aspects, from the design of roads, to the sweeping, cleansing, and even structural maintenance of the drainage outlets, scuppers, and roadside drains. This set-up clearly identified the parties responsible for finding solutions to the different parts of the problem, and hence there was ownership of the issue.

The Task Force met regularly and established an approach to tackle cases of localized flash floods as soon as they occurred. First, they would identify roads that were prone to ponding or localized flooding, and investigate all potential causes. They would then seek practical (engineering) solutions to the problems, and formulate implementation plans for the improvement works that would generally fall into one of five key strategies:

1. *Raising of low-lying roads:* For roads that were below or marginally above high tide levels, improving the drainage outlet facilities would not solve the flooding problems, especially when heavy rains coincided with high tides. Such roads had to be raised.
2. *Patching up of localized depressions in roads:* Sometimes, only isolated stretches of road were low-lying and simple patching up of the localized depressions would suffice.
3. *Improvement of road drainage facilities:* Even if the roads were well above the high tide level, if high intensity rainfall occurred, this could pose problems. The rapid accumulation of the run-off from the roads could cause ponding if the road drainage facilities were inadequate, in which case the drainage facilities would be improved to allow rainwater to drain away more quickly.
4. *Improvement of outlet drains:* In cases where the downstream outlet drains could be overloaded, they would be enlarged to the required capacity.
5. *Cleansing of road drainage facilities:* One common cause of ponding and localized flooding was the blockage of scuppers, roadside drains, and other road drainage facilities by leaves, litter, or debris from structural damages. Such problems could easily be overcome by increasing the frequency of inspection, cleansing, and maintenance of the drainage facilities.

Another example of close cooperation within the task force was the sharing of information. The Roads Division, for example, would send images from its extensive network of traffic cameras and highlight cases of ponding on roads to ENV in real time. ENV would then send officers to investigate and clear any blocked drainage outlets.

The Task Force proved to be so effective that it still exists today. Although the Ministry of the Environment and Water Resources, as ENV is now known, has since passed on its drainage functions to PUB, and its environmental health functions to the National Environment Agency (NEA), and the Roads Division has been restructured under LTA, the various agencies continue to work together with a common objective — to ensure minimal disruption to traffic during heavy rains. Since its inception, the task force, headed by the Drainage Department of then ENV (now known as the Catchment and Waterways Department of PUB), has tackled about 800 cases of flash floods over the past twenty-four years. The number of cases has dwindled in the past few years due to PUB's ongoing efforts both in preventing and alleviating floods. Nevertheless, the task force continues to meet every one or two months to coordinate activities, and resolve flash flood occurrences. This remains relevant today as flash floods can still occur for a number of reasons, including the blockage of drainage outlets by errant contractors, inadequate road drainage facilities, and wear and tear with the ageing of Singapore's drainage and road infrastructure.

Platform Levels and Requirements

Apart from specifying drainage requirements, the Drainage Department also stipulated the platform levels required for new buildings and infrastructural facilities for flood protection purposes. Vulnerable underground facilities such as rail and road tunnels had to comply with more stringent requirements. For example, all ground openings (including ventilation ducts) and accesses of subterranean facilities, such as Mass Rapid Transit (MRT) tunnels and stations, underground roads, and building basements, would have to be at least one metre above the highest recorded flood level. The effectiveness of these measures was put to the test in May 1988, when heavy rains caused flooding in various parts of Singapore. Although the floods resulted in traffic jams and disrupted bus services, the MRT trains continued to run smoothly as the stations and tunnels were well protected.

High sea levels also pose a challenge for drainage to the sea. Higher tide levels can aggravate inland flooding during rainstorms or storm surges, where the seawater is pushed to the shore by the force of the wind. In view of this, since 1991, all reclamation projects had to be built at least 125 centimetres above the highest recorded tide level. This was deemed by experienced drainage engineers to be a prudent measure, given the tendency for reclaimed land to settle over time. With hindsight, this requirement has put Singapore in a stronger position to deal with any future increases in sea levels arising from climate change as the requirement exceeds the Intergovernmental Panel on Climate Change's projection of the highest sea level rise in the region — 59 centimetres — by the end of the twenty-first century.

Dealing with Land Constraints: Opera Estate Outlet Drain Project

In land-scarce Singapore, drainage engineers often found themselves having to find creative solutions to drainage problems so as to minimize the use of land or develop conjunctive uses for the land. One example of the innovative use of land was the Opera Estate Drainage Improvement Scheme.

Houses lined the banks of the Opera Estate Outlet Drain and used to be hit by frequent floods. During flood events, residents were greatly inconvenienced and roads were made impassable to traffic. The conventional approach was to widen the drain, but this would require expensive and disruptive land acquisitions. Instead, in 1996, the Drainage Department's engineers came up with the solution of a Pump Drainage System, which comprised a two-tier drain (an upper tier and lower tier), a storage pond, and a pumping station.

During normal rainfall, rainwater would be channelled (by gravity) via the upper tier of the outlet drain to the sea. In a heavy storm, excess rainwater would overflow into the lower tier and be stored in an underground pond next to the outlet drain. After the storm, the rainwater would then be pumped back into the outlet drain. This two-tier system ensured minimal electricity consumption as the pump was only operated during heavy storms.

To maximize land use, the engineers designed a storage pond underneath a school field, with the pumping station sited above it in a small corner beside the field. The old outlet drain was replaced with a new covered drain which enabled a landscaped park connector with benches, and jogging and cycling tracks to be built on it for community enjoyment, and provided improved connectivity between both banks of the drain as well. Hence, besides a flood-free estate, residents of Opera Estate can now enjoy a picturesque stroll or ride to East Coast Park on top of the covered drain.

FLOOD CONTROL TODAY

Since 1973, more than S$2 billion[3] has been spent on the construction of new drains and canals in Singapore. These have helped to reduce flood-prone areas significantly by more than 95 per cent over the last few decades, even as urbanized areas have increased over the same period. By the early 1990s, basic drainage infrastructure had been provided almost all over Singapore, and by 2000, widespread flooding had become virtually unheard of.

On 19 December 2006, Singapore experienced its third heaviest storm recorded. A total of 366 millimetres of rain fell over a 24-hour period. Despite the intense rainfall, there were no major floods and only a few isolated spots (totalling 15 hectares) were affected. This is a strong testimony of the effectiveness of the drainage system.

Nevertheless, flash floods and pondings still occur in isolated locations around Singapore, and some low-lying areas experience localized flooding during heavy rains. PUB is now targeting its flood alleviation projects in these areas. As some of the older canals, drains, and outlet drains approach the end of their useful lifespan, PUB will also improve and upgrade them, as well as others that may still be functioning well, but will become inadequate when new developments take place in the near future.

Integration of Storm Water Management with the Water Loop

With the transfer of the Drainage and Sewerage Departments in ENV to PUB in 2001, the drainage functions are now integrated with the water supply catchment functions. Reservoirs such as Kranji, Pandan, Bedok, and Lower Seletar had been constructed within urban catchments and received urban run-off from the drainage network. This close relationship between drainage networks and water catchments was further enhanced in June 2006, when the planning, development, and management of reservoirs and waterways for water supply and flood control were integrated under one department in PUB — the Catchment and Waterways Department. This underscores the important role that storm water management plays in the water loop.

Marina Reservoir

Not long after the cleaning up of the Singapore River in the 1980s, the government began to seriously consider the Marina and Kallang Basin as a potential reservoir. Parts of the Marina Catchment, particularly those within the city centre, were notoriously low-lying, and a reservoir with a controlled water level could help to alleviate flooding.

Touted as a three-in-one project that would provide water storage, flood control, and lifestyle attractions, the Marina Reservoir would be formed by the building of a dam across the Marina Channel. This dam, known as the Marina Barrage, would act as a tidal barrier so that high tides would not be able to advance further inland, preventing the flooding of low-lying city areas in the Marina Catchment. At the same time, a 240-hectare freshwater reservoir would be created behind the dam, Singapore's fifteenth reservoir. In addition, the Marina Reservoir would have the potential to become an integrated water sports hub and premier tourist attraction with its constant water level all year round, making it conducive for recreational activities such as sailing, canoeing, dragon boating, fishing, and river cruises. Its location and synergies with other key attractions and developments such as the Gardens-by-the-Bay, Marina Sands Integrated Resort, and the Downtown Marina would also reinvent the city centre, creating a unique and vibrant Singapore.

The Marina Barrage, comprising nine steel crest gates and seven pumps, would isolate the urban rivers and canals from the sea and its tidal influence. To serve a flood control purpose, the barrage would be operated based on rainfall and tidal conditions. Under normal conditions, the crest gates will remain upright so a constant water level is maintained throughout the reservoir and the inland rivers of the Marina Catchment, regardless of the tide level. If a heavy rain coincides with a low tide, the crest gates can be lowered. As the water level of the Marina Reservoir is above the tide level, the water will flow out to the sea. When a heavy rain coincides with a high tide, the crest gates will be kept upright to keep the high tide out. Pumps will be activated to remove the excess water from the reservoir, keeping the water level in the reservoir and its upstream catchment fairly constant.

When fully operational, the barrage will alleviate flooding in the low-lying areas in the city centre, and is expected to reduce the size of flood-prone areas in Singapore to less than 100 hectares.

The Remaining Areas

Despite these efforts, it is impossible to eradicate floods in Singapore completely. The drainage system is built to a design norm of one-in-five year storms, a widely adopted standard. Should there be storms that are more intense than this, the drainage system may have difficulty coping. It would be costly (in monetary terms as well as opportunity cost in land-scarce Singapore) to upsize drains to cater to the most intense storms, nor is it possible to predict when the heaviest storms would occur and their maximum intensities, given the vagaries of the weather.

There are also low-lying flood-prone areas in Singapore where raising the ground level is the only way to alleviate flooding. Since tearing down buildings just to raise the ground level is extremely expensive, highly inconvenient, and a waste of resources, the only cost-effective option is to raise the ground in conjunction with redevelopment plans. In such cases, the drainage master plan earmarks such areas, so that when developers submit their development plans for approval, the requirements to raise the ground can be made known to them at an early stage and incorporated prior to development.

PUB has set up a database to track these areas. It shows, for example, the remaining depressed roads to be raised in conjunction with future road or drainage improvement works. A similar database is maintained on public buildings with a history of flooding.

Flood Response

Where flood alleviation projects have not been put in place, PUB will issue advisories to all building occupants in the flood-prone areas in October, prior to the wet season. These advisories will remind the residents of the high tide periods, the radio flood warning system, and the flood prevention measures they can take.

To cope with flood situations, PUB also has teams on standby to tackle them. A flood response room has been set aside as a command centre. When intense rain is forecasted, NEA's meteorological services will alert PUB via fax and mobile text messages, and the mobile teams are then deployed immediately to designated "hot spots" before the rain begins. Any drain obstructions observed at the sites are cleared immediately to prevent flooding, and if need be, the maintenance contractors are mobilized. If flooding does occur, flood investigation officers will be deployed to the site to ascertain the cause of flooding. Should the situation escalate, PUB will activate a "Combined Operations Room" to monitor the flood situation, ensure a suitable distribution of resources, and mobilize additional manpower where necessary to address the floods.

After heavy rain, PUB will review any floods that have occurred and look into how a repeat flood in the same location can be prevented. Where the cause of the flood is insufficient drainage outlets, local constrictions, or damaged drains, PUB will plan and carry out the improvements or repairs within two weeks where possible. If the works are more substantial and outside the scope of its regular maintenance contracts, the drain will be included in PUB's ongoing drainage improvement plans.

Maintenance Regime

PUB maintains an extensive network of some 990 kilometres of drains and canals and 7,000 kilometres of public roadside drains. To keep them free-flowing and without silt or debris, PUB engages private contractors to carry out physical cleansing, maintenance, and minor structural repairs of drains and canals. It spends about S$10 million a year to keep drains and waterways clean and in good functioning condition. Nevertheless, cleaning contractors can only do so much, and a lot more depends on the public playing their part to keep Singapore litter-free. For example, litter thrown from cars along roads and expressways find their way into roadside drains and the chokage can pose flooding risks. As such, PUB works closely with NEA and non-governmental organizations such as the Waterways Watch Society to raise public awareness and educate Singaporeans on the importance of keeping Singapore clean.

While the waterways are clean most of the time, they turn brown during and after rain. This is due to sediments that are washed into the rivers by the rainwater. They can remain suspended in water for a long time, resulting in murky-coloured water. These sediments are not only unsightly, but also increase the risk of floods as the build-up of silt reduces the conveyance capacity of the drains. Silt sediments also increase the cost of water treatment. To prevent the discharge of silty water and to keep storm water in the drainage system clean, a Best Management Practice (BMP) approach is adopted.

A major source of sediments is construction sites as construction activities tend to expose bare surfaces which are easily eroded and washed into the waterways during rain. In view of this, the construction industry is actively engaged in the sharing of BMPs and implementation of earth control measures at construction sites. To drive home the importance of earth control measures, PUB has instituted the need for all construction projects to employ a Qualified Earth Control Professional (QECP). The QECP designs a detailed earth control management plan for all stages of the project and supervises the implementation of the plan. Enforcement actions are taken against construction sites that do not abide by their earth control management plans and cause silty water to enter the waterways.

Integration of Drainage with Other Uses

Given the extensiveness of the drainage system and limited land in Singapore, PUB constantly explores the potential integration of drainage with other land uses. To a large extent, the integrated use of the drainage system for flood alleviation and water catchment purposes has been done. Another way to optimize land use lies in the design of covered drains, so that the top of the drains can be used as pedestrian walkways. Land developers are also encouraged to integrate the drainage infrastructure within their developments to optimize land use. The Stamford Canal serving the Orchard Road area, for example, was built as a series of covered drains and integrated within adjacent commercial developments to provide a wide and continuous pedestrian mall, which serves as an important public space in the shopping district. PUB also worked in tandem with NParks and URA to create "park connectors" (jogging or cycling tracks) from drainage reserves on either side of canals or monsoon drains. Going forward, PUB has also embarked on the Active, Beautiful and Clean (ABC) Waters Programme to tap the potential of waterways and reservoirs to develop more social and recreational opportunities, and community spaces.

CREATING NEW VALUE

In most parts of the world, waterways are designed primarily for storm water conveyance purposes. Nevertheless, as early as the 1970s, Singapore realized that there is much value that can be created from clean flowing waterways. In 1977, then Prime Minister Lee Kuan Yew put forth an ambitious goal to clean up the Singapore River and Kallang Basin. Both were badly polluted from heavy traffic along the river, and the disposal of garbage, sewage, and other by-products of industries located along the river's banks. Cleaning up the rivers involved reviewing land-use planning for the area and re-siting pollutive industries, workshops, and street hawkers, amongst others, from the banks of the rivers. Ten years on, in 1987, the rivers were transformed into pleasant and flowing waterways that were even able to attract marine life back (see Chapter 3 for more details of this river clean-up). The success of the river clean-up together with URA's rejuvenation efforts led to pubs, restaurants, and shops sprouting up along the river banks, showing Singaporeans the value of clean and flowing rivers, and the potential for the development of waterfront activities.

In the 1970s and 1980s, the government made a concerted effort to develop new housing estates in previously undeveloped parts of Singapore, which required a corresponding expansion in the drainage system to deal with the increased surface run-offs. These canals were large and often empty during dry weather, which was not a pretty sight. Following the success of the Singapore River clean-up, MND decided to set up a multi-agency Waterbodies Design Panel (WDP) in 1989, involving a multi-agency taskforce led by URA and comprising representatives from HDB, NParks, Maritime and Port Authority (MPA, then known as the Port of Singapore Authority), then PWD, PUB (then ENV's Drainage Department), as well as the private sector to evaluate and advise on improvements to the designs and aesthetics of all major waterways so as to integrate them into the urban landscape.

ENV worked closely with the WDP to identify key waterways which could be aesthetically developed in a manner that would enhance the natural charm and beauty of their surroundings while retaining their core functions. These waterways included Sungei Punggol, Sungei Api Api, and Alexandra Canal. For example, at Sungei Punggol and Sungei Api Api, mangrove saplings were replanted along the banks to restore part of the natural greenery and ecosystem. The rivers were also deepened to increase their conveyance capacity and to maintain a minimum water level in the rivers for the mangroves to thrive.

Ten years after its inception, the WDP was dissolved to encourage more innovative ideas from the private sector. Unfortunately, this did not take off with the private sector, in part due to the economic downturn of the late 1990s and early 2000s. Without the WDP, aesthetic improvements to waterways would lie dormant for several years.

PARKS AND WATERBODIES PLAN

In 2002, URA, working in collaboration with NParks, introduced a new Parks and Waterbodies Plan under the Singapore Master Plan. The Parks and Waterbodies Plan aims to transform Singapore beyond a "Garden City" into a "City in a Garden" with the vision to evolve Singapore into a bustling metropolis, nestled in a lush mantle of tropical greenery. Provisions have been made for an islandwide network of green spaces and to create more opportunities for people to gain better access to its waterways and waterbodies for recreation. The intent is to make greenery, nature, and the waters more accessible to all, and to provide a variety of recreational choices.

With limited land area for recreation, enabling people to make use of water "spaces" was an important strategy to meet recreational needs. PUB worked with URA and NParks to open up selected waterways and waterbodies such as the Kallang River, Lower Seletar, Pandan, MacRitchie, and Bedok Reservoirs, for water-based activities such as rowing, kayaking, wakeboarding, or just for people to sit and picnic by the waters in the parkland fringing the reservoirs. At the same time, working with the Singapore Sports Council (SSC) and National Sports Associations (NSAs) such as the Singapore Canoe Federation, Singapore Dragon Boat Association, and Singapore Sailing Federation, PUB introduced new activities such as sailing, dragon boating, and canoeing in Singapore's reservoirs in 2004. Today, a myriad of activities are carried out in and around nine of fourteen reservoirs.

To enhance the accessibility between the green spaces, park connectors — green, landscaped jogging and cycling paths that connect people from park to park — were developed along the many waterways and drainage reserves around the island. The target is to build a total of 300 kilometres of park connectors by 2015, covering seven closed loops for recreational activities. To date (2008), about 100 kilometres have been built, including the first complete loop of 42 kilometres, known as the Eastern Coastal Park Connector Network.[4]

In addition to park connectors, the Parks and Waterbodies Plan provides for a hierarchy of parks distributed throughout Singapore. Founded in 1859, the Singapore Botanic Gardens is one of the icons of Singapore's green network. Now spread over 63 hectares close to the centre of the city, it offers some of the most luxuriant landscaped grounds in Singapore, welcoming about 3 million visitors annually. More than just a public park for recreation, the Botanic Gardens is internationally recognized as a leading institution of tropical botany and horticulture with its Library and Herbarium collections of over 600,000 preserved specimens.[5]

The latest major addition to Singapore's green spaces is the Gardens-by-the-Bay, which will feature three world-class gardens on 101 hectares of prime land around the Marina Bay waterfront. This is truly an expression of the vision for a City in a Garden, and will anchor Singapore's new downtown. The first phase of the project involves the development of a 52-hectare garden at Marina South and is due to be completed by 2011. The Gardens-by-the-Bay will be a "green" garden in every sense of the word. To this end, the planners and designers have looked at the latest technologies available and are designing a system that will be as energy and water efficient as possible.

CONCEPTUALIZING THE ABC WATERS PROGRAMME

In 2004, seeing the untapped potential of reservoirs and waterways, the Ministry of the Environment and Water Resources spearheaded the opening up of these waterbodies both for their aesthetic value and for community activities on the water. As the waterways are often located close to, and run through, residential heartlands, they could potentially be developed as focal points for community activities, enhancing the value of surrounding properties. The use of the waterways for community activities will be further enhanced by the park connectors, which will increase accessibility to these sites, and invite even more residents to visit and participate in activities.

There is also great potential in utilizing the pervasive "blue network" of reservoirs and waterways (as shown in Map 5) for experiential-based public education on the need to keep the waters clean. Prior to this, PUB had conducted with mixed success several public campaigns over the years to get Singaporeans to value and conserve water. Adopting a bold mindset, PUB felt that the best way to get people to internalize these values was for them to enjoy and appreciate waterbodies and waterways, and in so doing, bond with water. At a national level, Singapore could be transformed into a unique "City of Gardens and Water".

The Active, Beautiful and Clean Waters Programme (or ABC Waters) is the umbrella programme that embodies this vision of unlocking the hidden potential and opportunities in waterbodies and waterways. The ABC acronym encapsulates the fundamental objectives of the programme:

Active: Providing new community spaces and bringing people closer to water through recreational activities. With more opportunities for interaction, it is hoped that people will connect with the water, developing a sense of ownership and valuing it better.

Beautiful: Developing reservoirs and waterways into vibrant and aesthetically pleasing lifestyle attractions that integrate with parks, estates, and even commercial developments.

Clean: Improving water quality by incorporating features such as aquatic plants, retention ponds, fountains, and recirculation to help remove nutrients. The aim is also to minimize pollution in the waterways through public education and by building closer people-water relationships.

Developing the ABC Waters Master Plan

To kickstart the programme, PUB initiated demonstration projects at three of the most popular waterbodies — MacRitchie Reservoir, Bedok Reservoir, and a stretch of Kallang River. These projects would be showpieces of what could be achieved through ABC Waters.

With experience gained from implementing the demonstration projects, PUB began to develop a master plan to identify potential projects across the island, for systematic implementation over the next ten to fifteen years. The map of Singapore was divided into three "watersheds", each with its own themes and projects. For each watershed, a consultant team known as the watershed manager (Black & Veatch, CH2M Hill, and CPG Consultants for the Western, Central and Eastern Catchments respectively) was appointed to develop the plans together with other planning agencies such as URA, HDB, JTC, and NParks. Such an integrated approach allowed various agencies to pool ideas and resources and to synergize the planning of infrastructure. For example, PUB's plans to redevelop the stretch of Kallang River running adjacent to Bishan Park were tied in with NParks' plans to overhaul the park. Concurrently, PUB consulted non-governmental organizations and interest groups that had specialist knowledge in particular areas. For example, the Nature Society was invited to share its expertise on plant and animal life.

The ABC Waters Programme will be implemented in phases, starting with the first five-year plan (2007–2011) comprising twenty-eight projects at an estimated cost of S$300 million. Subsequent projects will be further evaluated based on the evolving needs and aspirations of the community.

Engaging the 3P Partners

From the outset, PUB recognized the importance of actively engaging the public, private, and people sector (3P) partners in all aspects of the ABC Waters programme. On its own, PUB lacked the expertise in master planning and landscape design, the knowledge of what residents wanted, and the ability to maintain the projects in the long run. Working closely with the 3P sectors was the best solution to plugging these gaps.

The Public Sector

An inter-agency working committee (IAWC) was set up to coordinate the planning of projects among planning agencies such as PUB, HDB, and NParks. The agencies were also invited to review some of their existing projects to incorporate ABC Waters elements. HDB has done this for some of its estate redevelopments, for instance, at Whampoa Estate along Kallang River. Meanwhile, NParks is working with PUB on several projects, such as the Gardens-by-the-Bay, to integrate adjacent waterways with their parks and park connectors.

Aside from providing technical input, the IAWC has also served as a very useful source of feedback. The agencies involved have had plenty of experience in public consultation, and were aware of what the community wanted. NParks and HDB, for example, had knowledge of the common complaints and requests, as well as the profile of residents who live in various neighbourhoods. These in turn affected the concepts for each project, the facilities proposed, and the way the public education messages were presented to the community.

The Private Sector

To woo the private sector, multiple workshops and seminars were organized to introduce the concept of ABC Waters and to present successful overseas examples of waterfront transformation. Meanwhile, PUB continues to persuade developers to consider installing ABC Waters features. Additional incentives come in the form of "Green Mark"[6] points — that is developers could gain Green Mark points for incorporating ABC Waters elements. Private sector projects have started to come in, mainly from businesses that see the benefits of integrating water elements into their developments.

From a technical standpoint, PUB's Code of Practice on Surface Water Drainage was modified to encourage ABC Waters elements such as water-sensitive landscaping. PUB also developed a set of ABC Waters Design Guidelines, which include design ideas and considerations for the treatment of water edges, and technical guidelines for water sensitive landscaping.

Besides persuading professional engineers and architects on the ground, PUB has also been tapping the experience of renowned experts in the design field. Together with URA and other government agencies, PUB has formed an ABC Waters Review Panel, comprising top local architects, engineers, and developers. In a set-up not unlike the WDP, the panel meets on an *ad hoc* basis to review the ABC Waters Master Plan and the design of strategic ABC Waters projects, providing valuable insights and advice on the ABC Waters Programme.

The People Sector

The most critical group of stakeholders for the ABC Waters programme is the community itself. A week-long public exhibition was held in 2007 featuring the ABC Waters Master Plan. The opening ceremony was officiated by Prime Minister Lee Hsien Loong. In a show of support for the programme at the highest levels, he declared that Singapore would strive to become "a City of Gardens and Water", a significant acknowledgement of the waterways becoming part of the new image of Singapore.

PUB engages the community by encouraging them to develop sustainable projects around the enhanced water features in their neighbourhood. For instance, a community workshop was conducted prior to the launch of the Kolam Ayer project, with participants from grassroots organizations, schools, and interest groups taking part. At the workshop, participants selected the best ideas and were excited about developing them into sustainable projects that would be run by the community itself.

For people to participate enthusiastically in water activities, they have to feel comfortable and safe with water. Hence, all ABC Waters projects are designed with safety as a top priority. PUB has developed an alternative of bringing water closer to people in a safe manner, such as the carving of rivulets and water playgrounds away from the main canal channels, where people can interact safely with water, out of harm's way. Metal railings are replaced by earth mounds, boulders, or shrubs to form a natural barrier along the river bank.

Developing New Dimensions and Capabilities

To unlock the opportunities of the "blue network", a change in mindset was needed from all stakeholders to see drains, canals, and reservoirs not only as utilitarian facilities, but as potential areas for fun-filled community activities and aesthetic appreciation. For PUB, this meant that the water activities had to be managed in a way that safeguards the water quality standards. In addition, drainage engineers were also charged with the task of ensuring that with the introduction of new aesthetic designs for drains and canals, the waterways would still be capable of fulfilling their core functions of flood alleviation and speedy conveyance of surface run-offs. The scale of the ABC Waters Programme also added a more challenging dimension to the project.

In developing the ABC Waters programme, PUB engineers had to utilize new skill sets such as urban planning, environmental engineering, and landscape design. To address this, PUB leveraged both the public and private sectors through the engagement of the Watershed Managers, who worked in consultation with other planning agencies such as URA, HDB, JTC, and NParks. PUB engineers were also able to learn quickly from an NParks senior landscape architect, who was attached to PUB in an advisory capacity for six months.

CONCLUSION

Singapore has done much to turn floods into a thing of the past. The success of its flood management strategy stems from the long-term approach adopted. This is exemplified in the Bukit Timah Flood Alleviation Scheme, where the foresight of the British to earmark land for drainage reserve safeguarded the option to construct a diversion route. Long-term planning continues to underpin the work that is done today. To ensure that new flood areas do not occur with more urbanization, PUB proactively plans for and puts in place early drainage schemes for new developments.

In addition, some of the safeguards and measures that were instituted previously have stood Singapore in good stead to address emerging issues such as rising tide levels due to climate change. Scientists predict that climate change will bring with it more intense rain in Singapore. PUB is taking part in a vulnerability study to understand the impact and implications of climate change on the drainage system and to develop ways to ensure the robustness and efficiency of the system.

Even as PUB enhances drainage efficiency and flood response, it is moving beyond just flood control and flood management to transform utilitarian reservoirs and waterways into Active, Beautiful and Clean Waters. Developing this Programme and realizing its full potential may take a few decades, and the journey promises to be an uncertain but exciting one. Some regard it as a risky and expensive gamble, as allowing people to come close to canals and reservoirs could dirty them. However, PUB is prepared to challenge this mindset, so instead of keeping people away, it is now encouraging them to come closer to water so that they will learn to keep the waters clean. This stems from the strong belief that long-term sustainability for Singapore can only be achieved if the people become stewards of the environment.

PART IV

APPLYING ECONOMICS AND WORKING WITH THE COMMUNITY

9

APPLYING ECONOMIC PRINCIPLES TO ENVIRONMENTAL POLICY

The environment has often been neglected in the early stages of growth, leaving air thick with particulates and water contaminated with effluents. We believe this is a mistake, and one that is extremely expensive to fix in the future.

The Growth Report 2008: Strategies for Sustained
Growth and Inclusive Development; Commission on
Growth and Development

While it values the environment, the government makes decisions on the basis of stringent analysis as it has to prioritize competing demands in the face of limited resources. The full environmental cost of a certain initiative should be factored into the decision making process in order to arrive at the correct decision. In practice, this is seldom straightforward, due to the inherent complexity of environmental issues, such as quantifying intangibles and externalities, managing subjectivity in the value or cost that different individuals attach to the same outcome, and dealing with long timescales over which future scenarios may be uncertain. However, this does not negate the importance of rigorous analysis. In fact, given the subjectivity, there is a greater need to apply sound economic principles when developing environmental policy, to provide clarity on the choice of economic tools and models, as well as the assumptions and scenarios.

In Singapore, the formulation of environmental policies and legislation has benefited from the judicious use of economic principles. Here, we focus on four key areas in which economics has played a key role in guiding environmental policy: (i) in deciding between which projects or options to implement; (ii) in setting appropriate prices or user fees; (iii) when introducing market competition; and (iv) how market failures should be dealt with. Each of these situations is elaborated in the sections that follow.

GUIDING DECISION MAKING

Long-Term Cost Effectiveness

When decisions have to be made on whether to proceed with specific environment projects, a long-term view has to be taken. This means applying economics to evaluate long-term cost effectiveness. While a project might have higher upfront cost, it needs to be balanced against lower lifetime operating cost, potential savings from other related operations, and lower forgone revenue. Low cost projects that are cost-effective in the short term could compromise longer-term cost effectiveness.

Deep Tunnel Sewerage System

This was the basis upon which Singapore decided to embark on the Deep Tunnel Sewerage System (DTSS) project. The growing economy and population in the twenty-first century would impose increasing pressures on the existing used water infrastructure. To cope with the expected increase in used water flow, the options available were to continue expanding the conventional water reclamation plants, or explore a totally novel approach employing new technologies to replace the existing infrastructure. The latter was found to be cost-effective in the long term, albeit more expensive in terms of upfront costs. Hence, despite costing S$7 billion, the option of DTSS was adopted as it would free up scarce land for higher-value economic uses. Moreover, it presented a more sustainable solution that could meet Singapore's needs in the twenty-first century.

Land is a scarce and precious resource in Singapore. The existing sewage treatment works, pumping stations, and buffer zones around them occupy a total land area of 880 hectares. By implementing deep tunnel sewers that convey sewage flows by gravity, the existing sewage treatment facilities will be phased out, with only the two large wastewater works at Changi and Tuas occupying a total of 110 hectares remaining. The resulting savings and enhancements in land value were estimated in 1998 at S$1.5 billion.

If the government had decided not to proceed with the DTSS, the existing treatment facilities would still have to be replaced when worn out, and expanded to cope with the increasing volume of waste water. At the ground breaking ceremony for DTSS on 8 July 2000, then Minister for the Environment Lee Yock Suan mentioned that savings from lower capital and operating cost were estimated at S$3.7 billion. The total savings from both land and facilities were thus estimated at S$5.2 billion. While the upfront cost of DTSS is S$7 billion, with these savings, in the long term, the government is effectively paying S$1.8 billion to provide sewerage infrastructure for Singapore's growing needs.

Unaccounted-for-water

The example of DTSS illustrates how lower operating cost and potential land savings have to be balanced against higher upfront cost. In managing the water distribution system, the government also takes into account foregone revenue in its cost computations, as in the case of reducing unaccounted-for-water (UFW). UFW represents water loss due to leaks, illegal draw-offs in the distribution system, meter inaccuracies, and improper accounting. It is usually regarded as a measure of the efficiency of a water supply system. In Singapore, UFW has been reduced by using good pipe materials (such as cement-lined ductile iron, copper, and stainless steel pipes), optimizing pipe pressure, replacing old and problematic pipes systematically, and actively detecting underground leaks. UFW leaks result in lost value since water is lost from the system, but undertaking measures to prevent leakages can be quite costly too. Though the key consideration in managing UFW is to ensure service reliability, the cost of reducing UFW leakages still has to be weighed against that of supplying more water by developing new water resources.

In the period from 1990 to 2007 when UFW was reduced from 9.5 per cent to 4.4 per cent, about S$200 million was generated through the sales of water which would otherwise have been unaccounted for and, therefore, forgone. Going forward, the government expects to generate additional revenue of S$24 million each year (based on projected water sales and on maintaining UFW at about 4.4 per cent as opposed to 9.5 per cent). This additional revenue generated would be able to recover more than the costs of the various programmes and measures implemented as part of PUB's network maintenance regime, which cost about S$20 million per year currently. Another significant benefit of reducing UFW is the conservation of a scarce resource of strategic importance.

The Next Best Alternative

As part of the government's decision making process, evaluating long-term cost effectiveness is not only confined to individual projects, but also applies across different types of projects. Comparing the merits of different projects requires questioning what the next best alternative is at the national level, particularly if this cuts across different agencies. If land utilization for a specific project can be reduced, what is the benefit of the alternative use? How does the government decide whether a piece of land should be used as a disposal site or for residential development? In economics, exploring the next best alternative essentially means including the implicit opportunity cost. Examples of how opportunity cost shapes decisions are those of reducing buffer zones around water reclamation plants and choosing a landfill site.

Buffer Zone for Water Reclamation Plants

Water reclamation plants (WRPs) that treat used water were previously located in rural areas. Open tanks were used and, given the tropical climate, odour nuisance was inevitable. Hence, a 1-kilometre buffer zone was imposed on these WRPs, within which only limited development was allowed. As the urban area expanded, demand for more land resulted in higher land prices and greater development opportunities for the vacant buffer land. This led to an examination of how the buffer zone around WRPs could be reduced. While it had previously been expensive to cover up the treatment facilities and install odour control facilities, it now made economic sense to do so, since the resulting reduction in buffer zone allowed land to be freed up for other developments, and the value thus created was more than sufficient to compensate for the cost of upgrading the WRPs.

When the project was initially undertaken, reducing the buffer zones around WRPs was projected to have released a total land area of 1,276 hectares with an enhanced value of about S$3,750 million. In comparison, the total cost of covering up the treatment facilities and installing odour control facilities came up to about S$380 million. Hence, the Environment Ministry proceeded to cover up four of the six WRPs, as well as adopt more compact designs for extensions to WRPs and install special odour control facilities. As a result, the buffer zone for WRPs was reduced from 1 kilometre to

500 metres. Land around the WRP could then be released for higher value developments.

Landfill Sites

Projections indicated that existing dumping grounds would be exhausted by the late 1990s. When the Environment Ministry first looked for a new landfill site, the initial intention was to build the next landfill at Punggol. However, with increasing housing demand, HDB had plans to use Punggol for a coastal residential project — this would fetch greater value relative to a landfill due to its waterfront location and its distance away from major industrial developments. Factoring in the opportunity cost of this alternative development, the government took the decision to earmark Punggol as a new housing estate while an alternative site was sourced for the next landfill. After taking into consideration the competing needs for land space on the mainland and the experiences of other countries with similar land scarcity problems, the government conceived the idea of an offshore landfill. This led to the development of Semakau Landfill, which is featured in Chapter 4.

Optimal Timing

In addition to deciding whether to undertake a project, another crucial aspect of the decision making process is determining the best time to initiate the project. In this respect, public sector agencies keep a close eye on global technological developments so that when innovations result in prices becoming economically viable, they are ready to move in. Singapore's NEWater and desalination projects illustrate the need to appreciate the impact of technology on the evaluation of cost effectiveness.

NEWater

Attempts to reclaim water from used water date as far back as the early 1970s. In 1974, the first pilot water reclamation plant was built. However, within a year, the plant was decommissioned, as the 14-month trial concluded that producing potable water from secondary treated effluent was technically achievable, but not cost-effective. Nevertheless, ENV and PUB continued to monitor developments in membrane technology so that when major improvements were made by the late 1990s, they were able to capitalize on this opportunity to reinitiate the water reclamation project. In 1998, a demonstration-scale NEWater plant was commissioned in Singapore, which proved that the cost of water reclamation had indeed come down substantially, making it economically viable to produce NEWater on a large scale. Following a successful trial and extensive testing of water quality, full-scale NEWater factories were progressively rolled out, and NEWater will supply 30 per cent of Singapore's water demand by 2011. The NEWater produced caters primarily to industries demanding ultra pure water such as wafer fabrication, petrochemical plants, and commercial air-conditioning cooling towers.

Desalination

For Singapore, which is an island, desalination is a natural solution to its water needs. Desalination provides a steady source of water, unaffected by variations in rainfall. However, up to the 1990s, desalination technology consisted mainly of evaporating seawater to separate fresh water and dissolved salts, that is, via a distillation process. As this process was highly energy intensive, it was only adopted by oil-rich Middle Eastern countries. Like NEWater, recent technological advancements allowed desalination to be effected using an alternative method — reverse osmosis via membranes, which is estimated to cost about 20 per cent lower than traditional distillation methods. PUB recognized the potential for this new development to bring down the cost of desalination, and decided to call a tender for the private sector to design, build, own, and operate (DBOO) a desalination plant. SingSpring Pte Ltd, a wholly-owned subsidiary of Hyflux, was awarded the contract for the first desalination facility in Singapore. The 30-mgd SingSpring desalination plant at Tuas was successfully delivered and commissioned in September 2005.

Apart from being a lower-cost production method, another major advantage of using membranes for NEWater and desalination is easy scalability. Traditional fractional distillation plants entailed large-scale investments, which locks in a particular technology. In comparison, membrane-based solutions can be implemented in modules and can easily accommodate technological advances.

SETTING APPROPRIATE PRICES

Cost Recovery

Using economic principles to guide the decision making process helps in determining whether to go ahead with a particular project, following which a decision has to be made on who should pay for the project. Unless market failures exist or public goods are being provided, the user is generally made to pay the full-cost recovery price for the goods or services provided to ensure that market forces work to determine the right allocation of resources. In the next few examples, we highlight sewerage services as a public benefit where the government does not charge full-cost recovery. This is in contrast to the treatment of used water and waste incineration services where charges are set at cost recovery.

As a large infrastructural project, the used water distribution infrastructure required large capital investments. Among these, the sewerage network has been regarded as a public benefit and access to proper sanitation deemed a basic necessity, since the public health benefits that stem from a good sewerage system, such as the control of water-borne diseases, do not diminish with more users, nor is it practical to exclude non-paying users. Therefore, the sewerage network is owned and funded entirely by the government. The same reasoning does not apply to other parts of the used water distribution infrastructure, such as the treatment of used water in water reclamation plants, as consumers have discretion over the amount of used water that they discharge and send to the water reclamation plants for treatment. Hence, the water reclamation plants are owned by PUB, with their capital and operating costs recovered through user fees.

The provision of waste incineration services is costly due to the capital intensive nature of constructing and operating incineration plants. Apart from bearing the financing risk of paying the upfront cost, the government also had to bear the design and operational risk for the first few incineration plants since the concept of incinerating mixed waste in a tropical setting had not been tested on a large scale before. As in the case of the treatment of used water in water reclamation plants, incineration services are not considered a public good since consumers have discretion over the waste disposed. The gate fees at these facilities are reviewed yearly and are set on a cost recovery basis, which includes the recovery of capital cost, to ensure economic sustainability in the waste disposal sector.

Setting Prices to Reflect Other Policy Considerations

Although cost recovery is a primary consideration in setting prices, the government does not always adhere rigidly to this if there are good reasons to deviate from it. In the previous section, we touched on the provision of public good as a reason for deviation. However, there are also other policy considerations for not setting prices at cost recovery such as promoting conservation of scarce resources, helping consumers adjust, and keeping cost affordable.

Pricing of Potable Water

In a fundamental review of water pricing conducted in 1997, the price of potable water had two clear components. The water tariff was explicitly set to recover the full cost of production and supply, while the water conservation tax (WCT) was intended to reflect the higher cost of alternative water supply sources. The former ensured that the true cost of supplying water today would be properly accounted for — this was important because experiences in other countries had shown that under-recovery of water charges could lead to deteriorating services and under-investment in future capacity. Neither was it right for PUB to collect more revenue than it required for its operations.

While charging cost recovery rates would cover the cost of meeting water demand today, it would not be an accurate reflection of the marginal cost of supply, since water is a scarce resource. This means that the next available source of water would be more expensive than the current sources, hence pricing at cost recovery alone would result in over-consumption of the scarce resource. To ensure that consumers are conscious of this, they have to pay an additional levy known as the WCT, which is pegged to the cost of the marginal source, which at the time was desalinated water. Unlike the water tariff which is collected by PUB, WCT revenues are channelled directly to the Ministry of Finance, which can then be used to fund other worthy expenditure.

Gate Fees at Incineration Plants

Another instance in which prices deviated from cost recovery rates was in the setting of gate fees at the incineration plants. Before April 1991, gate fees were deliberately priced far below cost recovery levels to discourage illegal dumping. For the same rationale, trucks used to be able to bring one load of refuse a day of less than half a tonne for disposal without having to pay any fees.

However, this was not sustainable. The actual cost of disposing refuse borne by the government was going up as the growing volume of waste from an expanding economy meant that a fourth incineration plant and a larger landfill site (constructed offshore at Semakau due to a lack of alternatives on the mainland) were needed. In tandem with economic growth, land prices were also going up. Furthermore, subsidizing refuse disposal inhibited the waste recovery and recycling industry, as waste generators would find it cheaper to dispose of their waste rather than go for recycling.

It was increasingly not feasible to continue subsidizing waste disposal in order to discourage illegal dumping. Instead, punitive measures such as fines of S$10,000 and tighter enforcement were put in place to reduce the incidence of illegal dumping.

Even when the government decided to move towards cost recovery, the adjustment process was gradual. It took more than ten years to bring the gate fees on par with costs — from S$15 per tonne in 1991 to S$77 per tonne in 2002. Prices were not adjusted by more than S$10 per tonne each year. Disposal companies were also encouraged to absorb the initial increase. The gradual approach was adopted to ensure that the impact on households would be gradual. For every S$10 increase in incineration gate fees, a typical household in HDB flats would incur an increase of 90 cents a month for refuse collection fees. Apart from adjusting prices, fee exemptions for trucks disposing less than half a tonne of waste were also removed after a nine-month grace period. The grace period was to allow some forty small contractors who had been taking advantage of the exemption to rework their contracts with the waste generators to whom they were providing services.

Differential Pricing

Apart from setting fees and charges at cost recovery, the government also ensures that there is sufficient differentiation and flexibility in the fees and charges, so that price signals can optimize the allocation of scarce resources. Such examples can be found in Singapore's waste management industry.

Solid Waste Disposal Fees

In the incineration industry, Ulu Pandan Incineration Plant (in the central part of Singapore) and Senoko Incineration Plant (in the northern part of Singapore) are sited at more accessible locations.

Hence, differential gate fees were used to divert some of the waste to less accessible plants in the west (Tuas and Tuas South), so as to even out the loads arriving at each plant and avoid overcrowding. For this reason, Senoko's gate fee in 2007 was S$81 per tonne while Ulu Pandan's gate fee was S$87 per tonne for peak hours (between 7.30 a.m. to 2 p.m.) and S$81 per tonne for off-peak hours (after 2 p.m.), compared with S$77 per tonne in less accessible plants such as Tuas and Tuas South.

Since about half the waste disposed of in Singapore comes from the industrial and commercial sectors, a framework has been put in place to encourage recycling among the industries. The waste disposal fees for industries are pegged to the volume of waste they produce. Through market forces, industries would be incentivized to recycle if the cost of recycling is lower than waste disposal.

INTRODUCING MARKET COMPETITION

The previous section discusses how prices are set when the good or service is provided by the government. Increasingly, the government is allowing the market to provide goods and services wherever possible, in line with the economic tenet that free markets are usually more efficient in the allocation of resources. This has been Singapore's experience in introducing market competition in three areas: waste collection, incineration plants, and NEWater.

Waste Collection

In the mid-1980s, there had been many calls to privatize refuse collection services for domestic premises. However, the government decided not to go ahead with privatization on the following grounds: (i) refuse collection was considered an essential service; (ii) private companies could lock in their collection system and make it difficult and costly to switch; and (iii) service quality could deteriorate as profit maximizing companies cut corners.

In the 1990s, the privatization plan for waste collection was reviewed again and a cautious two-step approach was adopted. First, in 1996, the government waste collection arm was incorporated into a separate entity and given a three-year monopoly. This allowed the government time to monitor and convince itself that service quality and fees were not affected. Subsequently, in 1999, Singapore was divided into nine sectors where domestic waste collection was competitively tendered. Previous concerns over privatization were addressed through licensing conditions and a transparent fee structure. Efficiency gains have been realized from greater competition. In the second round of tender, the average refuse collection fee fell by approximately 30 per cent for flats and 15 per cent for landed premises, resulting in lower waste collection fees for residents.

Incineration Plants

Following the privatization of the refuse collection services in 1999, the Environment Ministry decided to liberalize the incineration plant (IP) industry with the objectives of: (i) further increasing efficiency and innovation in the sector by injecting competition; and (ii) developing the environmental engineering industry by transferring environmental engineering expertise residing with the government to the private sector.

In 2001, an open tender was called to develop the fifth IP on a design, build, own, and operate (DBOO) basis under a free market model with the potential developer taking the financial, design, and demand risk. The tender was, however, not well received by the market, with only one non-compliant bid submitted. The primary reason for the poor response was that potential bidders were unable to bear the demand risk associated with uncertain waste growth and a non-guaranteed waste stream, plus the high capital outlay required for IPs.

Learning from the experience, the Environment Ministry then decided to adopt a DBOO scheme under a full take-or-pay approach.

In this structure, the government would bear the demand risk of refuse throughput, by giving the DBOO operator full capacity payment regardless of the actual utilization rate of the IP. In return, the DBOO operator bears the operational risk. This meant that the DBOO operator would receive payments for availability of incineration capacity, the actual amount of refuse incinerated, and for the generation of electricity. In addition, the DBOO operator was required to meet two other performance indicators on quality of the incineration process (measured in terms of ash carbon content) and service quality level to waste collectors (measured in terms of turnaround time). If any of these specified performance levels are not met, the DBOO operator is required to take immediate remedial measures. Financial penalties can also be imposed.

Because of the heavy capital investment involved, a twenty-five-year contract was provided to the DBOO operator. Due to the long-term nature of the contract, payment variations based on changes in the consumer index were built into the fixed and variable components of the payment mechanism to take into account changes in inflation rates. Bidders are required to indicate the variable rates in their bid prices. Payment adjustments and profit sharing were also allowed in cases of changes in law, step change in technologies, refinancing gains, and third-party revenues arising from alternative uses of the plant's assets.

With this approach, a more equitable sharing of risk was achieved, which was well received by the market, with more competitive bids submitted by various companies. The fifth IP DBOO tender was successfully awarded to Keppel Seghers Engineering Pte Ltd in November 2005. This plant is currently being constructed and scheduled to be ready for commercial operation in mid-2009. From the experience gained through this tender and with support from NEA, Keppel managed to secure S$1.7 billion worth of solid waste management contracts in Qatar in 2006. This was followed in 2007 by another contract of a S$1.5 billion wastewater treatment and reuse plant in Qatar. With more private sector involvement in the waste management industry, the government's role is evolving from being a provider of services to being the overall regulator of the industry. This will provide opportunities to tap the private sector's expertise and maximize efficiency.

NEWater Plants

From the two earlier examples on privatization, one can see that a key success factor is the efficient allocation of risk. Private sector companies, being smaller than government as a whole, tend to be more risk averse. Therefore, it is important to allocate risk to the party that is in the best position to bear it. In the case of incineration plants, demand risk was a crucial consideration. In the next example on NEWater, not only was there some demand risk, but there was also technology risk in implementing the project, as the NEWater production process was still in its infancy.

Given the risk involved, PUB took the lead in developing Singapore's first NEWater plants at Bedok, Kranji, and Seletar. This helped to facilitate collaboration with global water companies such as General Electric Water & Process Technologies,Veolia Water, and Siemens Water Technologies, together with local companies such as Hyflux, as they worked together to implement various technologies at the NEWater plants. This allowed the private sector to gain confidence in the reliability and effectiveness of the new technologies, and build up its capability in operating a NEWater plant through working with PUB on-site. At this stage, PUB decided to offer private sector companies the opportunity to build and operate a NEWater plant through a DBOO model.

In 2007, about five years after PUB completed its first plant at Bedok, the fourth NEWater plant was commissioned. This plant at Ulu Pandan was built by Keppel Seghers and would supply PUB with 32 mgd of NEWater for twenty years. The payment structure for the Ulu Pandan project was fairly similar to that for the incineration plant. A two-part tariff based on availability and output was used. The availability payment, based on available capacity, covered the fixed cost of capital, overheads, maintenance, and energy. The output payment, which was dependent on the actual quantity of water output, covered the variable part of overheads, maintenance, and energy.

Contractual measures were also structured to ensure that the quantity and quality of water supply meet required standards. To do so, the DBOO agreements included clauses to impose penalties on non-performance such as not maintaining required capacity, or inadequate emergency product water storage. Other measures to mitigate potential impact on service continuity include "step-in" provisions in the event the concession company failed or was in default. For example, PUB could step in to manage the concession company's staff and equipment, or allow private financiers to identify other potential service providers that could take over operations. In addition, a comprehensive monitoring and audit system was put in place for all projects to allow PUB to check regularly on water quality, operation, and maintenance of the plants. This included linking the plant's key online water quality monitoring system to PUB's monitoring systems and having water sampled and analysed regularly at an accredited laboratory.

To meet the growing demand for NEWater, PUB in 2008 further embarked on the construction of a 50 mgd NEWater factory at Changi Water Reclamation Plant under a twenty-five-year DBOO arrangement with Sembcorp Utilities. With economies of scale, productivity gains, and more competitive membrane technologies, PUB was able to bring down the cost of NEWater production over the last few years.

Public-private partnership arrangements through DBOO are not just about reaping efficiency gains. Such arrangements are valuable and highly strategic learning opportunities for private companies to interact with government agencies over an extended period of time, tapping each others' amassed expertise and experience. Keppel had invited PUB to be actively involved in the Ulu Pandan NEWater project from the design and construction phase. In fact, Keppel had attached their plant manager and operators to PUB's Bedok NEWater factory for on-the-job training. PUB also invited Keppel's staff to attend in-house training courses to build up capabilities in construction, commissioning, and the subsequent operation of NEWater factories. Similarly, staff from Keppel Seghers are also receiving training on incineration plant operations at NEA's IPs. Such unusually close collaborations with industry partners help them build up technical expertise and process know-how. The government benefits as it ensures that services outsourced to the private sector will continue to be as reliable and efficient as before.

DEALING WITH MARKET FAILURE

Whilst market solutions are explored wherever possible, free markets generally work well only when there is perfect competition and information. In reality, market failures are common for a variety of reasons. Here, government intervention through grants, price mechanisms, or legislation is required to correct the market failure.

Correcting Externalities

Externalities occur when actions taken by economic agents during a transaction have cost and benefit implications on other parties that are not part of the initial transaction. Common examples of negative externalities include smoking and noise pollution, while positive externalities include good forest management and clean air. Broadly, externalities are dealt with in two ways. One is to get the polluter to face the true cost of the impact imposed on others. The other is through a quota system.

Air Pollution

In terms of air pollution, lead concentration levels in Singapore were rising due to strong growth in vehicle population in the first half of the 1980s. Studies have shown that lead can affect the proper functioning of the brain and lungs. Motorists contributing to lead pollution in the air create a negative health externality among pedestrians and those living or working near roads, which motorists themselves do not internalize since most vehicles are air-conditioned.

This market failure was corrected through legislation and by pricing the externality. To control the emission of lead from motor vehicles, lead in petrol was progressively reduced from an uncontrolled level of about 0.84 g/l to 0.15 g/l in 1987. In addition, the use of unleaded petrol was promoted through a differential tax system which made unleaded petrol about 10 cents per litre cheaper than leaded petrol. These measures led to significant improvements in the air quality. The lead level in ambient air dropped to 1.2µg/Nm^3 in 1990 and then to 0.1µg/Nm^3 in 2000. Leaded petrol was totally phased out by 1998.

Water Pollution

Another common externality is water pollution from industrial plants. Singapore deals with this externality through a combination of legislation and pricing. As rainwater is channelled to the reservoirs and eventually treated to potable quality, catchments need to be protected from pollution resulting from the illegal discharge of trade effluent, which is defined as liquid discharges from any trade, business, manufacturing, or construction site. Regulations have been put in place to control the discharge of trade effluent, both under the Environmental Protection and Management (Trade Effluent) Regulations for the control of trade effluent discharged into watercourses and land, as well as the Sewerage and Drainage (Trade Effluent) Regulations for the control of trade effluent into public sewers. The former is administered by NEA, whilst the latter by PUB.

Under the Environmental Protection and Management Regulations, trade effluent has to be treated before it is discharged into watercourses or land. Any effluent released must not be a hazard to human health or a public nuisance (such as of a foul odour). The party who discharges the effluent is required to install and make available the results from test points, inspection chambers, flow meters, and other recording apparatuses at the point of discharge. First time offenders can be fined up to S$10,000, while subsequent offenders face double the fine.

The Sewerage and Drainage (Trade Effluent) Regulations controls the discharge of used water from domestic, industrial, agricultural, and other premises into the public sewers. The Regulations allow certain industries that produce biodegradable waste water to discharge their effluent into public sewers, as long as they are in accordance with specified water quality limits. These Regulations ensure that trade effluent collected can be treated by water reclamation plants to levels that comply with discharge standards into the watercourses. The Trade Effluent Tariff Scheme was also introduced to allow applicants to discharge slightly lower quality effluent into the public sewer for a fee. The fee is meant to recover the costs incurred in treating the additional pollution load at water reclamation plants.

Ozone Depleting Substances

The two above examples tackle externalities through the price mechanism. Another means is through using quotas. A tender and quota allocation system is used to control the amount of ozone depleting substance (ODS) imported for use in Singapore. On 5 January 1989, Singapore became a party to the Montreal Protocol, which is an international treaty to phase out ODS such as chlorofluorocarbons (CFCs) and halon. With an economy highly dependent on the electronics and chemical industries, policies to phase out ODS had to be handled with care.

Singapore's transitional experience was rather unique as it was among the first to regulate the use of ODS with a market-based allocation mechanism. Launched on 5 October 1989, the Tender and Quota Allocation System (TQS) allowed market forces to determine the price that industries had to pay for ODS. The system achieved two desirable outcomes, namely, the distribution of the limited quantity of available ODS to those with the highest replacement costs, and a strong market signal to induce ODS users to look into substitutes, conservation measures, and recycling.

To help companies make the transition, the Singapore Productivity and Standards Board offered technical consultancy and services to firms who wanted to recycle controlled ODS or to switch to substitutes. A sum of S$1.6 million from the Public Sector R&D fund was granted to the Board to initiate the various ODS alternative and conservation programmes. The scheme allowed for the hiring of experts in ODS alternative technologies. Many local SMEs, which generally lacked in-house expertise, benefited from this scheme.

As a result, Singapore successfully phased out the consumption of ODS by January 1996, well ahead of the time frame set for developing countries, which was 2010. For its contributions, Singapore was presented the Outstanding Ozone Unit Award by the United Nations Environment Programme (UNEP) at the 9th Meeting of Parties in Montreal in 1997.

Remedying Information Asymmetries

Another common cause of market failure is information asymmetry, which occurs when economic agents do not have the same amount of information or have imperfect and incomplete information. Information asymmetries are dealt with by passing legislation that facilitates the sharing of more information with those who are making consumption decisions.

One example is the introduction of a water efficiency labelling scheme (WELS), which aims to empower customers by allowing them to make informed choices. WELS was introduced in 2006 on a voluntary basis, covering taps, showerheads, dual-flush low-capacity flushing cisterns (LCFCs), urinals, and clothes washing machines. As WELS was voluntary, most suppliers and manufacturers registered only the more water-efficient models, constituting only 16 per cent of the market. Because of the ineffectiveness of a voluntary approach, the Mandatory Water Efficiency Labelling Scheme (MWELS) will be launched in 2009 for taps, LCFCs, and urinals.

Similarly, NEA mandated energy labelling for two major energy-using devices — air-conditioners and refrigerators — starting in 2008, to make consumers aware of the potential savings of the devices. Informal feedback from retailers suggests that this has spurred increased sales of four-tick (most efficient) air-conditioners, even though these cost more upfront. Labelling endorsed by the government is seen as independent and helps to reduce "search" costs, which is the opportunity cost of the time spent by consumers in finding out about energy and water consumption of the appliances. This also reduces information asymmetry, since manufacturers or retailers can no longer make unsubstantiated claims about their products' resource efficiency.

Public Goods

Public goods are defined as products that are non-rival (consumption of the good by one individual does not reduce the amount available for consumption by another individual) and non-exclusive (difficult to limit consumption to paying individuals). Examples of public goods are beautiful water landscapes and a clean living environment. Since the private sector is unable to recover the cost from those who enjoy a public good, it either does not have any incentive to produce the good or produces an amount that is below the social optimum. Government intervention either through enforcement or direct provision is often needed in the optimal provision of public goods.

Cleanliness, in the form of a pleasant environment and the absence of foul odours and diseases can be considered a public good. One's consumption of cleanliness does not reduce the benefit another person gets from enjoying it. It is also difficult to exclude non-paying individuals from enjoying the benefits of cleanliness. Hence, the government has to help bring about public cleanliness by setting standards and enforcing them. Those caught littering are made to pay a fine or carry out corrective work orders (by cleaning up a public place) as a deterrent. (Details on how the government addresses the issue of public cleanliness are given in Chapter 3.)

Related to public cleanliness is the ABC Waters programme. This programme seeks to transform waterways and waterbodies into beautiful rivers and lakes so that people can enjoy water based activities such as canoeing and sailing, and in so doing, appreciate the value of having clean waters. (More details on ABC Waters are in Chapter 8.) As the benefits of ABC Waters accrue to the general public, the government has taken the lead in transforming waterways, as this will create a better living environment and improve quality of life in Singapore.

Split Incentives and Bounded Rationality

An emerging form of market failure stems from split incentives and bounded rationality. A good example to illustrate this concept can be drawn from the initiatives to promote energy efficiency in buildings. Developers bear the initial upfront cost of constructing a building, while occupants face the recurrent cost of living or operating in the building. When it comes to the incorporation of energy-efficient features and fixtures, there is a split incentive. Developers tend to build in features and fixtures that minimize the initial upfront cost, even if this means higher recurrent cost imposed on occupants. Compounding this problem, occupants are rationally bounded, that is, they often do not have the time and resources to demand energy-efficient features and fixtures as the benefits are relatively small.

This combination of split incentives and bounded rationality has resulted in a market failure, which calls for government intervention.

The government is beginning to deal with this by setting standards. For instance, in 2007, the Building and Construction Authority (BCA) enhanced current legislation requiring new buildings and existing ones undergoing major retrofitting to meet certain environmental sustainability standards (termed Green Mark) in several areas such as energy efficiency, water efficiency, project management, indoor air quality, and building innovation.

CONCLUSION

This chapter highlights the role economics plays in guiding environmental policies and legislation in areas such as decision making, setting prices, introducing market competition, and dealing with market failures. When used in setting prices, economics helps allocate limited goods and services to consumers who value them the most as charging helps to reveal what the consumer is prepared to pay. Market competition helps in determining the most efficient and effective means of providing a good or service. With market failure, economics helps correct the failure and enables markets to work better.

Economics is used as a tool to arrive at the best decision in the interest of the public. The rigour of economic analysis ensures that decisions made can stand the test of time and scrutiny. However, there may be occasions when prices have to be calibrated to take into account other policy considerations, such as in meeting social needs. Pricing can be a powerful tool to shape public behaviour and consumption when the correct costs and incentives are in place. To complement the pricing mechanism, targeted help can also be made available to the lower-income groups, for example, in the form of Utilities Save rebates (see Chapter 6).

Applying economic principles alone may not provide all the answers, and it is important to understand and appreciate their limitations too. Evaluating issues that stem from social or environmental concerns may not be as straightforward as simply carrying out a cost-benefit analysis, since quantifying these concerns would depend on the values and perspectives of different individuals. Nevertheless, economics is a constantly evolving field, and there has been increasing interest in applying economics to the environment, such as in valuing the cost of pollution or the loss of certain habitats. This will offer even more avenues in which economic analysis can be used to guide environmental policy.

In the final analysis, economics is only a tool. It can support and complement, but not replace, a clear vision and strategic priorities.

10

WORKING WITH PEOPLE AND THE COMMUNITY

Let us resolve today to do our part, no matter how modest our contribution may appear. Let us bear in mind that the quality of our living environment will depend not only on grand future decisions but on many modest decisions we take each day.

Minister for the Environment Mah Bow Tan,
at the Closing Ceremony of the Clean and Green Week,
12 November 1994

While most people want a good and clean environment, many may not be sufficiently motivated to act in the interest of the public good to achieve such an outcome. Government intervention is, therefore, necessary to ensure that there is adequate provision of environmental goods and services, as well as to shape individual and organizational decisions to be in line with the desired environmental outcomes. In addition to government investment in environmental infrastructure and government provision of basic environmental services such as public cleansing, other levers which the government employs to ensure a quality environment are the enactment of legislation, coupled with effective enforcement, to make sure that minimum standards are complied with, and the provision of incentives to influence behaviour.

That said, government action alone is insufficient to deliver and sustain a high-quality environment. For instance, while the government can provide infrastructure such as recycling facilities or information on the water or energy efficiency of household appliances, these will come to nought if the public does not use the infrastructure or make informed decisions in support of the environment. Ultimately, the public has to appreciate the importance of the environment and play its part in contributing towards achieving a good environment. This requires not just awareness about environmental challenges, but a mindset and behavioural change towards shared ownership and responsibility.

The Ministry's approach towards working with people and the community is encapsulated in the phrase "3P Partnership", where the 3Ps represent the Public, Private, and People sectors or the various stakeholders in the environment. The premise of 3P Partnership is that environmental sustainability can only be achieved through a multi-stakeholder approach. The desired outcome of 3P Partnership is to build a community that takes ownership of the environment and is willing to contribute to achieving a good environment. 3P Partnership comprises three key thrusts: (i) communicate, (ii) engage, and (iii) empower.

COMMUNICATION

The first step in galvanizing the community towards environmental ownership is to make its members aware of the issues at hand, as well as how they can contribute towards addressing the challenges. Communication is also the first step towards creating a sense of interest and ownership over the environment, which will then motivate people to take action to sustain it.

Keep Singapore Clean Campaign[1]

The 1968 "Keep Singapore Clean" campaign was the first national campaign dedicated to the creation and maintenance of a healthy and sustainable environment in Singapore. The campaign was born out of the government's recognition that public cooperation and participation were crucial if it wanted to improve the living environment and state of cleanliness in Singapore. While government provision of public cleansing services was one part of the cleanliness equation, the other part was to make the public aware of the importance of cleanliness, educate them on appropriate social behaviour, and inculcate in them a sense of civic-mindedness.

To ensure that the Keep Singapore Clean message was driven home to the general public, the mass media was enlisted to provide maximum publicity for the campaign. Feature articles and programmes were published in the press. Jingles, newsreels, documentaries, filmlets, and slides were broadcast daily over television and radio. Hundreds of thousands of posters and banners were displayed in shops, restaurants, offices, factories, community centres, bus shelters, and public notice boards. "Keep Singapore Clean" rubber stamps, seals, and postal franking of all correspondence and postal articles were used. All letters and bills from government and statutory boards, and even cinema tickets, were stamped with the slogan "Keep Singapore Clean". Even petroleum companies distributed "Keep Singapore Clean" car stickers to consumers at petrol stations. Never before was the public subjected to a publicity blitz on such a massive scale.

Key to the success of these early efforts was the commitment of government leaders. The campaign was launched by then Prime Minister Lee Kuan Yew himself. Following the launch, Members of Parliament, together with community leaders, brought the government's messages down to the constituency level through house-to-house visits, rallies, competitions, and exhibitions, to get as many of their constituency members involved as possible. The seeds of community volunteerism were sown through the formation of "broomstick brigades", comprising volunteers to clean up the common areas of their constituencies, often with the Members of Parliament rolling up their sleeves and leading the way. These positive demonstrations of leadership by example widened the reach of the national campaigns from mere rhetoric to actual action.

In addition, competitions were held to select the ten cleanest schools, community centres, markets, government offices, and restaurants. Besides applying the "carrot" approach to reward people for their exemplary conduct, the government also used the "stick" to very good effect. Films and photographs of places and establishments found to be dirty as well as members of the public caught in the act of littering the streets were broadcast on television and published in the press. The ten dirtiest premises were also named and publicized. Social pressure thus became a tool both at the individual and organizational levels to "Keep Singapore Clean".

The Keep Singapore Clean Campaign also marked the first time that fines were used as a means to regulate and enforce social behaviour. People caught littering public areas after the campaign were fined to a tune of up to S$500, not a small sum in those days. Those issued fines had to bear public scrutiny and suffer the inconvenience of queuing for hours in front of City Hall to pay the fines, which had a further deterrent effect against other would-be offenders.

Water Is Precious Campaign

National crises also provided the impetus and opportunity to effect change. The images of water rationing in 1963 and 1964 were fresh in people's minds when another similar water shortage crisis loomed in 1971. That year, PUB launched the first "Water is Precious" campaign. The campaign focused on reminding the public of the inconveniences of water rationing in the 1960s so they would make a concerted effort to cut down water consumption. Not only were "save water" messages broadcast on TV and radio, but the newspapers also reported Singapore's daily water consumption, indicating the increase or decrease from the previous day so citizens could see the result of their efforts. The young were not forgotten, with PUB handing out colourful posters and stickers to school children through the Ministry of Education (MOE). All in all, the efforts succeeded in bringing down water consumption by 4.9 per cent.

The "Water is Precious" campaign helped to tide the country through the drought without the need for water rationing. The campaigns not only encouraged people to adopt water saving habits through small but practical ways, but at the same time drove home the message that saving water had to become a daily habit for Singaporeans.

Environmental Education

In addition to national-level campaigns to communicate to the general public the importance of caring for the environment, a more targeted approach was adopted to raise the awareness of the young through schools, so as to inculcate in them good environmental habits from a young age.

Since the 1980s, the Environment Ministry has worked with the MOE to incorporate environmental elements into the formal curriculum for schools, in subjects such as social studies, geography, and biology. Ministry officers also regularly conducted talks during school assemblies on issues ranging from littering to recycling to water conservation, and provided collaterals and educational materials such as posters and exhibition panels for display in the schools.

To help students develop a greater appreciation for the pervasiveness of environmental issues and the challenges involved in ensuring a good environment, programmes were designed to take them "behind the scenes" and immerse them in what goes into the making of the environment they enjoy. For example, "Learning Journeys" or experiential and hands-on learning through site visits, are organized to key installations such as incineration plants, Semakau landfill, meteorological stations, water treatment plants, and nature parks.

ENGAGEMENT

Following on from communication, the next thrust under the 3P Partnership approach is engagement. As a two-way process, engagement allows the government to seek views and feedback from the private and people sectors and tap their expertise. This injects additional perspectives to the environmental policy making process and also helps to develop a close partnership with the private and people sector over time. In addition, the two-way dialogue allows the government to convey the considerations behind specific policies, including the various options considered and the trade-offs involved, thereby increasing the level of public acceptance and support.

Clean and Green Singapore

The new series of annual public education campaigns, under the banner "Clean and Green Week" (CGW), which took off from 1990 onwards, was characteristic of the engagement approach. For instance, environmentally committed organizations and businesses were roped in to co-organize and even take the lead for various activities during the campaign. From 2004, the Community Development Councils (CDCs) took turns to co-organize the launch of the CGW in partnership with NEA. This helped to establish the CGW as an integral part of building strong community bonds. In 2007, the CGW was further revamped into a year-long initiative called Clean and Green Singapore (CGS), to signal the importance of environmental ownership. The new CGS initiative aims to inspire individual

Singaporeans to care for and protect the living environment by making green practices and green consumerism an integral part of their daily lives.

Singapore Green Plan

The first United Nations Conference on Environment and Development (UNCED), or the Earth Summit as it is more popularly known, was held in Rio de Janeiro, Brazil, in June 1992. This historic conference was convened by the U.N. General Assembly with the intention of elaborating on the strategies and measures needed to halt and reverse the effects of environmental degradation and to promote sustainable development in all countries.

In the lead-up to the Earth Summit, the Environment Ministry formulated a comprehensive environmental master plan for Singapore called the Singapore Green Plan (SGP). The aim of the SGP was to capture Singapore's efforts in environmental sustainability, and demonstrate its commitment towards shaping Singapore into a model Green City in the twenty-first century, thereby providing a high-quality living environment for its residents.

The Ministry realized that for the plan to be effective, it had to resonate with the people that it was intended to benefit. Hence, a key consideration in the formulation of the SGP was to involve and consult as many people as possible. Besides internal consultations within the government, draft copies of the SGP were circulated widely amongst the public for comments.[2] Public forums were held to explain the goals and targets and further publicize the plan, thereby garnering much support and feedback.

The extensive public consultations sparked the interest of many who had previously been ambivalent towards the environment. In fact, more than 100,000 people visited the Singapore Green Plan Exhibition, held in tandem with the launch of the SGP action programmes during Clean and Green Week in 1993. In his speech at the opening of the Singapore Green Plan Exhibition, then Minister for the Environment Mah Bow Tan underscored the critical role played by the individual: "For the Green Plan to succeed, we will need the strong support, commitment and participation of Singaporeans from all walks of life. The man in the street can, and should, through his simple, everyday actions, help to translate the vision under the Green Plan into reality."

The SGP was subsequently reviewed and updated in 2002 and 2005 to ensure that it remained relevant and up to date. The 2005 review involved eight months of widespread public consultation through a variety of platforms, including Internet surveys, a round table discussion, a public exhibition, and the formation of focus groups which comprised about sixty 3P sector representatives. The focus group discussions were not confined to these representatives, but also reached out to the relevant industry and interest groups.

The approach taken in the SGP formulation and reviews is but one example of the many steps that the government started taking to engage individuals in becoming members of a more environmentally proactive Singapore society.

Opening up of Reservoirs

Another significant step taken to move beyond public education is through the opening up of reservoirs to the public for non-pollutive recreational activities such as canoeing, kayaking, wakeboarding, and sailing. The intention is to get more people closer to water to build a relationship with it, as the Ministry realized that besides showing how everyone can be water wise, there is also a need to educate people on the need to value Singapore's waterbodies and keep them clean. This is especially important for Singapore today since much of Singapore already serves as water catchments.

Engaging Schools

The move towards engaging schools involves organizing joint initiatives with schools as well as other partners. Going beyond raising awareness, engagement places more emphasis on getting teachers and students involved in developing and implementing environmental initiatives, creating greater buy-in, participation, and ownership of the programmes.

The NEA has established a network of Environmental Education Advisors (EEAs) within the schools since 1994. This network acts as a key point of contact and facilitates better communication between teachers and NEA, making both parties more accessible to each other. Regular networking sessions are organized for EEAs to gather feedback from teachers, generate ideas to improve existing or develop new initiatives, and allow teachers to share experiences and best practices with one another.

MOE's Community Involvement Programme, which involves students contributing their time and services to the community beyond their regular curriculum, is another avenue used to engage teachers and students in environmental areas such as water, resource conservation, public hygiene, and recycling. An example is the Seashore Life Programme, launched in 1997, where students learn about seashore life and the harmful effects of pollution on the marine environment. At the same time, they help to clean up the beach as their contribution to the community and to protect the ecosystem of the beaches. The programme was jointly developed by NEA and HSBC and includes the development of teachers' guides and students' activity sheets/books. Another example is PUB's Our Waters programme, which allows 3P partners to pick a waterway or reservoir and care for it for at least two years. In recent years, more schools are participating in the programme. St Andrew's Secondary school was the first "adopter" of the programme. With the support of PUB, the school has organized activities such as clean-ups along Kallang River and the development of an educational story board on the history of Kallang River.

EMPOWERMENT

By engaging its partners to conceptualize and organize environmental initiatives jointly, there is greater buy-in and contribution to the success of Ministry-initiated schemes and programmes. More importantly, engaging partners also helps to build up their capacity and paves the way to empowering them into implementing their own initiatives. These self-initiated actions and programmes are ultimately what is necessary to achieve environmental sustainability for Singapore.

Schools

Some schools have begun to spearhead environmental initiatives, for instance, implementing their own environment education modules and organizing environment-themed seminars. Nanyang Girls' High School, for example, has been hosting a Biennial Regional Environmental Science Conference since 2005, whilst Nan Hua High School has been holding an annual Youth Environmentalist Forum since 2006. These forums have provided the younger generation with invaluable opportunities for the cross-fertilization of ideas, and broadened their environmental perspectives. Beyond just talk, students have also rolled up their sleeves to do their bit for the environment. For example, students have been trained as guides for the Sungei Buloh Wetland Reserve and the Climate Change Exhibition at the Singapore Science Centre. Schools also participate in the Water Volunteer Group Programme and go out to their neighbouring constituencies to encourage residents to adopt water saving habits and practices.

Since 2004, the NEA has started the Student Environment Champions (EC) programme to equip students with knowledge and skills to be proactive environmental agents of change in their schools. This was done through customized workshops and networking sessions. The empowered students assist their teachers in implementing schoolwide environmental initiatives and also conduct talks in their schools on environmental topics. To date, there are some 2,000 ECs within primary and secondary schools, as well as junior colleges.

As an extension to the EC programme, the NEA developed the Youth Environment Envoy (YEE) programme to train mature youths to conceptualize and implement environment projects and serve as catalysts for environmental change within the community. To date, more than 100 youths have been trained as YEEs. By grooming environmentally proactive individuals, the NEA is empowering them to take up environmental causes independently in future. Some YEE graduands have since gone on to found their own NGOs.

Corporate and School Partnership (CASP) Programme

The Corporate And School Partnership (CASP) Programme was started to provide companies with an avenue to demonstrate their environmental stewardship. Under the programme, participating companies groom young leaders from educational institutions through initiating joint environmental programmes and transferring technical knowledge through a mentoring system. An active supporter of the CASP is Senoko Power, a local power generation and retail company. The company started out by adopting eight schools to educate the students on cleaner power generation technologies and energy conservation. One year on, Senoko Power was so convinced of the benefits of the engagement that they contributed S$1 million to fund a national initiative, the National Weather Study Project (NWSP), to raise awareness among students on how climate and weather patterns can impact daily lives and the environment.

For the schools, participation in this programme provides their students with exposure to real-life applications beyond the classroom, and challenges them to think of innovative solutions to environmental problems. For the companies, participation not only allows them to take on some corporate social responsibility, but also allows their own staff to understand the importance of conserving the environment better. It is, therefore, no wonder that the number of partnerships has risen over the years, from forty-three in 2004, when the programme was launched, to over 160 in 2008.

City in a Garden[3]

Engaging and empowering the public is also key to realizing Singapore's vision of a "City in a Garden" (described in Chapter 8).

Through its Community in Bloom (CIB) programme, the National Parks Board (NParks) involves the community in gardening projects to enhance their appreciation for the environment. Since its inception in 2004, the response to the programme has been encouraging. To date (2008), there are some 250 active gardening groups throughout Singapore, tending flower, herb, and vegetable gardens in public and private residential estates, schools and public places such as hospitals.[4] In addition to generating community involvement in gardening, the CIB programme has also had a positive impact on the living environment and community relations. For instance, neighbours, young and old, are mingling in outdoor green spaces, and school gardens are being used as outdoor classrooms.

Singaporeans are also encouraged to contribute to greening efforts by participating in the Plant-a-Tree programme, initiated by the Singapore Environment Council (SEC) and the Garden City Fund (GCF). The GCF was incorporated as a registered charity in 2002 to allow individuals and corporations to donate to the greening efforts of Singapore. Traditionally, tree-planting activities in Singapore were catered more for organizations or groups, for instance, through the annual tree planting day. The Plant-a-Tree programme opens opportunities for tree planting to all those who are interested. Under the programme, individuals as well as organizations are encouraged to plant trees at designated parks or nature reserves for a nominal donation of S$200.

Dengue Prevention Volunteer Group (DPVG)

A joint initiative by MEWR/NEA and grassroots organizations, the DPVG is a community engagement programme which provides residents with a platform to learn more about dengue prevention and allows them to volunteer to champion the cause of dengue prevention.

Dengue Prevention Volunteers help to raise their fellow residents' awareness of the dangers of dengue and why and how they need to keep their homes and neighbourhood mosquito-free. The volunteers man dengue prevention exhibition booths during community events, organize door-to-door visits, surveillance checks and talks, and participate in source reduction exercises to get rid of potential mosquito-breeding grounds. They also actively recruit new members from their neighbourhood. NEA equips the volunteers with the necessary knowledge and skills through the provision of training and advice.

The first DPVG was formed in Serangoon Gardens in 1998. Today, there are more than 6,200 DPVG members islandwide in both private and HDB communities.

The Waterways Watch Society

NGOs and other civic groups can be said to capture the spirit of empowerment since they comprise a group of like-minded individuals working together to further a specific cause. Some examples of local NGOs are the SEC, the Waterways Watch Society (WWS), the Nature Society (Singapore), the Restroom Association (Singapore) and ECO Singapore. Many of them have grown from strength to strength and have established programmes targeting a wide range of environmental issues and catering to different spectrums of the public.

The WWS is a non-profit, volunteer organization which helps to keep Singapore's waterways at their scenic and pristine best. Its founding in 1998 was inspired by the government's efforts to clean up the Singapore River. The society has grown over the years from having an original membership of twenty-five members to over 150 now. Their volunteers come from all age and ethnic groups, and diverse backgrounds.

WWS volunteers patrol the rivers, collect debris, and record data on the type of debris collected. The patrols help to promote public awareness and identify "hot spots" that require constant monitoring. Over the years, their activities have expanded to include school programmes that educate students on the consequences of pollution in rivers, and anti-pollution measures, as well as beach clean-ups along the Kallang River.

When the PUB launched its Our Waters programme, WWS was one of the first to come on board the programme by adopting the Kallang Basin. Going beyond just taking care of their adopted location, WWS helps in training the rest of the adopters under the programme. The WWS has also embarked on a programme to cultivate and groom potential youth leaders as environmental ambassadors, and takes the lead in facilitating local participation in worldwide annual events such as World Water Monitoring Day.

Giving Recognition

A pat on the back is always a welcome gesture that not only motivates the one given the recognition to do more and do it better, but also conveys to others that such efforts are indeed appreciated.

Over the years, various awards have been introduced to honour worthy individuals and organizations for their significant environmental contributions to Singapore. To encourage continued commitment, national awards are tiered, with top honours for significant achievements given out by the President himself. One of the inaugural recipients for the President's Award for the Environment is Singapore's Ambassador-At-Large, Professor Tommy Koh, for his active involvement internationally in work to protect the environment, and on sustainable development. The other two inaugural recipients were Dr Geh Min, for having championed environment protection and nature conservation issues in Singapore for many years, and the WWS, for its efforts in keeping Singapore's waterways clean and free of pollution.

To complement the President's Award, the Watermark Award and the EcoFriend Award were introduced by PUB and NEA respectively in 2007. The Watermark Award gives recognition to individuals and organizations that have gone the extra mile in raising awareness about water and what it takes to sustain Singapore's water supply. Similarly, the EcoFriend Award acknowledges proactive individuals such as school teachers, NGO volunteers, and grassroots members who have made personal contributions to protecting, promoting, and enhancing the environment through efforts beyond their immediate job scope.

CONCLUSION

As new generations of Singaporeans take their place in society and new challenges come to the fore, one thing remains certain — creating and sustaining a good environment for Singapore requires the support and participation of the entire community. The government will also need to keep its engagement efforts contemporaneous with the changing social landscapes and the issues at hand. To do this successfully requires nimbleness and a willingness to take a step back to review and refresh strategies, all the while keeping channels of communication open, welcoming feedback and involvement, and building trust.

The government seeking to engage the public and various stakeholders first needs to gain their trust with the assurance that it has done its part in making a sound analysis of the key issues and realizable outcomes, before proposing the adoption of new behaviours and attitudes.

Beyond gaining public acceptance, however, is an even steeper hill to climb — building new and active citizens who not only understand and accept the issues, but take it upon themselves to get involved and even lead such efforts. The summit beckons, and slowly but surely, Singapore is on its way.

11

LINKING WITH THE GLOBAL COMMUNITY

While we strive for a cleaner and greener Singapore, we must remember that we live in an interdependent world and Singapore is only one tiny island in this great wide world. Many environmental issues today cannot be resolved by any one country alone. As a responsible member of the international community, Singapore must continue to play her part by cooperating with others in the effort to resolve emerging regional and global environmental problems.

Minister for the Environment Teo Chee Hean,
Earth Day, 22 April 1995

Global environmental challenges will continue to confront the world. From pollution by hazardous industrial waste in the 1970s to ozone layer depletion in the 1980s and climate change in the 1990s, the importance of environmental management has grown and become more transboundary in nature, in tandem with increased urbanization and population growth.

Singapore firmly believes that global environmental responsibility must first begin at home. The government's priority thus lies in ensuring that domestic environmental issues are well managed, which provides the foundation for moving beyond Singapore's shores to collaborating with the international community on global environmental issues.

In the early years, Singapore lacked the necessary expertise in the environmental sector and relied on international assistance for its capacity building needs. In developing infrastructure and experimenting to find workable solutions for its environmental and water challenges, Singapore has gained useful best practices and experiences along the way. It is now thus able to contribute and share its experience with other countries that may be facing similar environmental challenges.

As Singapore built up its domestic environmental track record, it also became party to key Multilateral Environmental Agreements (MEAs) to partner the international community in solving shared environmental challenges. On accession to, or ratification of, these treaties, Singapore takes its obligations very seriously and puts in place systems and infrastructure to ensure that its responsibilities under these MEAs can be fulfilled. Despite being an export-oriented economy, Singapore did not pursue its trade interests at the expense of its environmental commitments, even if that meant foregoing certain economic opportunities. In seeking progress, every effort was made to balance the demands of economic development, social progress, and environmental sustainability.

At the regional level, Singapore participates actively in ASEAN environmental forums, joining hands with its neighbours to overcome issues of common concern, such as the perennial transboundary haze. It also collaborates bilaterally with partners such as Australia, China, and Germany on joint projects to facilitate capacity building and technology transfer. Singapore has over the years facilitated dialogue and exchange of environmental experience through the hosting of various high-profile environmental and water-related events such as the Singapore International Water Week, International Desalination Association's (IDA) World Congress, and EnviroAsia.

LEARNING FROM OTHERS

After independence in 1965, Singapore was left to fend for its own environmental 'protection needs. The government then had little expertise and resources to commit to the hefty investments required for environmental infrastructure. Assistance from the global community was thus needed, both in terms of expertise and financing. The country also started building up its environmental systems and regimes by studying the best expertise and technology from various developed countries, and adapted these technologies to fit the local context.

Import of Technology

Incineration

In the area of solid waste management, Singapore has benefited much from the experience of developed countries. When the government was considering the various alternative means of waste disposal, such as refuse compaction and composting, it shortened the learning curve by sending a fact-finding team to Japan and Europe to learn from their experiences of operating compaction and incineration facilities. This led to the selection of incineration as the most appropriate option for waste disposal in Singapore (as described in Chapter 4).

In 1971, following the construction of Singapore's first refuse incineration plant at Ulu Pandan with a throughput of 1,200 tonnes/day, M/s Fichtner Consulting Engineers from Germany were appointed as consultants, as the Germans were the front-runners in incineration technology. It was also the first time that Singapore embarked on a large incineration project, and the government looked to the World Bank (International Bank for Reconstruction and Development loan) for funding. The World Bank started the appraisal of the project in March 1975 and loan negotiations were completed in May 1975 for a sum of US$25 million partially to finance the construction, and to procure 200 refuse collection vehicles and dump trucks.

The contracts were subject to international competitive bidding under procedures consistent with the Bank's procurement guidelines. The main contractor for the mechanical contract was a German company called Deutsche Babcock, which supplied the incineration roller grate system, and their subcontractor for the boiler parts was Kawasaki Heavy Industries (a Japanese company). The electrical equipment contract was awarded to a Swiss company, Brown Boveri Corporation (BBC), which supplied and erected the turbine generator, switch gears, and control and monitoring equipment. Assisted by international partners, the plant was ready for commissioning in December 1978.

Semakau Landfill

Likewise, in planning for the offshore landfill in Semakau Island in the early 1990s, a U.S. company, Camp Dresser McKee (CDM), was contracted as consultant. The Environment Ministry conducted study trips to the United States to understand the various technologies that were available in the market better, and this led to the use of impermeable membranes from the United States to line the landfill. The study team had learnt that such membranes were a key feature of well-planned landfill sites in the world so no waste or leachate would leak into the surrounding waters.

The logistics of transferring waste from the mainland to Semakau proved to be a challenging task. Semakau is about 8 kilometres away from the mainland at its closest point. It thus did not make economic sense for Singapore to construct a land route solely for the transfer of waste, unlike for many landfills in the world that are served by land routes. The only cost-efficient option available was to transport waste via the sea with barges over a span of about 30 kilometres, which translates to a three-hour journey. Owing to the long journey, Singapore could not duplicate the experience in some parts of the United States, which was to put the waste in containers, and then transport them in barges. This would require massive facilities such as container-handling yards and cranes, and a logistic chain comprising containers being hauled from the incineration plants to the Tuas Marine Transfer Stations, and barged to Semakau, which would have required some 400 people to operate due to the complicated logistics and handling. Instead, 3,000-tonne barges were deployed, so as to maximize the load for each barge trip and lessen the logistic demands.

To enhance safety along the long sea route, Singapore engineered its own push-tug and coupling system, instead of the typical pull-tug system employed in the United States which tended to be less stable in stormy conditions. The barges were further fitted with a hydraulic metal fly ash cover, instead of just a netting that was deployed in some landfills, so as to ensure that the waste did not get wet during the long journey or be blown away in transit.

For conveying waste at the transfer station from land onto the barge, the initial intention was to operate existing overhead cable cranes, similar to those used in the incineration plants. However, the engineers who made the study trip to New York witnessed a more efficient manner of deploying huge long-arm, mining-type excavators to transfer the waste. Based on engineering estimates, deployment of the excavators proved to be the superior option as it cut down the time required for the transfer by half. Singapore has since adapted the U.S. experience of using excavators and giant mining trucks for waste transfer operations, which is in practice till this day.

Singapore had thus adopted some of the U.S. technologies and methods while modifying others to fit its unique context, such as adapting incineration technologies to the wetter refuse composition in Singapore. This led to the development of a successful waste management model and modern infrastructure to handle solid waste.

Water Reclamation

Given the scarcity of natural water sources in Singapore, it had to turn to water reclamation, i.e. NEWater, to supplement existing water supplies. NEWater is essentially treated used water that has undergone stringent purification and treatment processes using advanced dual-membrane (microfiltration and reverse osmosis) and ultraviolet technologies. When assessing the feasibility of NEWater, Singapore first studied the use of reclaimed water in various parts of the United States, including Orange County Water District in Southern California. PUB/ENV found this to be a particularly interesting case study as it had been producing high-quality water, reclaimed from treated used water, since 1976. Another region that had an established history of using reclaimed water is Virginia where high quality reclaimed water has been discharged into Occoquan Reservoir since 1978. Occoquan Reservoir is a source of water supply for more than one million people in the vicinity of Washington, D.C. A study team from Singapore visited these facilities to learn more about their water reuse experiences. Based on two decades of experience in the United States, it was evident that planned indirect potable use (IPU) was viable and technological options were available to achieve the treatment objectives for IPU purposes. The fact that IPU had been safely used before was instrumental in giving confidence that IPU was a viable option for Singapore. The study trip yielded valuable learning points which led to the conceptualization of the subsequent NEWater demonstration-scale study, which, in turn, culminated in the successful launch of NEWater as Singapore's third "national tap".

Manpower Training

Apart from environmental and water-related infrastructure, Singapore also relied on its international friends for assistance in training its people. When incineration was first embarked on and there was no existing plant in Singapore, engineers were sent overseas to learn how to run such facilities. In 1975, the first batch of fresh graduate engineers and technicians were recruited for familiarization training on steam and power generating equipment at local power stations. Five of the engineers were further trained in West Germany in similar incineration plants built by Deutsche Babcock. Staff supervising the construction and commissioning activities of the incineration plants were also sent to Japan for training in plant process control, operation, and maintenance. They quickly learnt the best practices and work ethic of the Japanese, and adapted them locally on their return to train other staff in the safe operation and maintenance of the incineration plants.

With the experience gained from their European and Japanese counterparts, ENV officers liaised closely with international consultants at the outset to specify the parameters and performance standards of the new incineration plants. These officers would continue to supervise the construction and commissioning of the equipment, and ultimately, stay on to operate and maintain the plants.

In terms of capacity building and the upgrading of its people, Singapore was a beneficiary of fellowship programmes and scholarships offered by developed countries, the World Health Organization (WHO), and the Commonwealth in the 1970s–90s. These gave its officers the opportunity to gain greater exposure to various environmental systems and the regimes of other countries. The scholarships were offered to engineers working in the then Ministry of the Environment to pursue Master's programmes in Public Health Engineering (subsequently termed Environmental Engineering). Most of the engineers completed their one-year Master's programmes in U.K. universities, while others did so in Australia, the Netherlands, and the United States.

Singapore has also sought to learn from the Dutch who have a sound reputation in water management. With about half of the Netherlands less than 1 metre above sea level, the Dutch have built up a vast experience over the years in the areas of flood control, as well as water quality and ecology. PUB has thus been sending its engineers to the Netherlands to learn about their flood management strategies and infrastructure. As recently as 2006, PUB engaged the Dutch consultant, Delft Hydraulics (now part of Deltares), to study water quality issues pertaining to the Marina Reservoir. In the process, five PUB officers were trained by Deltares in various components of the hydraulic and hydrological catchment model, the pollution emissions model, the hydrodynamic model, and the three-dimensional water quality model. With this knowledge, PUB officers can now use the water quality model for scenario planning and analysis, as well as apply their expertise to other reservoirs in Singapore.

SHARING SINGAPORE'S EXPERTISE AND EXPERIENCE

Through the process of learning and adapting from the experience of others in developing environmental and water infrastructure and management systems, Singapore has acquired some useful best practices and experience that can be shared with friends from both the developing and developed world.

Technical Assistance Programmes

At the 19th Special Session of the United Nations General Assembly in June 1997, Prime Minister of Singapore, Goh Chok Tong, launched the "Singapore Technical Assistance Programme for Sustainable Development", aimed at promoting sustainable development amongst developing countries. During its three-year run, the programme benefited more than 1,100 officials from eighty-one developing countries. The programme dealt with various themes of sustainable development, ranging from urban management to wastewater engineering. Since 1999, Singapore has launched other technical assistance programmes, such as the Small Island

Developing States Technical Cooperation Programme, to provide training opportunities to other government officials from the Small Island Developing States, such as Barbados, Mauritius, and Papua New Guinea.

Institutions of Learning

Singapore Environment Institute

In 1993, the Centre for Environmental Training (CET) was set up as an internal training arm of the Ministry. Besides meeting the training needs of ENV staff then, the CET also provided training to government officials from other countries as and when requested. Between 1997 and 2002, CET conducted more than fifty regional environmental training programmes for some 700 participants from more than fifty countries. Building on the strong foundation of CET, the in-house training arm was transformed into a full-fledged education and training institute called the Singapore Environment Institute (SEI) in February 2003.

SEI is actively engaged in the process of knowledge transfer through competency and capacity building programmes such as courses, workshops, training attachments, and technical visits to public and private organizations. Working with various governmental agencies, key industry players, the academia, and local and international organizations such as Singapore's Ministry of Foreign Affairs, Civil Service College, WHO, the United Nations (UN), Asian Development Bank (ADB), Hanns Seidel Foundation, and various foreign governmental training agencies in China, India, Japan, Korea, and ASEAN, SEI delivers close to 200 training programmes in Singapore and overseas to more than 6,000 policy-makers, industry professionals, and conscientious members of the public annually. SEI's training areas span across varying themes such as Pollution Control Management, Solid Waste Management, Environmental Public Health Management, Urban Environmental Management, Climate Change, and Energy. Since its inception in

2003, SEI has conducted more than 130 regional training programmes for some 2,700 international participants from more than sixty countries.

WaterHub

In the effort to contribute towards the water industry both internationally and locally, WaterHub was formally launched in December 2004 by PUB. WaterHub seeks to bring together all the elements of water technology development, learning, and networking for members of the water industry, under one roof. It collaborates with local governmental agencies and water industry players, namely the Singapore Water Association (SWA), as well as international water organizations and aid agencies such as the International Water Association (IWA), WHO, ADB, and United States Agency for International Development (USAID), to host capacity building programmes, seminars, symposiums, and exhibitions. Through these initiatives and training tie-ups, PUB hopes to build a vibrant water industry through knowledge sharing and quality exchange of expertise in water-related areas. WaterHub has trained some 1,000 participants mainly from ASEAN, Middle East, China, India, and various Asia-Pacific countries. It has also received more than 20,000 delegates and visitors at its facilities to date.

WaterHub now houses the IWA Regional office that serves its network of members, stakeholders, and collaborators in the Asia-Pacific region. The close partnership between IWA and Singapore has led to a number of collaborations such as the inaugural IWA Leading Edge Technology Conference and Exhibition 2007, amongst other activities, which provide platforms for water professionals to develop effective and sustainable methods of water management. In addition, the set-up of corporate research institutes such as Siemens, Nitto Denko, and Konzen at WaterHub has supported PUB's effort in helping to develop R&D clusters and broaden the spectrum of technologies for the water industry.

As one of the lead agencies in the Asia-Pacific Water Forum (APWF), PUB partners ADB and the United Nations Education, Science and Cultural Organization (UNESCO) to improve coordination and promote the sharing of water knowledge in the Asia-Pacific region through the development of a network of knowledge hubs. The APWF, the Governing Council of which is chaired by Singapore's Ambassador-At-Large, Professor Tommy Koh, aims to boost investments, build capacity, and enhance cooperation in the water sector at the regional level so as to contribute to sustainable water management in Asia and the Pacific. It is the desire to share that has led to the establishment of the Asia Training and Research initiative for Urban Management by International Enterprise Singapore and ADB, to promote knowledge sharing in urban infrastructure and water management by Singapore's governmental agencies. More than sixty Chinese and Indian policy-makers have since attended the capacity building workshops on urban water management conducted by PUB at the WaterHub.

BEING A RESPONSIBLE GLOBAL CITIZEN

Apart from sharing its environmental experience, Singapore also contributes as a global citizen towards the protection of the environment by partnering international bodies in tackling transboundary issues of common concern. Singapore thus takes its obligations under the Multilateral Environmental Agreements (MEAs) that it is a party to very seriously.

Montreal Protocol

The "Vienna Convention on the Protection of the Ozone Layer" and the "Montreal Protocol on Substances that Deplete the Ozone Layer" are treaties aimed at preventing further damage to the ozone layer through the elimination of the production and consumption of ozone-depleting substances (ODS). Singapore has been a party to the 1985 Vienna Convention and the 1987 Montreal Protocol since January 1989. It has also been party to all further amendments to the Protocol, which have been made to ensure that efforts to prevent ozone layer depletion are on track.

In particular, Singapore successfully phased out the consumption of controlled ODS such as chlorofluorocarbons (CFCs) and halons within a span of only six years (1990–95). This did not come easily. When Singapore took the decision in 1989 to accede to the Montreal Protocol, intensive inter-agency consultations were conducted to consider the trade-offs between its environmental concerns and the impact on trade. In fact, the ozone problem would not have been immediately felt in Singapore as it is fortunate enough to be sited in the equatorial region, some distance away from the Antarctic Ozone Hole.

On the other hand, there were significant trade implications as the economy was highly dependent on chemical industries. Although Singapore had never produced any ODS, significant quantities were used in electronics manufacturing operations, refrigeration, and air-conditioning applications. Nonetheless, as a responsible global citizen, Singapore decided to commit to the Montreal Protocol. This required the cooperation of the industries. Extensive consultations were carried out with the industries to phase out the use of controlled CFCs by the year 2000, in accordance with the Montreal Protocol.

To take into account the interests of various stakeholders and smoothen out the potential trade impact, Singapore was one of the first to regulate the use of ODS with an innovative market-based mechanism. Instead of legislating an outright ban, the then Trade Development Board (TDB) introduced a Tender and Quota System in October 1989 to control the consumption of CFCs in Singapore, which helped the industry wean itself off the use of CFCs at a manageable and economically feasible pace. This helped prepare the industry for the eventual ban on the import and manufacture of non-pharmaceutical aerosols and also polystyrene sheets and products made using the controlled CFCs in 1996.

These efforts produced prompt results. Consumption of the controlled CFCs in 1986 was about 4,000 tonnes in Singapore. By 1990, this was reduced to about 3,500 tonnes, and further to 1,900 tonnes in 1992. Singapore's success in phasing out CFCs and halons consumption in 1996 was way ahead of the schedule prescribed by the Montreal Protocol, leading to its winning an award for "Outstanding Ozone Unit" in 1997 from the United Nations Environmental Programme (UNEP).

Basel Convention

The Basel Convention is another MEA that Singapore is party to. The Convention was adopted in March 1989 and came into force in 1992 in response to concerns about toxic wastes from industrialized countries being dumped in developing countries. It dictates that transboundary movements of hazardous wastes be reduced to a minimum, consistent with their environmentally sound management; and that movements of such wastes be subject to the prior informed consent of the importing and transit states. The Convention also calls for the generation of hazardous wastes to be reduced and minimized at source, and for the wastes to be treated and disposed of close to their source of generation.

As a small country with a substantive manufacturing sector, it is, therefore, pertinent that Singapore has a robust pollution control regime to protect its environment, and ensure that it does not become the source of pollution to another country. With this in mind, Singapore became a party to the "Basel Convention on the Control of Transboundary Movements of Hazardous Waste and their Disposal" in January 1996.

The Hazardous Waste (Control of Export, Import and Transit) Bill was passed by Parliament in November 1997 to ensure sound and effective management, transportation, and disposal of hazardous wastes in Singapore. Under the Hazardous Waste (Control of Export, Import and Transit) Act and its Regulations, any person who wishes to export, import, or transit hazardous wastes will require a permit from the Pollution Control Department (PCD) of NEA, the national competent authority for the Basel Convention. NEA will only issue a permit if it is satisfied that all the relevant competent authorities of the other countries have given their consent to the movement. NEA will prevent the import of hazardous and other wastes if it has reasons to believe that the wastes in question will not be managed in an environmentally sound manner. It also does not permit hazardous and other wastes to be exported to, or to be imported from, a non-Party/State.

To ensure that the government has full control over any transboundary waste and its disposal in a manner that does not pose any health and environmental hazards, all new industries are required to obtain clearance from NEA before they operate in Singapore. As part of the process of obtaining the clearance, NEA will require them to furnish full details of the chemicals they use in the process, the process itself, and the chemicals that are released as a result of their manufacturing processes. In this way, NEA is able to track both toxic chemicals that have to be used or imported, as well as the toxic and hazardous substances that are generated. NEA will also require them to illustrate how they intend to treat the hazardous materials that are released. They can either do it in-house or will have to get the services of one of their licensed toxic waste collectors who will then dispose of the chemicals for them.

NEA will not hesitate to prosecute violators of the Act. Corporate entities may be subjected to a fine not exceeding S$300,000, while individuals have to pay a fine not exceeding S$100,000 or serve an imprisonment term not exceeding two years, or both.

To meet its obligations under the Basel Convention within Singapore, the government has thus diligently put in place strict regulations and enforcement regimes that are rigorous enough to withstand scrutiny by all, be it lobby groups or NGOs. In keeping to its obligations under the MEAs, some unintended benefits have also arisen. When one of the neighbouring countries blamed Singapore for dumping illegal waste in its territory, Singapore could rely on the regimes it had in place to ascertain that the allegation was unfounded. With the assistance of the Basel Secretariat, the matter was amicably resolved with the release of a joint press statement by both countries which stated clearly that Singapore did not breach the Basel Convention. Singapore's strong reputation in meeting its obligations under the MEAs had helped in a major way in convincing the international body of Singapore's arguments in this particular case.

United Nations Framework Convention on Climate Change

In the area of global warming, Singapore has ratified the United Nations Framework Convention on Climate Change (UNFCCC) in May 1997 as well as acceded to the Kyoto Protocol in April 2006 to demonstrate its commitment towards global efforts to mitigate climate change. Although Singapore is not obligated under the Convention or the Kyoto Protocol to take on emission reduction targets as a developing country, and despite being an energy disadvantaged country, it has adopted a climate change strategy to play its part in climate change mitigation, such as through implementing energy efficiency policies.

The country's leaders have also been advocating for more to be done on environment sustainability and climate change. At the UNFCCC meeting in Bali in December 2007, Prime Minister Lee Hsien Loong stressed the need for countries to pursue pragmatic and cost-effective ways to reduce greenhouse gas emissions by exploiting technologies to improve energy efficiency and reduce wastage. He also called on the global community to work together to protect the world's carbon sinks and set overall targets to reduce emissions.

Meeting obligations under various international MEAs is not without trade-offs for all countries, including Singapore. Before signing on to any MEA, Singapore carries out intensive consultations amongst the relevant ministries and agencies to ensure that it is able to meet the obligations and that the necessary measures and legislation are, or can be, put in place. The government also consults the business community and provides necessary assistance so that these businesses are not unfairly affected by Singapore's obligations towards the MEAs. The bottom line is that Singapore is prepared to take tough decisions, even at the expense of its trade interests, so that it can also do its part towards preserving and protecting the global environment.

FACILITATING INTERNATIONAL ENVIRONMENTAL NEGOTIATIONS

While Singapore may be a small country, it has no qualms about making its opinions heard in the international arena. When called upon, it also does not shy away from taking up crucial roles in facilitating international negotiations on environmental issues. In December 1989, the UN General Assembly passed Resolution 44/228 which called for the United Nations Conference on Environment and Development (UNCED) in 1992. The UNCED (also known as the Earth Summit) held in Rio de Janeiro in Brazil was attended by 116 Heads of State. More than 178 governments adopted Agenda 21, a programme of action to reverse the negative impacts of human activity on the environment, and to promote environmentally sustainable development. Two personalities were instrumental in facilitating and forging agreement during the intense negotiations that took place between 1990 and 1992, namely, the Secretary General of the Conference, Maurice Strong of Canada, and Singapore's Ambassador-At-Large, Professor Tommy Koh, as Chairman of the Preparatory Committee, and subsequently Chairman of the Main Committee.

Professor Koh was invited to steer the Preparatory Committee (Prepcomm) given his role in concluding the United Nations Convention on the Law of the Sea (UNCLOS) in December 1982, where an unprecedented 119 countries signed up to the Convention on the first day it was open for signature. Singapore was also a natural choice to chair the Prepcomm as it was seen as an honest broker in the North-South divide, and could play a useful role in reconciling the differences between the "Developed North" and the "Developing South".

In Singapore's efforts to join hands with its global partners in solving the world's environmental problems, it has been open in sharing with the world its state of the environment, the difficult trade-offs it has faced, and the solutions it has come up with in striving towards environmental sustainability. Singapore published its first Singapore National Report to the 1992 UNCED Preparatory Committee in 1991 and also formulated the first Singapore Green Plan 1992–2002, which is Singapore's blueprint for charting its long-term vision of attaining environmental sustainability. The second Singapore Green Plan 2002–2012 was subsequently released at the World Summit on Sustainable Development (WSSD) held in Johannesburg, South Africa, in September 2002.

REGIONAL AND BILATERAL COOPERATION

Apart from environmental issues that have a global reach, some transboundary and emerging environmental challenges may have a direct impact on Singapore and its surrounding region. Geographically, Singapore is a small island within the intricate ecosystem of ASEAN. It is inevitable, therefore, that environmental issues that affect neighbouring countries would have an effect on Singapore as well.

ASEAN Summit

ASEAN leaders have grown increasingly concerned about environmental issues that may affect the precious environmental heritage and natural resources in the region. Recognizing that attaining environmental sustainability is a key pillar of sustainable development, Singapore played its part in focusing ASEAN leaders' attention on environment issues when it hosted the ASEAN and East Asia Summits in November 2007. The Heads of States adopted three key declarations related to the environment and climate change, outlining the commitment of countries in the region towards environmental protection, and paving the way for more initiatives to be implemented in these areas.

In particular, two key challenges facing the ASEAN region are transboundary haze pollution and sprawling urban cities creating undue stress on the environment.

Transboundary Haze

Transboundary haze from land and forest fires has been a challenge confronting ASEAN since the 1990s. In the 1997 El Nino year, the ASEAN region suffered the worst case of transboundary haze pollution, which affected the health of the people, the business climate, as well as investors' confidence and tourism in the region. According to the ASEAN Secretariat's Environment and Disaster Management Centre, the 1997–98 haze cost regional economies US$9 billion.

The key source of smoke haze in the ASEAN region is fires, particularly in Sumatra and Kalimantan, caused by land clearing practices by farmers and plantation companies. The smoke haze situation was aggravated during El Nino years such as 1994, 1997, and 2006. In October 2006, the particulate matter level rose beyond alarming levels of 300 parts per million in Indonesia, resulting in reduced visibility and posing respiratory problems to its citizens. At the same time, the air pollutant index at its worst in Malaysia reached unhealthy levels of 160 in Kuala Selangor and 221 in Sri Aman, Sarawak. The 24-hour PSI levels in Singapore likewise hit the "unhealthy" range, that is, rising above 100, on three days in October 2006.

As transboundary haze had previously been viewed as a local and regional problem, international assistance to combat it has been limited. However, with new knowledge that the ASEAN land clearance and forest fires account for a significant amount of carbon emissions to the atmosphere contributing to climate change, the international community has come to realize that the ASEAN haze is more than just a local or regional problem. Consequently, international resources have begun to flow towards controlling the haze situation in ASEAN.

Fighting land clearance and forest fires is a long-term process that requires sustained effort from all parties involved. Indonesian authorities will need to step up enforcement actions against plantation owners and companies that carry out illegal land clearing practices by fires. This will be a long-haul process which will require a substantial amount of commitment from Indonesia, with assistance from ASEAN countries, regional, and international organizations.

Singapore has been working closely with the Indonesian Government to help mitigate the fires and smoke haze under the ASEAN mechanism. In December 1997, Singapore hosted the first ASEAN Ministerial Meeting on Haze (AMMH), which developed the Regional Haze Action Plan (RHAP). The Plan sets out measures to prevent and suppress land and forest fires as well as provide early warning and monitoring to detect smoke haze in the region.

Unfortunately, the ASEAN Haze Agreement signed in June 2002 has made little progress and the haze problem remains. As of August 2008, two countries — Indonesia and the Philippines — have yet to ratify the Agreement. Recognizing that a top-down approach of instituting broad regional mechanisms could not adequately address the haze problem, Singapore thus embarked on a bottom-up approach and took up Indonesia's invitation for ASEAN countries to work directly with its fire-prone provinces and districts.

Singapore has collaborated with the Jambi Provincial Government to jointly develop a Master Plan to deal with land and forest fires in the Muaro-Jambi Regency. The Master Plan focuses on the prevention of land and forest fires to mitigate transboundary haze pollution. Similarly, Malaysia has offered to work with the Riau Province. Since the signing of a Letter of Intent (LOI) in November 2007, Singapore has been assisting the Muaro-Jambi Regency of the Jambi Province in implementing selected action programmes under the Jambi Master Plan, such as the setting up of air and weather monitoring stations and the hosting of "Socialisation Workshops" on sustainable farming and zero-burning practices to assist villagers in adopting alternative methods of land clearing. The collaboration with Jambi also comprises efforts to help local villagers find alternative livelihoods such as through the fishery industry. By introducing alternative livelihoods to the local farmers, Singapore hopes to find a sustainable solution to prevent land clearing practices using fires. Singapore has committed S$1 million to assist the Muaro-Jambi Regency in implementing the Master Plan. If successful, the Jambi Master Plan can serve as a model that can be replicated in other fire-prone areas in the ASEAN region.

Apart from its work in Jambi, Singapore has also been deploying its advanced satellite imagery and weather monitoring technologies to help the ASEAN region in tracking the hotspot and haze situation. Singapore's Meteorological Services Division (MSD) under NEA has served as the ASEAN Specialised Meteorological Centre (ASMC) to provide weather forecast and monitoring of smoke haze, land, and forest fires in the region since 1995. Singapore Civil Defence Force firefighters and the Air Force's C-130 cloud seeding aircraft also joined their Indonesian counterparts in helping to combat the worst fires in Sumatra, Indonesia, in August 2005.

Environmentally Sustainable ASEAN Cities

Singapore has been proactive in bringing in foreign expertise and assistance to the ASEAN region. One example is through the ASEAN

Initiative on Environmentally Sustainable Cities (AIESC), which aims to promote environmentally sustainable cities in the ASEAN region. The ASEAN Working Group on Environmentally Sustainable Cities (AWGESC) was formed to develop strategies and action plans to drive and develop the AIESC.

Singapore chaired the AWGESC from 2003 to 2007. By focusing on experience sharing and capability building, it managed to successfully channel useful foreign expertise for the benefit of all in ASEAN. For instance, many international organizations and global partners contributed funding and technical support towards the work of the AWGESC. These include the UNEP, UNDP, USAID, United Nations Centre for Regional Development, Hanns Seidel Foundation, Japan-ASEAN General Exchange Fund, United Nations University-Institute of Advanced Studies (UNU-IAS), Asian Institute of Technology (AIT), Clean Air Initiative-Asia, GTZ (German Technical Cooperation Agency), and many others. Through the AIESC, Singapore also shares its experience with fellow countries, especially in areas such as urban environmental management, water technologies, pollution control, and solid waste management.

Germany-Singapore Environmental Technology Agency

To facilitate the transfer of environmental expertise from Germany and Europe to the Asia-Pacific region, the Germany-Singapore Environmental Technology Agency (GSETA) was set up in 1991 under a bilateral arrangement between the then Ministry of the Environment (ENV) and the German Federal Ministry for the Environment, Nature Conservation and Nuclear Safety (BMU). Both ENV and BMU jointly administer this Agency. Since its inception, the GSETA has successfully organized eighteen regional events such as seminars, workshops and conferences on environmental issues, including waste management, air and water pollution control, environmental protection strategies, environmental quality standards, and energy efficiency. These have benefited close to a thousand participants from the Asia-Pacific region.

The GSETA events have been well received by Asia-Pacific participants as good knowledge-sharing forums. To promote environmental sustainability, Germany and Singapore remain committed to the efforts of forging greater environmental partnership among Germany, Singapore, and the Asia-Pacific economies. The GSETA serves as an effective platform for information sharing and a vital link between Germany and Asia in the field of environmental protection.

Bilateral Sharing of Expertise

By adapting innovative technologies and environmental systems from the global community for the local context, Singapore has managed to leverage some of these state-of-the-art technologies to turn its limitations into strengths. Though Singapore is not well endowed with water supplies, it has creatively harnessed innovative technologies such as water reclamation (NEWater) and desalination to bolster its limited water supplies. Singapore's success in water technologies gained international recognition when its national water agency, PUB, won the Stockholm Industry Water Award in 2007. This has given Singapore further credibility and opportunity to share its experience with the global community, including various developed countries.

PUB has also been sharing its experience in water reuse with several states in Australia, which were plagued by droughts in recent years. PUB's Director for Technology serves as advisor on the Queensland Expert Advisory Panel set up by the State's Water Commission in 2007. PUB undertook advanced water analysis of effluent samples for Australian Capital Territory Electricity and Water (ACTEW) Corporation Limited from Canberra in June 2007, which is the water, sewerage, natural gas, telecommunications, and energy utility in Canberra, Australia. PUB was also involved in the testing and commissioning of the Bundamba Advanced Water Treatment Plant that is part of the Western Corridor Recycled Water Scheme in Queensland between August and November of 2007.

Singapore also has long-standing bilateral environmental cooperation with regional countries such as Brunei, Malaysia, and Indonesia. To take bilateral cooperation with Malaysia as an example, Singapore has been working closely with the Malaysian government in areas such as the reduction of smoky vehicles from Malaysia, monitoring of water quality in the Straits of Johor, and emergency response to chemical spills at the Second Link. Such collaborations have provided opportunities for sharing of environmental experience bilaterally, and also enhanced the friendship of environment officers between the countries.

Apart from joint environmental cooperation, Singapore also seeks to lend a helping hand where possible. Many coastal states in the Indian Ocean were caught offguard by the fateful tsunami that struck on 26 December 2004. During the initial difficult period, swift actions were undertaken by the authorities in the affected countries, and generous assistance poured in from the international community to help soothe the immediate needs of the affected people. Singapore launched a significant relief operation to render immediate assistance. As part of this relief effort and longer term reconstruction assistance, Singapore assisted the Maldives in its recovery efforts.

MEWR/PUB recognized that providing drinking water was a critical step that would help support the Maldives' reconstruction efforts, and PUB's desalination expertise could be put to good use in providing a sustainable supply of drinking water. PUB worked closely with private water companies in Singapore, such as Keppel Integrated Engineering, to send a 240-cubic-metres-per-day water desalination plant to the Maldives. In addition, GrahamTek also contributed a water desalination plant with a capacity of 200 cubic metres per day, and Hyflux Ltd dispatched its "Dragonfly" water generators to the Maldives. Singapore was able to provide relief assistance promptly because of the close partnership between PUB and private companies.

FOSTERING A CULTURE OF SHARING AND LEARNING

Singapore's success in environmental management and water supply systems has also attracted interest from many foreign officials who wish to learn from the Singapore experience. The country has hosted many visitors at its environmental facilities, such as its incineration plants and landfill, and in the process shared how it has been able to overcome its environmental challenges despite being a small island state devoid of resources.

Singapore International Water Week

To facilitate the sharing of experience and best practices on water management further, Singapore hosted the inaugural Singapore International Water Week (SIWW) in June 2008. SIWW is a platform for government officials, industry leaders, and water specialists to meet and discuss policies, business solutions, and water technologies. Comprising a Water Leaders Summit, Water Convention, and Water Expo, the SIWW culminates in the presentation of the Lee Kuan Yew Water Prize, a prestigious international award to recognize outstanding contributions in solving water issues.

Dengue Collaboration with WHO

In another example, Singapore has experienced a resurgence of dengue in recent decades and put in place a robust, integrated vector control programme to combat this. In so doing, Singapore has also accrued valuable experience and expertise that can be shared with other dengue-endemic countries. Singapore has, therefore, partnered the WHO in developing a strategic dengue control plan for countries located in the Southeast Asian and Western Pacific regions. The plan will serve as a blueprint for the countries to strengthen their dengue control programme. This programme provides a platform for mutual learning as it is implemented. Singapore has also entered into a Memorandum of Understanding with Cuba in September 2007 that would allow both countries to leverage each other's expertise and experience in dengue control.

Eco-City in Tianjin

As environmental challenges grow more complex with each passing day, more innovative solutions will also need to be formulated to overcome these challenges. Since 2007, Singapore, led by the Ministry of National Development, has partnered China, led by the Ministry of Housing and Urban-Rural Development and Tianjin Municipal Government, in a joint venture to build an Eco-City in Tianjin. With the support of government agencies such as NEA, PUB, HDB, LTA, BCA, as well as private sector companies such as Keppel and Surbana, through a Master Plan team led by URA, the project seeks to test bed and demonstrate environmentally sustainable and economically viable approaches for urban development. When completed, there will be some 350,000 residents living and working in energy and water efficient buildings in the Eco-City in Tianjin's Binhai New Area.

Setting high, yet realistic, targets will ensure that the Eco-City measures up to the high standards of other environmentally friendly cities in the world. Of particular note, the site for the Eco-City is in an area experiencing water shortages and poor surface water quality. These challenging circumstances provide greater impetus for the planners to devise innovative environmental solutions to ensure that the target of achieving more than 50 per cent of the water supply from non-traditional sources such as recycling, rainwater harvesting and desalination can be met and that the surface water system is rehabilitated.

When completed, the Eco-City will become a model of sustainable development for other cities in China. There will also be opportunities for Singapore to gain from the experience in the Eco-City partnership, and bring back some of the innovative environmental solutions and technologies to Singapore.

Zhangjiagang Water Supply Project

MEWR has also been working closely with China in the area of water management. Singapore signed an MOU with China's Ministry of Construction (MOC)[1] in July 2007 to collaborate in the area of integrated utilization of water resources in urban environments. In particular, the Zhangjiagang Water Supply Project was proposed between Sembcorp and the Zhangjiagang Government as a demonstration project between both countries to improve water supply, water treatment, and water conservation in China. Under Phase 1 of the project, SembCorp will focus on providing one-stop service to industries to treat industrial waste water, and recycle the treated industrial effluent for reuse. The project will also cover the management and operation of used water treatment in Zhangjiagang city.

CONCLUSION

Singapore's environmental interactions with international partners had humble beginnings. Options available to the young nation then were limited, which necessitated learning from the experiences of developed countries. Where relevant, overseas technologies were adapted to Singapore's local context. Through this continuous learning process, Singapore has managed to turn some of its constraints into strengths, such as overcoming its lack of water resources to become a leader in applying and adopting water technologies.

Singapore is committed to being a responsible global citizen and became party to MEAs in the hope of solving common environmental problems. This did not come easily as there were times when certain difficult trade-offs had to be made in order for Singapore to meet its obligations under the MEAs. Nevertheless, Singapore remains steadfast in its commitment and puts in place strict regulations and enforcement regimes to ensure compliance.

Singapore will not rest on its laurels, but will continue to share its expertise with others as well as to learn from others who are all taking this same journey in seeking environmental sustainability for their communities. It is keen to continue partnering international bodies in coming up with innovative policy and technical solutions to the ever-changing and complex environmental challenges. Moving forward, Singapore is happy to continue to share the expertise it has acquired over the years to the global community, as it firmly believes that it is only through joint action by all countries that the world can be an environmentally sustainable home for future generations to come.

PART V

LOOKING AHEAD TO FUTURE CHALLENGES

12

A SUSTAINABLE SINGAPORE, A SUSTAINABLE WORLD

The sustainable development of cities is one of the key challenges of our time. Good governance is vital in tackling this challenge, and achieving the right balance between economic growth, environmental protection, and high quality of life for urban dwellers. The stakes are high and we have to get it right early. The welfare of our peoples depends on how well we harness our collective ideas, knowledge and capabilities. Countries and cities should work together, so that we make progress towards cleaner, more resource-efficient, and more vibrant cities for the future.

Prime Minister Lee Hsien Loong at the joint opening of the Singapore International Water Week, World Cities Summit and East Asia Summit Conference on Liveable Cities, 24 January 2008

While some may view the economy as being a part of the environment, it does not mean that the environment is more important than the economy. However, while it is important to alleviate people's suffering from hunger, sickness, and poverty, economic development should not be the only consideration. The choice should never be between the environment or the economy. Instead, it should be both the economy and the environment.

Singapore has been successful because it did not regard environmental sustainability as being incongruous with economic development. Between 1965 and 2005, its GDP[1] grew from about US$5 billion to US$112 billion, an increase of more than 20 times. Per capita GDP grew from about US$1,500 to US$27,000. Alongside this rapid development, it continues to enjoy clean air, clean land, clean water, and good public health. This is possible as the government has consciously sought solutions that enabled the environment and the economy to progress in a compatible way.

While Singapore has achieved a good balance between economic growth and environmental sustainability, the work is far from over and the challenge is greater going forward.

On the domestic front, population size, density, and affluence are increasing. This means more demands on resources, more pollution, and more threats to public health unless greater efforts are made to keep Singapore clean. And ironically, as residents become richer and the city becomes cleaner and less heavily polluted, many people seem less willing to sacrifice consumption and convenience for the efforts needed to improve the environment. This indifference is compounded by the perception that it is the job of the government rather than a shared responsibility to keep Singapore clean and green.

At the global level, there are increasing demands on scarce resources such as energy, raw materials, and food in the face of growing population and accelerating economic development. The result is greater waste and pollution. Many of such environmental problems are transboundary in nature. Countries must therefore agree to act responsibly and assume a fair share of the efforts needed to protect the environment, or the well-being of everyone living on this earth will be threatened.

CLIMATE CHANGE AND ENERGY EFFICIENCY

The greatest environmental threat today is global warming, which, as shown by IPCC, is very likely primarily due to human actions. The direction of scientific consensus has also been towards higher probabilities of more significant climate change impacts, which will be exacerbated by the global trend towards more intense urbanization. Global warming will also likely reduce crop yields and water supplies in parts of the world. The climate change challenge underscores the need for the world to grow in a sustainable way. If unaddressed, it will have profound consequences for factors critical to socio-economic development — food, water, and energy security, as well as a healthy environment.

Climate change is a global problem, which by its nature requires the collective efforts of the international community to tackle. Singapore will, of course, not escape from the possible consequences of climate change and, as a responsible member of the global community, must play its part to solve the global problem. Singapore acceded to the Kyoto Protocol under the United Nations Framework Convention on Climate Change (UNFCCC), supports regional initiatives to deal with climate change, and is playing a constructive role in international negotiations to achieve a fair global solution, in ways that take into account differences in national circumstances. Given how countries differ in size, population, level of development, structure of their economy, level of exports, and access to renewable energy, an equitable solution cannot be a one-size-fits-all one. All countries can, however, try to push for higher energy efficiency as well as move towards cleaner fuels. Some of these measures not only mitigate climate change, but also ensure greater resource efficiency, thereby sustaining future growth.

Singapore is taking early steps to prepare for climate change. While there are existing measures in place, for instance the minimum platform levels specified by the PUB, it has commissioned a vulnerability study to understand the specific impacts of climate change on Singapore better. Singapore's approach towards mitigating the risks of climate change is to pursue pragmatic and economically sensible ways to reduce greenhouse gas (GHG) emissions. As Singapore has very limited renewable energy resources, energy efficiency is its main strategy to mitigate GHG emissions. The International Energy Agency (IEA) estimates that unexploited energy efficiency potential offers the single largest opportunity for emission reductions across all economies. Improved end-use energy efficiency can account for nearly two-thirds of total avoided carbon dioxide (CO_2) emissions, with fuel savings (achieved, for instance, through more efficient vehicles and industrial processes, and applications) contributing 36 per cent and lower electricity demand (achieved, for instance, through more efficient appliances, industrial motors, and buildings) contributing 29 per cent.[2]

Because energy use is pervasive, a holistic approach is necessary in order to improve energy efficiency successfully. Competency and expertise in energy efficiency has to be built up so that organizations have the capabilities for energy-efficient design and management. The targeted provision of incentives to overcome market barriers to energy efficiency is another lever. Finally, a robust regulatory framework that promotes energy efficiency and removes inefficient products from the market has to be put in place. These measures need to be adapted to, and adopted across all sectors of the economy.

In Singapore, energy efficiency is driven by NEA, which has adopted a multi-agency approach and formed an Energy Efficiency Programme Office (E²PO) to work with key agencies such as the Building and Construction Authority (BCA), the Economic Development Board (EDB), the Energy Market Authority (EMA), the Agency for Science, Technology and Research (A*STAR) and the Land Transport Authority (LTA). The E²PO has launched E² Singapore, an integrated Energy Efficiency Masterplan comprising a portfolio of programmes and measures which are gradually being rolled out to improve Singapore's energy efficiency across all key sectors.

Going forward, Singapore needs to do more through setting higher standards for energy efficiency, regulations, and finding the right mechanisms and incentives to achieve the desired improvements in energy efficiency. Singapore could learn from countries such as Japan and Denmark, which have attained a high standard of energy efficiency and conservation. This was achieved through strong legislation, monitoring and reporting of energy data, as well as efficiency measures and regulations, which were tightened over the years. Both countries have taxes on energy. Both have energy conservation laws. In both countries, the government took the lead, provided incentives to kickstart industry development and R&D, and these measures are beginning to pay dividends through strong export-oriented sectors. Both countries also have government-funded but independent non-state agencies dedicated to promoting energy efficiency. Over time, this led to the public developing greater awareness of and support for energy efficiency and conservation.

Singapore sees its energy and resource constraints not as a handicap, but as the impetus to be a leading energy-efficient economy, a position that confers both opportunity and advantage. Just as it has turned its strategic vulnerability in water to a source of economic advantage, it similarly hopes to turn its constraints in resources and energy into a new source of competitive advantage and growth. Energy efficiency will enable Singapore to continue succeeding — economically and environmentally — in an uncertain future.

THE IMPORTANCE OF CLEANLINESS

When juxtaposed against today's prominent environmental concerns such as sustainable development and global warming, cleanliness might seem like a relatively trivial matter that is not terribly challenging to achieve. However, the importance of cleanliness goes beyond just a visible manifestation of the lack of litter and other forms of grime. The state of cleanliness of a place is also a reflection of the values and mindset of its people. Widespread littering is a sign of a place that is not law-abiding and populated by people who lack civic-consciousness.

In reality, achieving a clean city, and, thereafter, maintaining it, is no simple task. Achieving cleanliness requires no less than the provision of sound infrastructure, investing in public education to inculcate the right attitudes and behaviour, enacting legislation to deter and target recalcitrant offenders, and being committed to firm but fair enforcement. All of these actions must be coordinated and executed well, and in a sustained manner, before cleanliness can be successfully achieved.

While Singapore may be known today as a Clean and Green City, the work in this area is not done. Littering and other inconsiderate acts that dirty public places have yet to be eradicated. While the government invests considerable resources to ensure that public places remain clean, cleanliness should not be achieved by an army of cleaners, but by people not littering in the first place. After forty years of public education through campaigns, Singapore continues to grapple with the problem of persistent littering, and the need for heavy enforcement and cleansing. To this end, more in-depth behavioural studies have to be undertaken. More innovative and effective means are also necessary to reach out to all Singapore residents and encourage them to translate awareness to behaviour. Singaporeans must themselves want to live in a cleaner city. Only then will there be a Singapore that is clean because Singaporeans are environmentally conscious, do not litter, and observe good environmental habits.

POLLUTION CONTROL

In addition to public cleanliness, pollution control is the other basic requirement to ensuring a clean and green city. A pollution-free environment is a public good, since no one can be excluded from enjoying its benefits once it is attained. As it is thus an externality, the government has to put in place the necessary pollution control standards and regulations to ensure that there is a certain minimum standard with which all industries must comply.

Standards must be set taking into consideration the availability and cost of measures to reduce emissions. While the additional cost of pollution abatement may be a cause for concern for some companies, in the longer run companies in Singapore will become stronger and more competitive globally. There is a fine balance to strike between economic growth and environmental protection. But it is necessary to strive for this balance. After all, the quality of the environment affects the quality of life enjoyed by the residents in a city. As Michael Porter and Daniel Esty have pointed out, "... we find no evidence that improving environmental quality compromises economic progress. To the contrary, strong environmental performance is positively correlated with competitiveness".[3]

RESOURCE CONSERVATION

To sustain both economic growth and environmental quality requires going beyond just being clean and green to conserving resources. Put simply, resource conservation is about adhering to the waste management hierarchy, also known as the 3Rs — Reduce, Reuse, Recycle. The first "R", Reduce, means consuming and throwing away less to begin with. This is the best since it prevents the generation of waste in the first place. The second "R", Reuse, also reduces waste. Reusing products where possible is better than recycling them because the item does not need to be reprocessed before it can be used again. The third "R", Recycling, turns materials that would otherwise become waste into valuable resources. To be most effective, recycling must be practised together with the first two "Rs".

As a small, island city state with no natural resources other than its people, Singapore is no stranger to the concept of resource conservation. In fact, while striking a balance between the economy and the environment often means accepting certain trade-offs, resource conservation is a practice that benefits both the economy and the environment. By practising the 3Rs, the amount of natural resources used can be reduced or utilized in a more efficient manner. This means cost savings to individuals and organizations. At the same time, using fewer resources also sustains its natural environment. In fact, resource conservation, specifically energy efficiency, is an important aspect of Singapore's strategy to fight climate change.

ENVIRONMENTAL SUSTAINABILITY

A city can only be said to be environmentally sustainable when it is clean and green with a population and community that conserve resources. Arriving at such an outcome and sustaining it in the long term is not easy. It calls for several key strategies, which are laid out in the following sections.

Technology Research & Development

As a small country with no natural resources, Singapore has always used knowledge creation as a key facet of its nation-building efforts.

Over the years, it has invested heavily in R&D and technology to seek innovative solutions to its challenges, including environment and water management and, relatively more recently, on climate change mitigation.

In 2006, the Singapore National Research Foundation (NRF) earmarked environment and water technologies (EWT) as a strategic area for R&D and committed S$330 million in funding to this endeavour.

While efforts to promote R&D activities, such as translational research and development work on technology products that are close to the market, are being stepped up, of utmost priority is the germination of new ideas through basic R&D. In this regard, the government has challenged the research community to come up with viable alternatives, for example, to address simultaneously the objectives of drinking water production and energy efficiency by developing methods to desalinate seawater at less than half the current energy cost.[4] This effort, if successful, will significantly lower the energy consumption and costs of water treatment, and bring benefits to Singapore and other countries.

Clean energy is another focus area in which Singapore is investing. Clean or renewable energy such as wind and solar can be an alternative to fossil fuels. But for many of these technologies, investments in R&D are required before they can be scaled up to a level that can meet growth and development needs cost-effectively.

The Solar Energy Research Institute of Singapore (SERIS) has been set up at the National University of Singapore (NUS) in partnership with the Clean Energy Programme Office (CEPO) of the EDB. This joint effort aims to build strong capabilities in solar technologies through the training of skilled manpower and high-quality research. Established with S$130 million over five years, SERIS will focus on three key areas of research for a start — silicon-based solar cells, novel photovoltaic devices, and innovative materials for solar and energy-efficient buildings.

Policy Research and Innovation

Aside from technology R&D, policy research and innovation will be essential for Singapore to stay on the leading edge of environment and water management and solutions. Developing expertise and thought leadership in this area will provide it with valuable inputs and alternative viewpoints on sustainable development policies, and also help it to flag out early upcoming challenges and emerging trends that need responding to. Singapore's initiatives in this area are described in the following sections.

Centres of Excellence

For water, MEWR/PUB are co-sponsoring the establishment of the Institute of Water Policy (IWP) at the Lee Kuan Yew School of Public Policy (LKYSPP). The IWP will be a centre of excellence focusing on research, education, and training on water policy and governance in Asia and the Pacific. It will also be a knowledge hub in Asia providing a forum for key water policy-makers to discuss and debate water policy and management issues.

For energy, the government has worked with NUS to set up the Energy Studies Institute (ESI), which is a multi-disciplinary energy research institution that will undertake policy research on energy economics, energy security, and the geopolitical and environmental impact of energy. The ESI is also Southeast Asia's first think-tank on energy issues and will provide a platform to promote greater awareness and dialogue on energy issues, both within the region, as well as in the global community at large.

Finally, to bring together existing capabilities in sustainable development and position Singapore for the next leap, the Centre for Liveable Cities (CLC) has been established to build up competencies and undertake policy research and planning on sustainable development, liveability of cities, and the related issues of governance. A holistic cross-disciplinary approach will be taken to study how policies, technology, behaviour, and regional/ international factors interplay to influence environmental and sustainability outcomes at the city level.

International Conferences and Summits

In addition to creating centres for thought leadership, Singapore has been organizing international conferences and summits to provide platforms for the sharing of best practices and insights among experts and practitioners from across the globe.

PUB launched the Singapore International Water Week (SIWW) in 2008 as an annual gathering of water policy-makers, industry leaders, experts, and practitioners from around the world. The event serves as a showcase of best practices in water management and the successful application of water technologies and aims to be the global platform for water solutions. The key highlights of SIWW include a Water Leaders' Summit, Water Convention, Water Expo, and the Lee Kuan Yew Water Prize. Named after Singapore's founding father and a strong advocate of sound environmental policy, the Lee Kuan Yew Water Prize is an international award that encourages and recognizes the outstanding work by an individual or organization in helping to solve the world's water problems through the application of innovative technologies or the implementation of policies and programmes that benefit mankind.

On the public health front, in support of WHO's efforts in building up regional capabilities for dengue prevention and control, NEA and WHO co-hosted the Asia-Pacific Dengue Programme Managers Meeting in May 2008. The meeting provided a platform for member countries, with Western Pacific and Southeast Asia regional offices finalizing the Asia-Pacific dengue strategic plan. The Asia-Pacific dengue strategic plan will serve as a blueprint to guide these countries in their efforts to address dengue prevention and control and is an important milestone for the region's dengue control efforts.

Engaging the Community

While investing in "hardware" such as infrastructure and R&D in technology and policy is important, the challenge of sustainability is ultimately about people. It is anchored in the many individual decisions made every day — in their work and personal lives. Thus the values and ethics surrounding environmental protection must continue to be addressed through education, so that environmental understanding and participation become an integral part of people's lives. Without this, the focus of environmental management will tend to be on repairs and temporary fixes, rather than longer-term solutions.

Crisis brings people closer together and rallies them to support new policies and make changes in their habits or even change their lifestyle. Singaporeans support water conservation and NEWater because they understand that the country is reliant on imported water, and they support the need to become self-sufficient in water. Singaporeans adopted a high standard of personal hygiene and kept public places clean during the SARS crisis in 2003, but lapsed into their pre-SARS behaviour when the threat receded. Many Singaporeans have not yet realized the looming crisis that climate change will bring to the future, and have thus not yet supported the efforts to use energy more efficiently and reduce carbon emissions. This is the time to act, rather than wait until the crisis is upon them.

The government must do more on educating the public and raising the awareness of the environment. The population at large must want a cleaner and greener environment and prepare to work for it, even sacrificing some current levels of consumption. When Singapore was poor and dirty, the public rallied behind the government and Singapore was able to invest heavily to improve its environment. Singaporeans must not be complacent and believe that they have arrived, or that there is no longer a need to pay for a better environment. The government, the private sector, the civil society, and every individual Singaporean all play an important role in improving the environment.

A SUSTAINABLE SINGAPORE;
A SUSTAINABLE WORLD

The constraints faced by Singapore from the early years such as land and water scarcity are challenges faced by many cities today, often exacerbated by industrialization and urbanization. With the continued growth of the global economy and population, resource constraints will get even tighter as each city competes for the resources necessary to support further development. Economic growth will remain vital as, otherwise, governments will not have the financial resources to deal with other pressing priorities such as alleviating poverty and improving the lives of their people. Cities will, therefore, have to find solutions to manage their limited resources more creatively and in a way which still allows them to grow.

Alongside these global developments, Singapore is refining its approach to sustainable development and positioning itself to do better. This means continuing to innovate and develop new, better, and more cost-effective solutions for sustainability, in tandem with nurturing an environmentally conscious population that will contribute to sustainable development through adopting environmentally sustainable habits and lifestyles, and championing ground-up efforts and programmes.

Furthermore, the United Nations estimates that between 2007 and 2050, the world population is expected to increase by 2.5 billion to reach 9.2 billion. Urban areas are expected to absorb almost all of this growth while also drawing in some of the rural population through rural–urban migration. Cities are particularly vulnerable to environmental challenges such as climate change as they have a large number of people living in a densely populated area without major green areas that could serve as buffer zones for heat waves, pandemics, and floods. In addition to the vulnerabilities of cities, the trend of increasing urbanization and the growing number of cities mean that dealing with world environmental problems requires dealing with environmental issues in cities.

Through Singapore's work on sustainable development solutions, it hopes to play a part in global efforts to deal with environmental challenges. It also hopes to demonstrate the benefits that can be derived from sustainable development, and that it is possible to achieve both sustained economic growth and a high quality environment. For example, the green cover (that is, the area covered by greenery) in Singapore grew from 35.7 to 46.5 per cent between 1986 and 2007 (as shown in Map 6), even as population grew rapidly from 2.7 million to 4.6 million over the same period.[5] Singapore will continue to share its experiences with other cities, while learning from the best practices of others, and jointly developing new and better ideas.

Singapore may be small, but its impact need not be insignificant. It can lead by example and ideas, and offer itself as a sustainable model of a vibrant urban city with a high quality of life. Singapore has the wherewithal to test bed new technology, implement effective policies and regulations, and attain higher standards of environmental and energy efficiency, in order to stay ahead of the curve.

The goal is sustainability and a good quality of life, not just for Singapore but for other cities and future generations to come. There will be a cost to improving the environment, but there is a greater cost to inaction. There is, after all, only one earth and our fates are linked.

APPENDICES

Key Statistics of Singapore

1.   Singapore has changed significantly over its forty-three years of independence. The tables below track the key economic and social indicators and provide a snapshot of Singapore's journey. From a port with a small population of about 1.9 million and GDP[1] per capita of S$4,668 (US$1,525) in 1965, Singapore has developed into a dense city state with more than 4 million people and GDP per capita of S$44,767 (US$26,897) in 2005 (Table AI.1).

2.   In tandem with economic and population growth, Singapore has also progressed in social and human development aspects such as health and education levels of its citizens (Table AI.1). Adult literacy rates have increased from about 70 per cent in the 1970s to 95 per cent today. The quality and standards of healthcare services have also improved, as shown by the reduction of infant mortality rates from 26.3 to only 2 per 1,000 live-births in 2005. Total life expectancy at birth for residents has increased from 64.5 to 79.7 years since 1965.

TABLE AI.1
Key Economic and Social Indicators of Singapore

Key Indicators	1965	1985	2005
Gross Domestic Product (GDP) (S$ million)	8,807.5	51,254.0	194,371.3
Total Population (thousands)	1,886.9	2,736.0	4,341.8
GDP Per Capita (S$)	4,667.7	18,733.2	44,767.4
Overall Unemployment Rate (%)	–	5.7*	3.1
Literacy Rate of Residents aged 15 years and over (%)	72.7**	85.7	95.0
Infant Mortality (per 1,000 live-births)	26.3	8	2
Total Life Expectancy at Birth (residents)	64.5	73.9	79.7

Notes: * Earliest data available is for 1986.
     ** Earliest data available is for 1970.
Source: Department of Statistics, Singapore, <http://www.singstat.gov.sg/>.

3. International Benchmarking:

(a) *Global Competitiveness Index*
The Global Competitiveness Report series produced by the World Economic Forum is widely regarded as the world's most comprehensive assessment of countries' competitiveness, providing a dataset on a broad array of competitiveness indicators for a large number of industrialized and developing economies. The World Economic Forum (WEF) ranked Singapore the 7th most competitive economy out of 131 countries under its Global Competitiveness Index (Table AI.2).

TABLE AI.2

Top 25 Ranking of Global Competitiveness Index (2007–2008)

Country/Economy	GCI 2007–2008 Rank	Score	GCI 2006–2007 Rank
United States	1	5.67	1
Switzerland	2	5.62	4
Denmark	3	5.55	3
Sweden	4	5.54	9
Germany	5	5.51	7
Finland	6	5.49	6
Singapore	**7**	**5.45**	**8**
Japan	8	5.43	5
United Kingdom	9	5.41	2
Netherlands	10	5.40	11
Korea	11	5.40	23
Hong Kong SAR	12	5.37	10
Canada	13	5.34	12
Taiwan, China	14	5.25	13
Austria	15	5.23	18
Norway	16	5.20	17
Israel	17	5.20	14
France	18	5.18	15
Australia	19	5.17	16
Belgium	20	5.10	24
Malaysia	21	5.10	19
Ireland	22	5.03	22
Iceland	23	5.02	20
New Zealand	24	4.98	21
Luxembourg	25	4.88	25

Source: World Economic Forum, <http://www.gcr.weforum.org/>.

(b) *Human Development Index (HDI)*

The HDI, published every year by the Human Development Report since 1990, provides a broadened prism for viewing human development and well-being beyond economic growth. It provides a composite measure of three dimensions of human development: living a long and healthy life, being educated and with a decent standard of living. The HDI for Singapore in 2005 is 0.922, which translates to a rank of 25th out of 177 countries with data (Table AI.3).

TABLE AI.3
2005 Human Development Index Rankings for High Human Development Countries

HDI Rank	Country	HDI Value	HDI Rank	Country	HDI Value
1	Iceland	0.968	21	Hong Kong, China	0.937
2	Norway	0.968	22	Germany	0.935
3	Australia	0.962	23	Israel	0.932
4	Canada	0.961	24	Greece	0.926
5	Ireland	0.959	25	**Singapore**	**0.922**
6	Sweden	0.956	26	Korea (Republic of)	0.921
7	Switzerland	0.955	27	Slovenia	0.917
8	Japan	0.953	28	Cyprus	0.903
9	Netherlands	0.953	29	Portugal	0.897
10	France	0.952	30	Brunei Darussalam	0.894
11	Finland	0.952	31	Barbados	0.892
12	United States	0.951	32	Czech Republic	0.891
13	Spain	0.949	33	Kuwait	0.891
14	Denmark	0.949	34	Malta	0.878
15	Austria	0.948	35	Qatar	0.875
16	United Kingdom	0.946	36	Hungary	0.874
17	Belgium	0.946	37	Poland	0.87
18	Luxembourg	0.944	38	Argentina	0.869
19	New Zealand	0.943	39	United Arab Emirates	0.868
20	Italy	0.941	40	Chile	0.867

TABLE AI.3 (*continued*)

HDI Rank	Country	HDI Value	HDI Rank	Country	HDI Value
41	Bahrain	0.866	56	Libyan Arab Jamahiriya	0.818
42	Slovakia	0.863	57	Antigua and Barbuda	0.815
43	Lithuania	0.862	58	Oman	0.814
44	Estonia	0.86	59	Trinidad and Tobago	0.814
45	Latvia	0.855	60	Romania	0.813
46	Uruguay	0.852	61	Saudi Arabia	0.812
47	Croatia	0.85	62	Panama	0.812
48	Costa Rica	0.846	63	Malaysia	0.811
49	Bahamas	0.845	64	Belarus	0.804
50	Seychelles	0.843	65	Mauritius	0.804
51	Cuba	0.838	66	Bosnia and Herzegovina	0.803
52	Mexico	0.829	67	Russian Federation	0.802
53	Bulgaria	0.824	68	Albania	0.801
54	Saint Kitts and Nevis	0.821	69	Macedonia (TFYR)	0.801
55	Tonga	0.819	70	Brazil	0.8

Source: Human Development Report, <http://hdrstats.undp.org/indicators/1.html>.

(c) *Mercer Quality of Living*

Mercer's Worldwide Quality of Living is an annual survey that measures livability of cities for expatriates based on factors that people consider representative of quality of living. Mercer's study is based on detailed assessments and evaluations of 39 key quality of living determinants, grouped in the following categories:

Political and social environment (political stability, crime, law enforcement, etc.)

Economic environment (currency exchange regulations, banking services, etc.)

Socio-cultural environment (censorship, limitations on personal freedom, etc.)

Health and sanitation (medical supplies and services, infectious diseases, sewage, waste disposal, air pollution, etc.)

Schools and education (standard and availability of international schools, etc.)

Public services and transportation (electricity, water, public transport, traffic congestion, etc.)

Recreation (restaurants, theatres, cinemas, sports and leisure, etc.)

Consumer goods (availability of food/daily consumption items, cars, etc.)

Housing (housing, household appliances, furniture, maintenance services, etc.)

Natural environment (climate, record of natural disasters)

In 2008, the top-ranked cities are mainly from the European Union, Canada and Australia. Singapore, at no. 32, was one of the few Asian cities that ranked among the top 50 (Table AI.4).

Note

1. All GDP data are based on 2000 market prices and U.S. dollar exchange rate of 3.0612 for 1965 and 1.6644 for 2005.

TABLE AI.4

Top 50 Cities: Quality of Living (Base City: New York, US (=100))

Rank 2008	City	Country	Index 2008	Rank 2008	City	Country	Index 2008
1	Zurich	Switzerland	108	25	Calgary	Canada	103.5
2	Vienna	Austria	107.9	27	Hamburg	Germany	103.4
2	Geneva	Switzerland	107.9	28	Honolulu, HI	United States	103.1
4	Vancouver	Canada	107.6	29	San Francisco, CA	United States	103
5	Auckland	New Zealand	107.3	29	Helsinki	Finland	103
6	Dusseldorf	Germany	107.2	29	Adelaide	Australia	103
7	Munich	Germany	107	32	Singapore	Singapore	102.9
7	Frankfurt	Germany	107	32	Paris	France	102.9
9	Bern	Switzerland	106.5	34	Brisbane	Australia	102.4
10	Sydney	Australia	106.3	35	Tokyo	Japan	102.2
11	Copenhagen	Denmark	106.2	36	Lyon	France	101.9
12	Wellington	New Zealand	105.8	37	Boston, MA	United States	101.8
13	Amsterdam	The Netherlands	105.7	38	Yokohama	Japan	101.6
14	Brussels	Belgium	105.4	38	London	United Kingdom	101.6
15	Toronto	Canada	105.3	40	Kobe	Japan	100.9
16	Berlin	Germany	105	41	Milan	Italy	100.8
17	Melbourne	Australia	104.8	42	Barcelona	Spain	100.6
17	Luxembourg	Luxembourg	104.8	43	Madrid	Spain	100.5
19	Ottawa	Canada	104.7	44	Washington, DC	United States	100.3
20	Stockholm	Sweden	104.5	44	Osaka	Japan	100.3
21	Perth	Australia	104.3	44	Lisbon	Portugal	100.3
22	Montreal	Canada	104.2	44	Chicago, IL	United States	100.3
23	Nurnberg	Germany	104.1	48	Portland, OR	United States	100.2
24	Oslo	Norway	103.7	49	New York City, NY	United States	100
25	Dublin	Ireland	103.5	50	Seattle, WA	United States	99.8

Source: Mercer, <www.mercer.com/qualityofliving>.

APPENDIX II

ORGANIZATIONAL STRUCTURE: MEWR AND ITS STATUTORY BOARDS

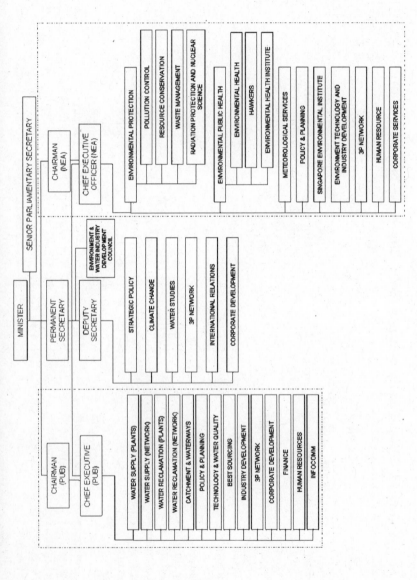

Environment Ministers and Permanent Secretaries; PUB and NEA Chairmen and Chief Executives

Environment Ministers

1.	Lim Kim San	September 1972 to January 1975
2.	E. W. Barker	January 1975 to February 1979
3.	Lim Kim San	February 1979 to January 1981
4.	Ong Pang Boon	January 1981 to January 1985
5.	Dr Ahmad Mattar	January 1985 to June 1993
6.	Mah Bow Tan	July 1993 to April 1995
7.	Teo Chee Hean	April 1995 to January 1997
8.	Yeo Cheow Tong	January 1997 to June 1999
9.	Lee Yock Suan	June 1999 to September 2000
10.	Lim Swee Say	October 2000 to August 2004
11.	Dr Yaacob Ibrahim	August 2004 to date

Permanent Secretaries of the Environment Ministry

1.	Lee Ek Tieng	September 1972 to March 1986
2.	Cheong Quee Wah	April 1986 to June 1992

3. Tan Guong Ching   July 1992 to March 1995
4. Tan Gee Paw   April 1995 to March 2001
5. Lam Chuan Leong   April 2001 to December 2003
6. Tan Yong Soon   January 2004 to date

PUB Chairmen

1. Fong Kim Heng   May 1963 to November 1963
2. Sir George E. N. Oehlers November 1963 to July 1965
3. Dr Ong Swee Law   August 1965 to December 1970
4. Lim Kim San   January 1971 to September 1978
5. Lee Ek Tieng   September 1978 to December 2000
6. Chiang Chie Foo[1]   January 2001 to April 2001
7. Tan Gee Paw   April 2001 to date

NEA Chairmen

1. Simon Tay   July 2002 to April 2008
2. Chew Gek Khim (Ms)   April 2008 to date

PUB Chief Executives

1. Lee Siow Mong   May 1963 to June 1965
2. Goh Teng Koon (AG)   June 1965 to July 1966
3. Kenneth Ying Doon Gin   July 1966 to September 1969
4. Z. K. Fiuczek (AG)   September 1969 to August 1970
5. Khong Kit Soon   August 1970 to March 1975
6. Wee Kian Kok (AG)   March 1975 to July 1978
7. Tay Sin Yan (AG)   July 1978 to August 1979
8. Lee Yong Siang   December 1979 to February 1995
9. BG Boey Tak Hap[2]   February 1995 to September 1995
10. Ong Ho Sim   October 1995 to April 2000
11. Khoo Chin Hean[3]   April 2000 to March 2001
12. Khoo Teng Chye   December 2003 to date

NEA Chief Executives

1. BG (NS) Lam Joon Khoi   July 2002 to April 2005
2. Lee Yuen Hee   May 2005 to date

Notes

1. In April 2001, PUB was restructured to become Singapore's national water authority, retaining its water supply functions and absorbing the sewerage and drainage departments from the Environment Ministry. The regulation of the electricity and gas industries, formerly undertaken by the PUB, was transferred to a new statutory board, the Energy Market Authority (EMA), formed under MTI. Chang Chie Foo was appointed Chairman of the EMA, while Tan Gee Paw was appointed Chairman PUB.
2. In October 1995, the electricity and piped gas undertakings of the PUB were corporatized. BG Boey Tak Hap was appointed the President and CEO of the newly formed company, Singapore Power Ltd.
3. Khoo Chin Hean was appointed Chief Executive of the newly formed EMA in April 2001. The PUB Chief Executive position for the period April 2001 to November 2003 was covered by Tan Gee Paw in his capacity as PUB's Executive Chairman.

Milestones

Year	Milestone
1963	• Public Utilities Board (PUB) formed as a statutory board under the Ministry of Trade and Industry (MTI)
1966	• Industrial Water introduced with construction of the Jurong Island Water Works
1968	• Annual "Keep Singapore Clean" Campaign launched • Environmental Public Health Act and Destruction of Disease-Bearing Insects Act enacted
1969	• Expansion of Upper Seletar Reservoir and eight stream abstraction stations
1970	• Formation of the Anti-Pollution Unit (APU) under the Prime Minister's Office (PMO) • A smoking ban was first introduced in Singapore in omnibuses, cinemas and theatres, and progressively extended to other outlets over the years, e.g., air-conditioned restaurants and entertainment outlets.
1971	• Clean Air Act passed • First hawker centre constructed • First "Water is Precious" Campaign launched

1972
- Formation of the Ministry of the Environment (ENV)
- First Water Master Plan
- Bukit Timah Flood Alleviation Scheme Phase 1 completed

1973
- Decision to build Singapore's first incineration plant at Ulu Pandan

1974
- First water reclamation plant constructed at Jurong (decommissioned after fourteen months)

1975
- Water Pollution Control and Drainage Act passed
- First estuarine reservoir with Kranji/Pandan Scheme completed
- Upper Peirce Reservoir and Chestnut Ave Waterworks completed

1976
- Control of fuel quality for vehicles commenced with limits set for sulphur content in diesel

1977
- Singapore River clean-up launched
- Trade Effluent Regulations introduced

1979
- Ulu Pandan Incineration Plant commissioned
- Bedok WRP commissioned

1980
- Kranji WRP commissioned

1981
- Seletar WRP commissioned
- Jurong WRP commissioned
- Western Catchment Scheme completed (Sarimbun, Murai, Tengeh, and Poyan Reservoirs) and expansion of Choa Chua Kang Waterworks
- First Water Conservation Plan

1982
- Singapore declared "malaria-free" by the World Health Organization
- Pig farming and open duck rearing phased out from all water catchments

1983   • APU transferred from PMO to ENV
        • Water Catchment Policy introduced to control
          developments within unprotected catchments

1984   • Vehicular exhaust emissions standards introduced for
          petrol vehicles
        • Inter-agency Road Drainage Improvement Task Force
          established

1986   • Tuas Incineration Plant and Kim Chuan Transfer Station
          commissioned
        • Completion of Sungei Seletar/Bedok Scheme and
          Bedok Waterworks

1987   • Singapore River clean-up successfully completed
        • Last night soil bucket phased out

1989   • Licensing for General Waste Collectors introduced
        • Acceded to the "Vienna Convention on the Protection
          of the Ozone Layer"
        • Acceded to the "Montreal Protocol on Substances that
          Deplete the Ozone Layer"

1990   • First annual Clean and Green Week
        • Bukit Timah Flood Alleviation Scheme Phase 2
          completed

1991   • Unleaded petrol introduced
        • Vehicular exhaust emissions standards introduced for
          diesel vehicles and motorcycles
        • Pollutants Standard Index (PSI) adopted to com-
          municate air quality information to the public
        • Water Conservation Tax introduced

1992   • Senoko Incineration Plant commissioned
        • Lim Chu Kang dumping ground closed

1993   • Establishment of the Centre for Environmental Training
          (which later became the Singapore Environment
          Institute in 2003)

1994   • Code of Practice on Pollution Control published
          • Telemetric air quality monitoring and management
          system introduced
          • Development of Semakau Landfill approved by Cabinet

1996   • Refuse collection function corporatized
          • Sewer Rehabilitation Phase 1 commenced (August)
          • Acceded to the "Basel Convention on the Control of
          Transboundary Movements of Hazardous Wastes and
          their Disposal"
          • CFCs and halons consumption phased out

1997   • Water Pricing Restructuring
          • Singapore 100 per cent served by modern sanitation
          system
          • Ratified the United Nations Framework Convention
          on Climate Change (UNFCCC)
          • Singapore hosted the first ASEAN Ministerial Meeting
          on Haze

1998   • Leaded petrol phased out
          • Control of Vectors and Pesticides Act passed to replace
          the Destruction of Disease-Bearing Insects Act

1999   • Lorong Halus dumping ground closed and Semakau
          landfill commenced operations
          • First tender called for provision of refuse collection
          services
          • Lifting of 1983 Water Catchment Policy's urbanization
          cap and population density limit
          • NEWater Study commences

- Commencement of DTSS Phase I
- Water Pollution Control and Drainage Act repealed and relevant powers streamlined into Sewerage and Drainage Act and Environmental Pollution Control Act

2000
- Emissions cap on major SO_2 emitters imposed (phased implementation)
- Tuas South Incineration Plant commissioned
- NEWater demonstration plant at Bedok commissioned

2001
- Hawker Centres Upgrading Programme launched
- National Recycling Programme launched
- PUB reconstituted to become Singapore's National Water Agency and transferred from MTI to ENV
- Sewer Rehabilitation Phase 2 commenced

2002
- National Environment Agency (NEA) formed as a statutory board under ENV
- Environmental Health Institute formed

2003
- PM Goh launched NEWater to the public
- NEWater Factories at Bedok and Kranji begin operations
- Ratified the ASEAN Agreement on Transboundary Haze Pollution

2004
- ENV renamed Ministry of the Environment and Water Resources (MEWR)
- Decision taken to adopt DBOO approach for construction of Singapore's fifth incineration plant
- Third NEWater Factory at Seletar begins operations
- Reservoirs opened for recreational activities
- WaterHub formed

2005
- Ultra low sulphur diesel introduced
- First Desalination Plant commissioned

2006
- Environment and Water Industry Development Council formed under MEWR
- Euro IV standards adopted for new diesel vehicles
- Private Sewer Rehabilitation Programme commenced
- Sewer Rehabilitation Phase 3 commenced
- Acceded to the Kyoto Protocol of the UNFCCC
- ABC Waters programme launched

2007
- Clean and Green Week rebranded as Clean and Green Singapore
- Voluntary Packaging Agreement launched for food and beverage industry
- PUB wins the Stockholm Industry Water Award
- Ulu Pandan NEWater Factory commissioned
- Reservoir Integration Scheme completed
- Energy Efficiency Master Plan launched

2008
- Inaugural Singapore International Water Week
- Formation of the Inter-Ministerial Committee on Sustainable Development
- Kim Chuan Water Reclamation Plant phased out

Environment and Water Regulations and Standards

Environment and water as well as public health issues in Singapore today are overseen by the Ministry of the Environment and its two statutory boards — the National Environment Agency (NEA) and the Public Utilities Board (PUB). In law, a statutory board is an autonomous government agency established by an act of Parliament that specifies the purpose, rights, and powers of the body. The NEA and PUB have been formed under the National Environment Agency Act and the Public Utilities Act respectively.

The National Environment Agency Act outlines the functions, duties, and powers of the NEA. The functions and duties of the NEA include monitoring, reducing, and preventing pollution, ensuring high standards of public cleanliness through the supervision of cleansing services and the prevention of littering, ensuring high standards of public health through vector control and research on vector-borne diseases as well as licensing food outlets, managing and regulating refuse collection and disposal, promoting resource efficiency, and the provision of meteorological services.

NEA administers the Environmental Protection and Management Act (EPMA), which provides a comprehensive legislative framework for the control of environmental pollution and the promotion of resource conservation. The EPMA was previously known as the Environmental Pollution Control Act (EPCA). The EPCA was amended and renamed the EPMA on 1 January 2008 to provide for additional provisions on the protection and management of the environment and resource conservation. The EPCA came into operation on 1 April 1999 and consolidated previous separate laws on air, water, and noise pollution, and hazardous substances control. In addition, NEA administers legislations under the Hazardous Waste (Control of Export, Import and Transit) Act, which governs hazardous waste. NEA also administers the Environmental Public Health Act (EPHA) and the Control of Vectors and Pesticides Act). Together, these Acts provide the legislative framework for ensuring high standards of public health and cleanliness. The EPHA covers areas such as public cleansing, refuse disposal, industrial waste, food establishments and hawker centres, and sanitary conditions.

The Public Utilities Act outlines the functions, duties, and powers of the PUB in relation to water. The functions and duties of the PUB include providing an adequate supply of water, regulating the supply of piped water for human consumption, supplying industrial and treated used water, and operating the public sewer systems and storm water drainage systems.

PUB administers the Sewerage and Drainage Act which provides for and regulates the construction, maintenance, improvement, operation, and use of sewerage and land drainage systems. The Act also regulates the discharge of used water and trade effluent.

Singapore Statutes are available at the Singapore Government Statutes Online website <http://statutes.agc.gov.sg>.

The details of the regulations under each Act are as follows.

ENVIRONMENTAL PROTECTION AND MANAGEMENT ACT

- Environmental Protection and Management (Boundary Noise Limits for Factory Premises) Regulations

- Environmental Protection and Management (Control of Noise at Construction Sites) Regulations
- Environmental Protection and Management (Fees for Licences) Regulations
- Environmental Protection and Management (Hazardous Substances) Regulations
- Environmental Protection and Management (Trade Effluent) Regulations
- Environmental Protection and Management (Vehicular Emissions) Regulations
- Environmental Protection and Management (Composition of Offences) Regulations
- Environmental Protection and Management (Air Impurities) Regulations
- Environmental Protection and Management (Ozone Depleting Substances) Regulations
- Environmental Protection and Management (Energy Conservation) Regulations
- Environmental Protection and Management (Prohibition on the Use of Open Fires) Order
- Environmental Protection and Management (Registrable Goods) Order

HAZARDOUS WASTE (CONTROL OF EXPORT, IMPORT AND TRANSIT) ACT

- Hazardous Waste (Control of Export, Import and Transit) Regulations
- Hazardous Waste (Extend Meaning of Hazardous and Other Wastes — Indonesia) Notification 2005
- Hazardous Waste (Extend Meaning of Hazardous and Other Wastes — Malaysia) Notification 2005
- Hazardous Waste (Extend Meaning of Hazardous and Other Wastes — Philippines) Notification 2005

- Hazardous Waste (Extend Meaning of Hazardous and Other Wastes — Thailand) Notification 2005

ENVIRONMENTAL PUBLIC HEALTH ACT

- Environmental Public Health (Burning of Joss Sticks and Candles) Regulations
- Environmental Public Health (Registration of Environmental Control Officers) Regulations
- Environmental Public Health (Public Cleansing) Regulations
- Environmental Public Health (Licence Fees) Regulations
- Environmental Public Health (Funeral Parlours) Regulations
- Environmental Public Health (Crematoria) Regulations
- Environmental Public Health (Cooling Towers and Water Fountains) Regulations
- Environmental Public Health (Cemeteries) Regulations
- Environmental Public Health (Swimming Pools) Regulations
- Environmental Public Health (Toxic Industrial Waste) Regulations
- Environmental Public Health (General Waste Collection) Regulations
- Environmental Public Health (Notice to Attend Court) Regulations
- Environmental Public Health (Corrective Work Order) Regulations
- Environmental Public Health (Food Hygiene) Regulations
- Environmental Public Health (Composition of Offences) Rules 2003
- Environmental Public Health (Employment of Environmental Control Officers) Order
- Environmental Public Health (Qualifications of Environmental Control Officers) Notification

CONTROL OF VECTORS AND PESTICIDES ACT

- Control of Vectors and Pesticides (Composition of Offences) Regulations
- Control of Vectors and Pesticides (Prescribed Form) Regulations
- Control of Vectors and Pesticides (Registration, Licensing and Certification) Regulations

PUBLIC UTILITIES ACT

- Public Utilities (Reservoirs and Catchment Areas) Regulations
- Public Utilities (Composition of Offences) Regulations
- Public Utilities (Tariffs for Water) Regulations
- Public Utilities (Water Supply) Regulations

SEWERAGE AND DRAINAGE ACT

- Sewerage and Drainage (Composition of Offences) Regulations
- Sewerage and Drainage (Trade Effluent) Regulations
- Sewerage and Drainage (Application Fees) Regulations
- Sewerage and Drainage (Sanitary Appliances and Water Charges) Regulations
- Sewerage and Drainage (Sanitary Works) Regulations
- Sewerage and Drainage (Sewage Treatment Plants) Regulations
- Sewerage and Drainage (Surface Water Drainage) Regulations

The legislations and regulations administered by NEA and PUB allow for the Singapore environment to measure up to the desired performance standards. The table below summarizes the standards which are tracked by NEA and PUB across the key environmental and water areas.

Area	*Standards*
Air Quality	Sulphur Dioxide (24-hour and Annual) Nitrogen Dioxide (Annual) Carbon Monoxide (1-hour and 8-hour) Ozone (8-hour) Particulate Matter 10 (24-hour) Particulate Matter 2.5 (24-hour and Annual) Lead (Quarterly average)
Environmental Health	No. of local dengue cases per 100,000 population No. of malaria cases (local and imported) No. of food outlet-related food poisoning outbreaks per 1,000 food outlets No. of licensed food outlets Total no. of hawker centres No. of upgraded hawker centres
Solid Waste Management	Percentage of population with access to waste collection services Waste generated (Total) Waste recycled (Total) Waste incinerated (Total) Waste landfilled (Total) Domestic waste disposed (Total and per capita) Non-domestic waste disposed (Total) Remaining landfill lifespan
Water Sustainability	*Water Resource Management* Drinking water (% access) Adequate sanitation (% access) Drinking water quality (meeting WHO standard) Unaccounted for Water

	Water Supply and Demand
	No. of raw water reservoirs in Singapore
	No. of desalination plants
	Sales of potable water in Singapore (domestic and non-domestic)
	No. of NEWater plants
Water Sustainability	Sale of NEWater
	Sale of Industrial Water
	Volume of used water treated
	Domestic water consumption per capita

Environment and Water Industry

Economic value add by water industry

Employment in water industry

	Absolute carbon dioxide emissions
	Carbon intensity
Climate Change and Energy Efficiency	Energy intensity
	Electricity generated from Natural Gas
	Number of approved projects in EASe[1]
	Household electricity use per capita

Note

1. The Energy Efficiency Improvement Assistance Scheme (EASe) is a co-funding scheme administered by the NEA to encourage companies in the manufacturing and building sectors to carry out detailed studies on their energy consumption and identify potential areas for energy efficiency improvement.

NOTES

Chapter 1: Reflections on Singapore's Environmental Journey

1. Ministry of Trade and Industry Website, Singapore's Economic History <http://app.mti.gov.sg/default.asp?id=545>.
2. *Singapore: My Clean and Green Home* (Singapore: Ministry of Environment, 1997).
3. Statutory Boards are organizations that have been given autonomy to perform an operational function. They report to one specific Ministry and specialize in carrying out the plans and policies of the Ministries. In law, a Statutory Board is an autonomous government agency established by an Act of Parliament that specifies the purpose, rights, and powers of the body. Its overall activities are overseen by a Cabinet Minister. In addition, it has its own Chairman and Board of Directors.
4. *Water: Precious Resource for Singapore* (Singapore: Public Utilities Board, 2002).
5. Mercer HR Consulting's Quality of Living Survey 2007 and 2008.
6. World Economic Forum's Global Competitiveness Report 2007–2008.
7. In petrochemical plants, flare systems are installed to provide a safe means of disposal for the gas streams from its facilities by burning them under controlled conditions such that adjacent personnel and equipment as well as the environment are not exposed to hazards.
8. These are water catchments that are not within the Protected Catchment Areas. Apart from MacRitchie, Upper and Lower Peirce, and Upper

Seletar, the rest are unprotected catchments. In the book, however, we have made a further distinction between unprotected catchments in general, and urban catchments, the latter referring to schemes such as Bedok and Marina Reservoirs.

9. This refers to the total land area that can be developed within water catchments.
10. Land was re-zoned to land use of higher value so as to encourage the redevelopment of sites.
11. 3P refers to Public Sector, Private Sector, and People Sector.

Chapter 2: Achieving Clean Air Quality

1. Anti-Pollution Unit Annual Reports (1970–72, 1974, 1975), Prime Minister's Office.
2. These pollutants were: ammonia and its compound, benzene, dioxins and furans, ethylene oxide, formaldehyde, styrene monomer, sulphur dioxide (non-combustion sources), and vinyl chloride monomer.
3. For more information, refer to the Code of Practice on Pollution Control by the National Environment Agency <http://www.nea.gov.sg/cms/pcd/coppc_2002.pdf>.
4. These facilities are subject to monthly checks on fuel usage and fuel quality to ensure that the cap is complied with.
5. The daily mean for SO_2 exceeded the WHO guideline of $20\mu g/m^3$ for 251 days in 2007.
6. Land Transport Authority. Electronic Road Pricing <http://www.lta.gov.sg/motoring_matters/index_motoring_erp.htm>.
7. Vehicle Quota System Review Committee (1999). Report of the Vehicle Quota System Review Committee (SNP Security Printing Pte Ltd).
8. Land Transport Authority. Land Transport Masterplan: A People-Centred Land Transport System.
9. More information on the efforts to address the challenge of transboundary haze can be found in *Linking with Global Community*, Chapter 11.
10. Tuan Haji Ya'acob bin Mohamed, Minister of State, Prime Minister's Office. Parliament No. 2. Session No. 2. Volume No. 31. Sitting No. 8. Sitting Date: 2 December 1971.

Chapter 3: Cleaning the Land and Rivers

1. This introductory section draws heavily from *Singapore Success Story: Towards a Clean and Healthy Environment* (Singapore: Ministry of Environment, 1973).
2. This subsection draws heavily from *Singapore: My Clean and Green Home* (Singapore: Ministry of Environment, 1997).
3. This subsection draws heavily from *Singapore Success Story*.
4. *Singapore: My Clean and Green Home*, p. 67.
5. A term which describes any litter thrown from a high-rise flat that may pose a danger to lives.
6. This subsection draws heavily from *Singapore Success Story*.
7. Patricia Schultz, *1,000 Places to See Before You Die* (Kindle Edition, 2003), pp. 495–96.
8. Joan Hon, *Tidal Fortunes: A Story of Change: The Singapore River and Kallang Basin* (Singapore: Landmark Books, 1990), p. 27.
9. COBSEA Workshop on Cleaning up of Urban Rivers, Ministry of the Environment, Singapore & UNEP, 1986.
10. *Clean Rivers: The Cleaning up of Singapore River and Kallang Basin* (Singapore: Ministry of the Environment, 1987), pp. 16–22.
11. Hon, *Tidal Fortunes*, p. 37.
12. *Clean Rivers*, p. 8.
13. *Singapore: My Clean and Green Home*, p. 30.
14. Ibid., p. 31.
15. Hon, *Tidal Fortunes*, p. 42.
16. Ibid., p. 43.
17. *Clean Rivers*, p. 24.
18. COBSEA Workshop on Cleaning up of Urban Rivers.
19. Hon, *Tidal Fortunes*, p. 73.
20. Regional Workshop on Area-Wide Integration of Crop-Livestock Activities, FAO Regional Office, Bangkok, Thailand, 1998.
21. Hon, *Tidal Fortunes*, p. 93.
22. Ibid., p. 91, and COBSEA Workshop on Cleaning up of Urban Rivers.
23. Hon, *Tidal Fortunes*, p. 82, and COBSEA Workshop on Cleaning up of Urban Rivers.
24. *Clean Rivers*, p. 28.
25. Naidu Ratnala Thulaja, "Clean Rivers Education Programme and

Clean Rivers Commemoration" (2004). Retrieved from <http://infopedia.nl.sg/articles/SIP_398_2004-12-23.html>.

26. *Singapore: My Clean and Green Home*, p. 32.

27. *Recipients*   *Appointment in 1987*

    Lee Ek Tieng   Permanent Secretary, Ministry of the Environment (ENV)

    Tan Gee Paw   Director of Environmental Engineering Division, ENV

    Daniel Wang Nan Chee   Commissioner of Public Health Division, ENV

    Loh Ah Tuan   Deputy Commissioner of Public Health Division, ENV

    Chiang Kok Meng   Head of Pollution Control Department, ENV

    T. K. Pillai   Head of Drainage Department, ENV

    Tan Teng Huat   Head of Sewerage Department, ENV

    Wong Keng Mun   Head of Hawkers Department, ENV

    George Yeo   Deputy Head of Environmental Health Department, ENV

    Chen Hung   Former Director of Environmental Engineering Division, ENV

28. Thulaja, "Clean Rivers Education Programme and Clean Rivers Commemoration".

29. Hon, *Tidal Fortunes*, p. 104.

30. Information from NParks.

31. K.L. Chan, *Singapore's Dengue Haemorrhagic Fever Control Programme: A Case Study on the Successful Control of Aedes Aegypti and Aedes Albopictus Using Mainly Environmental Measures as a Part of Integrated Vector Control* (Southeast Asian Medical Information Center, 1985).

32. K.T. Goh, ed., *Dengue in Singapore* (Singapore: Institute of Environmental Epidemiology, Ministry of the Environment, 1998).

33. Ibid.

34. Besides the risk of death, dengue causes ill health and serious adverse social and economic losses. The disease is often times a prominent news. The currently available tools in prevention and control of dengue even though not perfect have known to be effective for more than two decades. Dengue control efforts work if it becomes everyone's concern.

Several countries have succeeded in controlling the growing menace of emergence of dengue. Examples are Singapore and Cuba. However, the present dengue control programmes in some countries are inadequately resourced. WHO South East Asian Regional Office, Press Release, 14 February 2007.

Chapter 4: Integrated Solid Waste Management

1. Hazardous waste comprises all toxic chemicals, radioactive materials, biological, and infectious waste.
2. The Joint Coordinating Committee on Epidemic Diseases (JCCED) has been in existence for some time and meets regularly to review diseases with epidemic potential in Singapore. The JCCED is now chaired by the Director of Medical Services, MOH, and comprises representatives from major public health institutes, such as NEA, SAF (Medical Corps), and AVA.

Chapter 5: Ensuring Water Sustainability: The Supply Side

1. United Nations Educational, Scientific and Cultural Organization (UNESCO), 2nd United Nations World Water Development Report (2006).
2. United Nations Educational, Scientific and Cultural Organization, 1st United Nations World Water Development Report (2002).
3. Kwa, C.G. and J. Long, *Water: Precious Resource for Singapore* (Singapore: Public Utilities Board, 2002).
4. K.Y. Choong, *Natural Resource Management and Environmental Security in Southeast Asia: Case Study of Clean Water Supplies in Singapore* (2001), pp. 12–16.
5. K.Y. Lee, *From Third World to First, The Singapore Story: 1965–2000*, Memoirs of Lee Kuan Yew, Vol 2 (2005).
6. K.S. Goh, "Oral Answers to Questions — Punggol Pig Farmers (Dispossession)", on 3 December 1984. Singapore Parliamentary Reports. Accessed on 23 October 2007, from <http://www.parliament.gov.sg/parlwebgu/get_highlighted_content.jsp?docID=20440&hlLevel=Terms&links=PIG,FARM&hlWords=%20pig%20farming%20&hl

Title=&queryOption=1&ref=http://www.parliament.gov.sg:80/
reports/private/hansard/title/19820831/19820831_S0004_
T0026.htm#1>.

7. "Multi-storey Farms", *Primary Production Bulletin*, Primary Production Department [PPD], August 1971, p. 10.

8. The term sewerage treatment plant was changed to water reclamation plant following the development of NEWater. This is important to emphasize that used water is a resource.

9. Groundwater Replenishment System (2004). <http://www. gwrsystem.com/about/pdf/0312gwrs_whitepaper.pdf>.

10. Actew's Water2WATER: Global Experiences. <http://www.actew. com.au/water2water/GlobalExperiences.aspx#2>.

11. Estrogenic effects refer to actions or changes that are similar to that caused by the hormone estrogen.

12. Members of the initial EAP included Professor Joan Rose, Professor Ong Choon Nam, Professor Lee Hian Kee, Professor Thomas J.Grizzard, Mr Michael Wehner, and Professor Ng Wun Jern.

13. In fact, NEWater has also fared well in blind taste tests overseas In one such test conducted by Australia's *Sunday Mail* newspaper in 2007, a third of fifty-six blind-tasting participants in South Australia picked Singapore's reclaimed water as the best-tasting water, ahead of rainwater, bottled water, and desalinated water.

14. Paul Tan and Harry Seah, "Impact of Newater as Feedwater for the Production of Ultra-High-Purity Deionised Water and Manufacturing Process", *Future Fab International Issue 16 — Process Gases, Chemicals, and Materials*.

15. Message left by HE Professor Saifuddin Soz (Minister for Water Resources, India) following his visit to the NEWater Visitor Centre on 15 February 2008.

16. Asit Biswas, "Water — Managing a Precious Resource", *Pan IIT Technology Review Magazine*, December 2006.

Chapter 6: Ensuring Water Sustainability: Water Demand Management

1. Under this agreement, which will run until 2015, WHO will work with Singapore to strengthen and disseminate knowledge to

developing member states on the procedures for the safe use of wastewater in direct and indirect drinking uses; intra-urban water catchment management; the desalination and advanced chemical treatment of waste/seawater as a source of drinking water; and the ability of a country's drinking water infrastructure to withstand disruptions and restrictions in its water supply.

Chapter 7: Managing Used Water

1. Speech by Ban Ki-Moon, United Nations Secretary General at the Launch of International Year of Sanitation. "UN Launches International Year of Sanitation to Address Global Crisis", New York, United States, 21 November 2007. Accessed on 3 June 2008 from <http://www.unwater.org/iys.html>.
2. Excerpt of interview with Chiang Kok Meng, Project Director for Deep Tunnel Sewerage System, Public Utilities Board. *Public Utilities Board Annual Report 2005* (Singapore: Public Utilities Board). Accessed on 20 May 2008 from <http://www.pub.gov.sg/annualreport2004/Future_Lights_Tunnel.html>.
3. Speech by Dr Yaacob Ibrahim, Minister for the Environment and Water Resources, at the Deep Tunnel Sewerage System Pumping Station completion ceremony at Changi Water Reclamation Plant, 28 August 2006. Accessed on 20 May 2008 from <http://app.mewr.gov.sg/press.asp?id=CDS4176>.
4. A floor trap is an opening on the floor of the bathroom or kitchen to drain off floor washings to the sanitary pipe. Below the opening is a U-shaped bend that retains some water at its bottom. This retained water acts as an airtight seal (hence the name water seal) to prevent entry of foul air from the sanitary system.
5. "Inadequate Plumbing Systems Likely Contributed to SARS Transmission", Press Release WHO/70, 2003.

Chapter 8: From Flood Prevention and Flood Management to ABC Waters

1. L.Y. Tan, *Singapore's Worst Floods* (Singapore: National Library Board, 1999).

2. Under the Water Pollution Control and Drainage Act (predecessor to the Sewerage and Drainage Act), the Drainage Department was empowered to construct or require others to construct drainage systems.
3. This excludes the cost of drainage works undertaken by other public and private agencies.
4. NParks.
5. *From Garden City to City in a Garden*, MND Corporate Handbook (2008).
6. The Building and Construction Authority's Green Mark Award is a green building rating system to evaluate a building for its environmental impact and performance. It is endorsed and supported by the National Environment Agency. It provides a comprehensive framework for assessing building performance and environmental friendliness. Buildings are awarded the BCA Green Mark based on five key criteria: Energy Efficiency, Water Efficiency, Site/Project Development & Management (Building Management & Operation for existing buildings), Good Indoor Environmental Quality & Environmental Protection, and Innovation.

Chapter 10: Working with People and the Community

1. Peter Teo, " 'Clean and Green — that's the way we like it': A critical study of Singapore's environmental campaigns", Working Papers Series, Working Paper No. 121, Centre for Language in Social Life, Department of Linguistics and Modern English Language, Lancaster University.
2. This was before the Internet age, so there was none of the convenience of e-consultations.
3. Information from NParks.
4. *From Garden City to City in a Garden*, MND Corporate Handbook (2008).

Chapter 11: Linking with the Global Community

1. As of 11 March 2008, the Ministry of Construction has been restructured to form the Ministry of Housing and Urban-Rural Construction (MHURC).

Chapter 12: A Sustainable Singapore, A Sustainable World

1. All GDP data are based on 2000 market prices and U.S. dollar exchange rate of 3.0612 for 1965 and 1.6644 for 2005.
2. IEA World Energy Outlook, 2006.
3. Michael Porter and Daniel Esty, *National Environmental Performance: An Empirical Analysis of Policy Results and Determinants* (UK: Environment and Development Economics 10, Cambridge University Press, 2005).
4. At present, seawater desalination using reverse osmosis membranes requires 3.5 kWh/m^3.
5. This is based on a study conducted by the Centre for Remote Imaging, Sensing and Processing (CRISP), National University of Singapore [Source: NParks].

GLOSSARY

Agency for Science, Technology and Research (A*STAR)	A statutory board of the Ministry of Trade and Industry whose mission is to raise the level of science and technology in Singapore. A*STAR was established in 1991 as the then National Science and Technology Board.
Agri-Food and Veterinary Authority (AVA)	A statutory board of the Ministry of National Development which seeks to ensure a resilient supply of safe food, safeguard the health of animals and plants, and facilitate agri-trade for the well-being of the nation. The AVA was formerly known as the Primary Production Department.
aquifers	An underground layer of water-bearing permeable rock or unconsolidated materials (gravel, sand, silt, or clay) from which ground-water can be usefully extracted.
averaging time (for air pollution concentration)	The time period over which the air pollutant concentration readings taken are averaged.
brackish water	Water that has higher salinity than fresh water, but lower salinity than seawater.
brine	Water that is saturated or nearly saturated with salt.

Building and Construction Authority (BCA)	A statutory board of the Ministry of National Development, which champions the development of an excellent built environment for Singapore.
bumboat/lighter	A boat used to ferry goods to and from ships moored away from shore.
carbon monoxide (CO)	A colourless, odourless, and tasteless gas formed when there is incomplete combustion of fuels containing carbon.
catchment	Catchment or catchment area is the term used to describe the area which is drained by a river.
catchments (fringe)	Refers to catchments which are not drained by major rivers. It is, therefore, cost-ineffective to tap water from such catchments through the creation of estuarine reservoirs.
catchments (non-protected)	Refers to catchments outside of the protected catchments.
catchments (protected)	Refers to catchments within the Central Catchment Natural Reserve, where no developments are allowed.
catchments (urbanized)	Refers to catchments outside the protected catchments which are highly urbanized with residential, commercial, and industrial developments.
Chassis Dynamometer Smoke Test (CDST)	The CDST measures the smoke emission from a vehicle under simulated driving conditions. During the test, the vehicle is brought up to a specific speed on a chassis dynamometer and the power delivered by the engine is checked by a computer. Load is then gradually added to the engine to simulate actual driving conditions before smoke measurements at its exhaust are taken.
Chikungunya fever	A viral infection transmitted by infected *Aedes* mosquitoes. Symptoms include fever, rashes and arthritis affecting multiple joints.

cistern water-saving bags	Bags that are water displacement devices which, when installed in conventional 9-litre flushing cisterns, can help to reduce the amount of water used in each flush by about 1.5–2 litres per flush.
City Council	The City Council of Singapore, known as the Municipal Council before 1951, was the administrative council that was responsible for the provision of water, electricity, gas, roads and bridges, and street lighting in Singapore.
Code of Practice on Pollution Control (COPPC)	A publication that summarizes the environmental requirements for developments in Singapore and interprets the relevant legislation in a manner that can be readily referred to by industry players.
Common Services Tunnel	A network of tunnels that will house and distribute various utility services to the developments at Marina Bay in Singapore. The tunnels will house electrical and telecommunication cables, district cooling pipes, NEWater and potable water pipes, and will also provide for the future installation of a pneumatic refuse conveyance system.
Community Development Councils (CDC)	The CDCs of Singapore function as local administrations of their district, initiating, planning, and managing community programmes to promote community bonding and social cohesion, as well as provide various community and social assistance services.
conventional water treatment	Water treatment by the use of flocculation, sedimentation, sand filtration, and chlorination.
conveyance function	The effectiveness of a drain in collecting and conveying storm water away during heavy rain to prevent flooding.
culvert	A drain under a road or embankment.
Design, Build, Own and Operate (DBOO)	A form of public-private partnership (PPP) to achieve cost efficiencies. *See also* PPP.

Deep Tunnel Sewerage System (DTSS)	A long-term solution to meet the needs for used water collection, treatment and disposal to serve the development of Singapore through the 21st century. The project consists of two large, deep tunnels criss-crossing the island, feeding to two centralized water reclamation plants by gravity, deep sea outfalls and a link-sewer network.
dengue	A viral infection transmitted by infected female *Aedes* mosquitoes (principally *Aedes aegypti*). Symptoms include fever, with severe headaches, muscle and joint pain.
desalination	The processes by which salt and other minerals are removed from seawater to produce freshwater suitable for human consumption or irrigation.
diversion canal	A man-made drainage channel that conveys water during a storm event from one drainage catchment to another, usually to avert flooding.
Drainage capacity	The rate and volume of storm water that a drain can convey.
Drainage reserve	Any land set aside for drainage works as a result of development proposals approved by a competent authority.
Earth streams	A naturally formed earth-lined drain with flowing water and vegetation along its embankments.
Economic Development Board (EDB)	A statutory board of the Ministry of Trade and Industry that plans and executes strategies to sustain Singapore as a leading global hub for business and investment.
El Nino (1997)	El Nino is the result of the interaction between the surface layers of the ocean and the overlying atmosphere in the tropical Pacific. The El Nino in 1997 resulted in drought-like conditions in Southeast Asia in 1997.
Energy Market Authority (EMA)	A statutory board of the Ministry of Trade and Industry which regulates the electricity and piped

gas industries and district cooling services in designated areas. EMA is also responsible for ensuring the security, reliability, and adequacy of electricity supply, overseeing the operation of the wholesale electricity market, and facilitating competition in the electricity and piped gas industries.

Environmental Impact Assessment (EIA)
: An assessment of the likely positive and/or negative influence a project may have on the environment.

epidemiology
: The study of factors affecting the health and illness of populations.

estuary
: A semi-enclosed coastal body of water with one or more rivers or streams flowing into it, and with a free connection to the open sea. *See also* reservoir (estuarine).

first flush
: Refers to the first part of a run-off during a rainfall.

float-boom
: A floating structure that traps debris and flotsam.

fluidized bed incinerators
: Fluidized bed incinerators utilize a refractory-lined vessel containing inert granular materials with heated air and combustion gases blown through the material at a rate sufficiently high to cause the bed to expand and act as a fluid. Waste is then added to this fluid to be burned. The technology uses pre-separation and shredding to provide a more uniform feedstock.

Free Acceleration Smoke Test (FAST)
: FAST measures the smoke emission from a diesel-driven vehicle with the transmission disengaged, i.e., in neutral gear, with the accelerator pedal pressed down so that the engine increases to its maximum governed speed.

Geographical Information System
: A system for collecting, storing, managing, and analysing spatial (geo-referenced) data.

groundwater
: Water located beneath the ground surface in soil pore spaces and in the fractures of rock formations.

Hantavirus	A rodent-borne virus that is associated with the disease known as haemorrhagic fever with renal syndrome (HFRS).
Housing and Development Board (HDB)	A statutory board of the Ministry of National Development that is responsible for public housing in Singapore.
hydrocarbons	Chemical compounds that contain hydrogen and carbon. Most traditional fuel sources, such as oil, natural gas, and diesel are hydrocarbon-based. Hydrocarbon pollution occurs as a result of incomplete fuel combustion when unburnt or partially burnt fuel is released into the air, or when fuel evaporates into the atmosphere.
hydrological factors	Factors such as rainfall distribution, paved up surface areas, topographical and soil data used in the study of water occurrence, distribution, movement, and balances in ecosystems.
hydrophobic membrane	A membrane that only allows water vapour to pass through, and not water in the liquid state.
industrial water	A source of non-potable water for industries, which is produced by treating effluent. It is of a lower quality and grade compared with NEWater.
International Desalination Association (IDA)	A non-profit association of over 2,000 members in fifty-eight countries, committed to the development and promotion of the appropriate use of desalination and desalination technologies worldwide.
International Water Association (IWA)	A global network of water professionals, spanning the continuum between research and practice and covering all facets of the water cycle.
Japanese encephalitis	Acute inflammation of the brain caused by a viral infection transmitted by infected *Culex* mosquitoes.

Jurong Town Corporation (JTC)	A statutory board of the Ministry of Trade and Industry which executes the planning, promotion, and development of high quality industrial facilities in Singapore. JTC was originally founded in 1968 to develop the Jurong area of Singapore into an industrial area.
Jurong Island	A man-made island located to the southwest of the main island of Singapore. It was formed from the amalgamation of seven offshore islands, and serves as an industrial zone.
Land Transport Authority (LTA)	A statutory board of the Ministry of Transport that spearheads, plans, and develops the long-term public and private transport needs of Singapore.
leachate	Liquid that drains or "leaches" from a landfill.
lead	A toxic metal which is released into the air through the burning of fuels that contain lead.
Legionella	A bacterial species that causes a respiratory infection known as Legionnaires' disease and is transmitted through the inhalation of mist droplets or aerosols containing bacteria that are generated from cooling towers, domestic hot-water systems, and fountains.
malaria	A parasitic infection transmitted by infected female *Anopheles* mosquitoes. The parasites multiply within red blood cells, causing symptoms that include symptoms of anaemia (light headedness, shortness of breath, tachycardia, etc.), as well as other general symptoms such as fever, chills, nausea, flu-like illness, and in severe cases, coma and death.
Mass Rapid Transit (MRT) system	The MRT system is a rapid transit system that is fast, efficient, and comfortable, and forms the backbone of the railway system in Singapore, spanning the entire city state.

membrane technology	*See* microfiltration; ultrafiltration; reverse osmosis.
microfiltration	A filtration process which removes contaminants from water by passage through a microporous membrane of pore size range of 0.1 to 10 micrometres (μm).
Ministry of the Environment and Water Resources (MEWR)	The Ministry of the Environment (ENV) was established in 1972. It was renamed the Ministry of the Environment and Water Resources in 2004. Its mission is to deliver and sustain a clean and healthy environment and water resources for all in Singapore.
Ministry of Finance (MOF)	The Ministry of Finance ensures the government's long-term fiscal sustainability through the efficient allocation of government resources to achieve Whole-of-Government objectives and overseeing the optimal management of Singapore's reserves. The Ministry also seeks to put in place a pro-growth fiscal system and create a conducive business environment in Singapore.
Ministry of Health (MOH)	The Ministry of Health oversees health issues in Singapore. Its mission is to promote good health and reduce illness, ensure access to good and affordable health care, and pursue medical excellence.
Ministry of National Development (MND)	The Ministry of National Development directs the formulation and implementation of policies related to the national development of Singapore. Its mission is to develop world-class infra-structure, create a vibrant and sustainable living environment, and build rooted and cohesive communities.
Ministry of Trade and Industry (MTI)	The Ministry of Trade and Industry directs the formulation and implementation of policies related to the trade and industry of Singapore. Its mission is to promote economic growth and create

	jobs so as to achieve higher standards of living for all.
multiple-barrier	The production process of NEWater that includes microfiltration, reverse osmosis, and ultraviolet disinfection.
multi-stage flash distillation (MSF)	A desalination process that distills seawater by heating water into steam. Heated water from the first stage is sent through subsequent stages of lower ambient pressure where water boils at lower temperatures. Relatively little heat is lost as heat from the waste stream is used to heat cold seawater flowing into the process.
National Environment Agency (NEA)	A statutory board of the Ministry of the Environment and Water Resources which focuses on the implementation of environmental policies.
National Parks Board (NParks)	A statutory board of the Ministry of National Development which is responsible for providing and enhancing greenery in Singapore.
nature reserve (Central Catchment)	The largest nature reserve in Singapore, acting concurrently as a catchment area for four reservoirs within its boundaries.
New Towns	The town planning concept adopted in Singapore, where each new town is designed to be completely self-sustainable.
NEWater	Trade name for the high grade recycled water produced by PUB using a multiple-barrier process. *See also* multiple-barrier.
NEWater Expert Panel	Formed in January 1999 to provide independent advice to PUB and ENV on the NEWater Study, and consisting of both local and foreign experts in engineering, biomedical science, chemistry, and water technology.
NS1	A non-structural protein that is expressed on the surface of cells infected by a dengue virus; it is a

	target of the human antibody response to dengue virus infection.
outlet drain	A drain which conveys storm water from roadside drains to a major canal or river.
oxides of nitrogen	Chemical compounds containing a combination of oxygen and nitrogen. They are released into the air through high temperature combustion processes, fuel burning equipment, and motor vehicles.
ozone (O_3)	A molecule containing three oxygen atoms. It occurs naturally in the upper atmosphere where it filters harmful ultraviolet light from reaching the Earth's surface. Ozone near ground level, however, is an air pollutant with harmful health effects. It is formed by chemical reactions in the presence of sunlight, involving compounds such as nitrogen dioxide and chemically reactive hydrocarbons.
ozonation	An alternative disinfection process to chlorination. Ozone does not form organochlorine compounds, nor does it remain in the water after treatment.
Particulate Matter (PM)	Small particles in the air such as dust or soot. PM10 is particulate matter of size 10 microns in diameter or smaller. PM2.5, a subset of PM10, is very fine particulate matter of size 2.5 microns in diameter or smaller.
People's Association (PA)	The PA of Singapore brings people together to take ownership of and contribute to community well-being.
Pollutant Standards Index (PSI)	An index developed by the United States Environmental Protection Agency (USEPA) to provide accurate, timely, and easily understandable information about daily levels of air pollution. It takes into account the ambient concentrations of the key air pollutants such as

sulphur dioxide, particulate matter (PM10), ozone, carbon monoxide, and nitrogen dioxide, and translates them into an overall index ranging from 0 to 500. Based on the health impact of different concentration levels of the various air pollutants, PSI levels between 0 and 50 are considered to be good, and levels from 51 to 100 are moderate. Index levels above 100 are assessed to be unhealthy.

polymerase chain reaction
A technique widely used in molecular biology, which amplifies a single copy of a piece of DNA to generate millions or more copies of the DNA piece.

ponding
A stagnant pool of water that is formed in a localized depressed area.

Port of Singapore Authority (PSA)
A statutory board which regulated maritime and shipping activity in Singapore and operated Singapore's port and wharf facilities. PSA was corporatized in 1997. The corporatized entity, PSA Corporation, operates port infrastructure in Singapore and overseas. PSA's regulatory functions were transferred to a new statutory board, the Maritime and Port Authority (MPA), under the Ministry of Transport. The MPA promotes the use and development of the port, controls vessel movements and ensures navigational safety, and regulates marine services and facilities.

Primary Production Department
See AVA.

public-private partnership (PPP)
A government service or private business venture which is funded and operated through a partnership of government and one or more private sector companies.

Public Utilities Board (PUB)
A statutory board of the Ministry of the Environment and Water Resources (MEWR). PUB

	was set up to ensure an efficient, adequate, and sustainable supply of water for Singapore.
pumping station	A pumping station is a facility with pumping installation and pump sump to lift water from a lower level to a higher level, for boosting pressure and/or pressurized conveyance purposes.
pyrolysis	Pyrolysis is the thermal decomposition of organic materials (in the absence or near absence of oxygen) into simpler molecules or smaller molecular weights that can be more easily combusted than the initial waste. It works in a temperature range of between 150°C and 9,000°C.
reverse osmosis (RO)	A separation process that uses pressure to force raw water through a membrane that retains the impurities on one side and allows clean water to pass to the other side.
reservoir (estuarine)	A reservoir created by constructing a dam at the mouth of a river.
reservoir (impounding)	A reservoir created by forming an inland dam to store water.
run-off	The flow of water, from rain, snowmelt, or other sources, over the land.
rivulet	A small stream.
scuppers	Drainage holes along the road kerb that collect and discharge rainwater from the road into a roadside drain.
self-closing delayed action taps	A tap that automatically closes its valve after a preset period.
serotype	A classification of micro-organisms according to the difference in their surface proteins. The dengue virus, for example, has four serotypes.
Severe Acute Respiratory Syndrome (SARS)	A respiratory disease caused by the SARS-coronavirus (SARS-CoV)

Singapore Municipality	*See* City Council.
standpipe	A standpipe is a freestanding pipe fitted with a tap that is installed outdoors to dispense water in areas which do not have a running water supply to the buildings.
storage pond	A pond with sufficient storage capacity to retain excess storm water, which is subsequently released either by pumping, or by gravity flow through gates into a drain.
subsidiary drains	A network of drains that channel storm water to a major canal or river.
subsoil pipes	Perforated pipes that are laid in the soil lying immediately below the surface layer to channel water away and prevent sogginess.
sulphur dioxide (SO_2)	A colourless gas that smells like burnt matches. It is released into the air through the burning of fuels which contain sulphur and, to a lesser extent, from petroleum refining processes.
surface water drainage	A system of drains to carry away excess rainwater effectively and prevent flooding.
tide gates	Movable gates constructed in a drain or waterway that will close to prevent the ingress of sea water from inundating low-lying grounds during high tide. The gates will open to discharge storm water during heavy rain.
Town Council	A corporate body established to control, manage, maintain, and improve the common property of public housing estates.
toxicology	The study of the adverse effects of chemicals on living organisms, especially the poisoning of people.
treated effluent	Effluent that has been treated in used water treatment plants.

turbidity	The cloudiness or haziness of a fluid caused by individual particles (suspended solids). The measurement of turbidity is a key test of water quality.
ultrafiltration (UF)	A filtration process which removes contaminants from water by passage through a microporous membrane of pore size range of 0.001 to 0.1 micrometres (μm).
unaccounted-for water (UFW)	The difference between the amount of water supplied from the waterworks as measured through its meters and the total amount of water accounted for.
unconventional sources	Refers to water sources other than catchment reservoirs.
Urban Redevelopment Authority (URA)	A statutory board of the Ministry of National Development. The URA is Singapore's national land use planning authority.
USEPA	The United States Environmental Protection Agency is an agency of the federal government of the United States charged with protecting human health and safeguarding the natural environment: air, water, and land.
Utilities Save (U-Save)	A scheme designed specifically to help lower and middle-income Singaporeans with their utilities bills. Lower-income households living in smaller-type flats will get more help and receive higher rebates, which are credited to their utilities account.
vector	Any organism carrying or causing or capable of causing any disease to human beings.
Variable Salinity Plant	A plant that uses microfiltration and reverse osmosis membrane processes to treat feed water with varying concentrations of salt.
water conservation tax (WCT)	A tax imposed by the Singapore Government to encourage water conservation, and reflect the higher incremental cost of additional supplies.

Water Master Plan	A master plan prepared by PUB that sets out the long-term plan towards self-sufficiency.
waterworks	A facility to remove contaminants from a raw water source to produce water for human consumption (drinking water).
WHO	The World Health Organization (WHO) is a specialized agency of the United Nations (UN) that acts as a coordinating authority on international public health.
West Nile viral encephalitis	Acute inflammation of the brain caused by a viral infection transmitted by infected *Culex* mosquitoes.
yield (reservoir)	Refers to the amount of water that can be reliably extracted from a reservoir such that the reservoir does not fail.

INDEX

ABOUT THE AUTHORS

Tan Yong Soon is the Permanent Secretary of the Ministry of the Environment and Water Resources, Singapore. He also co-chairs the Executive Committees for Environment and Water Technology, and for the Inter-Ministerial Committee on Sustainable Development.

He began his career in the Singapore Armed Forces and rose to the rank of Brigadier General before joining the Singapore Administrative Service. He has served as Principal Private Secretary to the Prime Minister, Deputy Secretary in the Ministry of Defence and the Ministry of Finance, and CEO of the Urban Redevelopment Authority. He was awarded the Public Administration Medal (Military)(Gold) and the Public Administration Medal (Gold).

He studied in Raffles Institution and National Junior College, Singapore, and holds a BA(Hons) and an MA in engineering from Cambridge University, an MBA from the National University of Singapore and an MPA from Harvard University. He also attended the Advanced Management Program at Harvard Business School.

He is married with two children, and is the author of *Living the Singapore Dream*, a reflection on his life experiences and those of his childhood friends, which expounds the values that made Singapore — and these individuals — successful.

Lee Tung Jean is Director of Water Studies at the Ministry of the Environment and Water Resources, Singapore, where she is involved in the formulation and implementation of policies relating to the management of water resources and enhancement of Singapore's living environment. She holds a concurrent appointment as the Deputy Executive Director of the Environment and Water Industry Development Council.

In her previous postings within the Singapore Administrative Service, she has worked on sea transport and telecommunications policies at the Ministry of Communications, as well as governance, investment and fiscal policies at the Ministry of Finance.

She studied in Raffles Girls' School and Raffles Junior College, Singapore, and holds a BA(Hons) from Harvard University, an MA in Economics from Yale University, and a DPhil in Economics from Oxford University which she pursued on a Rhodes Scholarship. She is married with three children.

Karen Tan E-Ling is Deputy Director for Strategic Policy at the Ministry of the Environment and Water Resources, Singapore. Her portfolio covers the formulation and implementation of policies to ensure Singapore's environmental sustainability, including air pollution control.

She has previously worked at the Ministry of Transport and the Ministry of Finance and is an officer in the Singapore Administrative Service.

She studied in Dunman High School and Victoria Junior College, Singapore, and holds a BA(Hons) in Politics, Philosophy and Economics from Oxford University and an MA in Political Science from Columbia University. She is married.